Home Cooking

CONTENTS

COOKING DELIGHT

America's Best Homemade Recipes!

OVER *600* FAMILY-PROVEN RECIPES!

WOMEN'S CIRCLE Home Cooking

EDITOR
JUDI K. MERKEL

PRODUCTION
PATRICIA ELWELL
BEVERLY WEILAND
DARLENE ZEHR

PHOTOGRAPHY
RHONDA DAVIS
MARY JOYNT
NANCY SHARP

PUBLISHERS
CARL H. MUSELMAN
ARTHUR K. MUSELMAN

CHIEF EXECUTIVE OFFICER
JOHN ROBINSON

MARKETING DIRECTOR
SCOTT MOSS

(219) 589-8741
FAX: (219) 589-8093

Women's Circle Home Cooking cookbook is a collection of recipes obtained from *Women's Circle Home Cooking* magazine, published by House of White Birches, 306 East Parr Road, Berne, Indiana 46711.

Exclusively distributed by:

P.S.I. & Associates, Inc.
13322 SW 128th St.
Miami, Florida 33186
(305) 255-7959

Appetizers
TO SAVOR

BAKED TACO CHIPS

1 (6-1/4-ounce) bag taco-flavored corn chips
1 (4-ounce) can chopped, peeled, and seeded mild green chilies
1/4 pound Monterey Jack cheese, grated

Sprinkle chips on a pan sprayed with a release agent. Sprinkle chilies and cheese over chips. Heat 5-10 minutes in a 350-degree oven until cheese melts. Break apart, if necessary. Serve on platter or serving plate.

Leota Baxter, Ingalls, Kan.

SAVORY CHEESE BITES
Makes 7 dozen

1 cup water
1/8 teaspoon salt
4 eggs
1/2 cup butter
1 cup flour
1 cup shredded Swiss cheese

Combine water, butter, and salt in a pan; bring to a boil. Stir until butter melts. Add flour; stir vigorously until mixture leaves sides of pan to form a smooth ball. Remove from heat. Add eggs, one at a time; stir until well-blended. Return to heat and beat mixture until smooth. Remove from heat; stir in cheese. Drop batter by heaping teaspoonfuls onto a greased baking sheet. Bake 400 degrees for 20 minutes, or until puffed and golden brown.

Vickie Vogt, Kewaskum, Wis.

BRAUNSCHWEIGER BALL

1 (8-ounce) package cream cheese, softened
1 pound braunschweiger, at room temperature
1/4 cup mayonnaise
1/4 teaspoon garlic salt
2 tablespoons dill pickle juice
1/2-3/4 cup chopped dill pickle
1/4 cup (or more) chopped onion
3 drops Tabasco sauce
1 tablespoon Worcestershire sauce
1/2 cup salted peanuts, chopped

Combine half the cream cheese with the remaining ingredients, except peanuts; mix well. Spread in a mold. Chill for several hours. Unmold. Frost with remaining cream cheese. Garnish with chopped peanuts. Snack with assorted crackers or slices of party loaf bread.

Marcella Swigert, Monroe City, Mo.

CRACKERS TOASTED WITH PARMESAN CHEESE
Serves 8

1 tablespoon reduced-calorie mayonnaise
2 teaspoons margarine, melted
4 teaspoons Parmesan cheese
1/8 teaspoon garlic powder
1/8 teaspoon Worcestershire sauce
16 soda crackers (unsalted tops)
Paprika (optional)

Combine first 5 ingredients in small bowl; mix well. Spread 1/4 teaspoon mixture on each cracker. Place on baking sheet and sprinkle with paprika. Broil, 6-8 inches from heat, for 1 minute, or until lightly browned and bubbly. Serve immediately. (39 calories per 2 crackers)

Edna Askins, Greenville, Texas

DEVILED HAM AND CHEESE BALL

I sometimes put this in a cup or Christmas mug and give it as a gift.

2 (4¼-ounce) cans Underwood deviled ham
1 (8-ounce) package cream cheese, softened
1 (8-ounce) package shredded cheddar cheese
2 tablespoons freshly minced onion
1 tablespoon dried parsley flakes
1 tablespoon lemon juice
Liquid smoke to taste (approximately 1 teaspoon)
¾ teaspoon celery salt
½ teaspoon garlic powder
½ cup chopped nuts (or use pecan halves)

In a medium bowl combine all ingredients *except* nuts. Chill until slightly firm. Form into desired shape and garnish with nuts or pecan halves. Chill several hours or overnight. Serve with crackers.

Diantha Susan Hibbard, Rochester, N.Y.

HAM BALLS
Makes approximately 48 appetizers

4 cups ground lean ham
1/2 cup finely chopped onion
1/4 teaspoon pepper
2 eggs
1 cup plain bread crumbs

Combine and mix all ingredients. Shape into 1-inch balls. Place in a shallow pan and bake at 400 degrees for 25 minutes.

Sour Cream Gravy:
2 tablespoons shortening
2 tablespoons flour
1/4 teaspoon dill seed
1/4 teaspoon marjoram
1/2 cup water
1 1/2 cups sour cream

Melt shortening; add flour and seasonings. Cook until it bubbles. Add water and sour cream, stirring constantly. Cook until thick. Makes 2 cups sauce.

Serve *Ham Balls* with *Sour Cream Gravy;* provide toothpicks for dipping.

— Edna Peavy

DEVILED TURKEY BONBONS

1 cup cooked, finely chopped turkey
1 cup finely chopped nuts
1 tablespoon chopped onion
2 tablespoons chopped pimiento
1/4 teaspoon salt
Hot pepper sauce to taste
1/4 cup cream of mushroom soup.

Combine turkey and 1/2 cup nuts. Add remaining ingredients except remaining nuts; mix well. Shape into small balls and roll in remaining chopped nuts. Chill until serving time.

SIMPLE HORS D'OEUVRES

It's true that these tempting tidbits have a French name, may be very elaborate, and are usually met in hotels, but that's no reason for not serving them simply, in the home, for a little variety.

Try a bit of pink, moist salmon on a piece of rye toast . . . some ripe olives . . . celery, stuffed with cream cheese flavored with mayonnaise, salt and paprika, or filled with a mixture of equal parts cream cheese and Roquefort cheese which has been seasoned with Worcestershire sauce . . . slices of salami. . . . All these are as truly and delightfully "hors d'oeuvres" as the most elaborate arrangement of caviar and egg.

CHEESE SURPRISE APPETIZERS

2 cups grated sharp cheddar cheese
1/2 cup softened butter
1 cup flour
1 small jar green, pimiento-stuffed olives

Mix cheese, butter and flour to form dough. Shape into small balls about 1 inch in diameter. Flatten ball with hands; place one olive in center, wrap dough around it, sealing edges completely. Freeze until just before ready to serve. (These *must* be frozen.)

When ready to serve, place frozen appetizers on baking sheet and immediately place in 375-degree oven. Bake about 10 minutes, or until golden. Cheese will puff up and melt.

Eleonora R. Scholl, Glendale, Wis.

ASPARAGUS ROLLS
Makes 20 appetizers

20 slices bread
1 package frozen asparagus
1 5-ounce jar processed pimiento cheese spread

Trim crusts from bread slices; spread each with cheese. Cook asparagus until just tender. Chill. Lay one piece asparagus diagonally across slice of bread. Turn opposite corners over asparagus, overlapping. Press firmly to seal. Wrap several sandwiches together in waxed paper. Place in covered container and chill for several hours.

Dorrie Fortner

MEATBALL APPETIZERS
Makes about 8 dozen tiny meatballs and 2 cups sauce

1 1/2 pounds ground beef
2 eggs
1/4 cup milk
1 cup plain bread crumbs
1/4 cup chopped onion
1 1/2 teaspoons chopped parsley
1 1/2 teaspoons salt
1/8 teaspoon pepper
3 tablespoons oil
10-ounce bottle chili sauce
1/2 cup grape jelly
1 tablespoon instant coffee

Combine meat, eggs, milk, crumbs, onion, parsley, salt and pepper and mix well. Shape into tiny meatballs and brown well on all sides in skillet in hot oil. Remove meatballs from pan. Drain excess drippings, leaving just 2-3 tablespoons. Add chili sauce, jelly and instant coffee to pan drippings and simmer, stirring occasionally, until jelly melts (about 4 minutes). Add meatballs and simmer 10 more minutes. Serve on toothpicks.

Meatballs can be browned, refrigerated, then cooked with sauce just before serving.

Dorrie Fortner

ANTIPASTO

2 cans tuna fish, undrained
1 can anchovies, undrained
1 small jar stuffed olives, drained
1 small bottle cocktail onions, drained
1 medium can mushrooms, cut up and drained
1 jar sweet pickled cauliflower, drained and cut in small pieces
1 small jar tiny sweet pickles, drained and cut in small pieces
1 No. 2 can green beans, drained
1 cup carrots, cooked crisp, cut in small rings
1 bottle chili sauce
1 bottle catsup

Mix all ingredients. Add a little salad oil if not moist enough. Marinate in refrigerator for at least one day. Eat with crackers. Makes a delicious hors d'oeuvre.

Mrs. Dena Little, Bened, III.

RYE CRACKERS

2 cups rye flour
2 cups wheat flour
Salt to taste
1/4 teaspoon baking soda
1/2 cup vegetable oil
1 cup (or more) water
1 tablespoon caraway seeds

Mix together. Roll out thinly on floured surface. Cut into desired shapes. Bake on cookie sheets at 275 degrees for about 30 minutes.

Fay Duman, Eugene, OR

DILL CRACKERS

2/3 cup Wesson oil
1 envelope ranch-style dry salad dressing
1 teaspoon dill
1/2 teaspoon lemon pepper
1/4 teaspoon garlic salt
10 ounce package oyster crackers

Mix all together, except crackers. Coat crackers with mixture, tossing until well coated, about 5 or 6 minutes.

Edna Askins, Greenville, TX

NUT BALLS

1 stick butter
1 cup pecans
1 teaspoon vanilla
2 tablespoons sugar
1 cup flour

Mix all ingredients and roll into tiny balls and bake at 250 degrees for one hour. Cool slightly and roll in confectioners' sugar. Roll in sugar again about half-hour later.

Karin Shea Fedders, Dameron, MD

TUNA SPREAD

1 can tuna (water packed), drained

1 (8-ounce) package cream cheese, softened
1 small onion, finely chopped
Salt and pepper to taste

Blend all ingredients until smooth. Serve with crackers. This can be rolled into a log and used for all types of festive entertaining.

Mrs. John J. Jenkins, Steubenville, OH

NUTS, BOLTS AND SCREWS

1 pound pecans
1 large box Cherrios
1 medium box stick pretzels
1 tablespoon Worcestershire sauce
1 box Wheat Chex
2 tablespoons salt
1 tablespoon garlic salt
1 pound oleo or butter
8   8

Melt butter in large roaster. Pour in all cereals, nuts and pretzels and seasonings. set oven at 200 degrees. Stir every 15 minutes for 1 hour.

Sue Hibbard, Rochester, NY

WHEAT GERM CRUNCHIES
Makes 3-1/2 dozen

1/2 cup all-purpose flour
1/2 teaspoon soda
2 teaspoons baking powder
1/4 teaspoon salt
1 cup brown sugar, firmly packed
1/2 cup shortening
1 egg, beaten
1/2 teaspoon vanilla
1/2 cup coconut
1/2 cup uncooked oatmeal
1 cup wheat germ
1-1/2 cups corn or wheat flakes

Sift flour, soda, baking powder and salt. Cream shortening and sugar. Add egg and vanilla. Add dry ingredients and wheat germ. Mix well. Stir in coconut, oatmeal and cornflakes just enough to mix. Drop by teaspoons on greased cookie sheet or roll into walnut-sized balls with fingers and place on greased cookie

sheet. Bake 15 minutes at 350 degrees.

Barbara Beauregard-Smith, Northfield, South Australia, Australia

TAFFY APPLES

1 large can crushed pineapple (save drained juice)
2-1/2 cups miniature marshmallows
1 egg
1 tablespoon flour
12 ounces Cool Whip
3/4 cup cocktail or Spanish peanuts
1-1/2 tablespoons vinegar
1/2 cup sugar
4-6 apples, unpeeled and chopped

Combine drained pineapple and marshmallows; refrigerate overnight. Beat pineapple juice, egg, flour, vinegar and sugar; heat until thick, stirring constantly. Cool and refrigerate overnight, separate from pineapple.

Next day: Mix sauce and Cool Whip; add peanuts, marshmallow mixture and apples; stir. Refrigerate at least 2 hours before serving.

Debbie Jones, Walnutport, PA

CELERY PINWHEELS

1 medium stalk celery
1 (3-ounce) package cream cheese
2 tablespoons crumbled Roquefort cheese
Mayonnaise
Worcestershire sauce

Clean celery and separate branches. Blend together the softened cream cheese with the Roquefort cheese. Add mayonnaise to make the mixture of spreading consistency and season with a dash of Worcestershire sauce. Fill the branches of celery with cheese mixture. Press branches back into the original form of the stalk. Roll in waxed paper and chill overnight in refrigerator. Just before serving, slice celery crosswise forming pinwheels. Arrange pinwheels on crisp lettuce for serving.

Marcella Swigert, Monroe City, MO

Beverages
REFRESHING

ICED TEA A LA MODE
Serves 3

2 cups double-strength cold tea
1 pint vanilla ice cream

Blend tea and ice cream until smooth and pour into a tall glass.

PEANUT BUTTER SHAKE
Makes 4 cups

2 cups milk
1 pint vanilla ice cream
1/4 cup creamy peanut butter

Combine all ingredients in container of electric blender; process until smooth. Serve at once.

Bertha Fowler, Woodruff, S.C.

HIGH-CALCIUM BANANA SHAKE
Serves 6

2 cups non-fat milk
1/4 cup non-fat dry milk
1 tablespoon vanilla extract
2 tablespoons fructose
1 banana
1 cup ice cubes

Place all ingredients in a blender and blend until smooth. Serve immediately, preferably in a chilled glass. (90 calories per shake)

SWEET CHERRY SODA
Serves 2

1/3 cup ruby-red cherry sauce
2 scoops vanilla ice cream
Club soda
2 whole sweet cherries

In a blender container, combine cherry sauce and ice cream. Cover and process until smooth. Pour half of mixture into each of 2 tall glasses. Fill glasses with club soda. Garnish each serving with a whole cherry.

Annie Cmehil, New Castle, Ind.

SPICED PEACH PUNCH
Serves 12 (Hot drink)

1 (46 ounce) can peach nectar
1 (20 ounce) can orange juice
1/2 cup brown sugar, firmly packed
3 (3 inch) pieces stick cinnamon, broken
1/2 teaspoon whole cloves
2 tablespoons lime juice

Combine peach nectar, orange juice, and brown sugar in a large saucepan. Tie cinnamon sticks and cloves in a cheesecloth bag and drop into saucepan.

Heat slowly, stirring constantly, until sugar dissolves; simmer 10 minutes. Stir in lime juice; ladle into mugs. You may garnish with cinnamon sticks. Serve warm.

Mrs. C. Michele Mastindill, Calhan, Colo.

CRANBERRY COCKTAIL PUNCH
Serves 30

2 (32 ounce) bottles cranberry juice cocktail, chilled
2 cups orange juice, chilled
1 cup pineapple juice, chilled
1/2 cup sugar
1/2 cup lemon juice, chilled
1 (28 ounce) bottle ginger ale, chilled
1 tray ice cubes
Lemon slices for garnish

In large punch bowl, stir first 5 ingredients until sugar is dissolved. Add remaining ingredients, except lemon slices, which should be added just before serving.

Leona Teodori, Warren, Mich.

CAFE SWISS MOCHA

1/4 cup powdered non-fat dairy creamer or non-fat dry milk
1/4 cup instant coffee
1/3 cup sugar
2 tablespoons cocoa

Shake in jar to mix. Use 1 level tablespoon, to 6 ounces boiling water. Put 1 heaping teaspoon into 1 cup cold water; heat in microwave for 1 minute, 15 seconds; let sit a moment; stir.

Ann Stuzee, Lincoln, Neb.

COFFEE EGGNOG

2 eggs, separated
1/3 cup sugar
1/3 cup instant coffee
Dash salt
1 teaspoon vanilla extract
2 cups milk, chilled
3/4 cup water
1 cup heavy cream, whipped
Shaved unsweetened chocolate

In small bowl, beat egg whites at high speed until soft peaks form. Gradually, beat in sugar until stiff peaks form. In large bowl, beat egg yolks until lemon colored. Gradually beat in coffee, salt, vanilla, milk, and 3/4 cup water. Stir in egg-white mixture and whipped cream; mix well. Serve well chilled, with chocolate shavings sprinkled over each serving.

Alpha Wilson, Roswell, N.M.

EGGNOG
Makes 6 large glasses

4 eggs
4 cups milk
4 tablespoons lemon juice
1/2 cup cream
1/8 teaspoon nutmeg
1/8 teaspoon salt
1/3 cup sugar

Beat eggs until thick and lemon colored. Add sugar, salt, nutmeg, and lemon juice; add ice cold milk and cream. Beat with mixer until frothy.

Betty Klopfenstein, Waterman, Ill.

FRIENDSHIP TEA

1 pound 2 ounce jar Tang
3/4 to 1 cup instant tea
2 tablespoons cinnamon
1 pound package dry lemonade
2-1/2 cups sugar

Mix together; store in closed container. To use: add 2 spoonfuls of mixture to one cup of hot water.

Marcella Swigert, Monroe City, MO

SPICED TEA

1 cup instant tea
2 cups Tang
1/3 cup lemonade mix (crystals)
2 tablespoons sugar
1 teaspoon cinnamon
1 teaspoon ground cloves

Mix thoroughly. Keep in airtight container. Use 1 rounded teaspoonful per cup hot water.

Florence Kloss, Lebanon, Ore.

SPICED TEA

1-1/2 cups instant tea
1 cup Tang
1 (3-ounce) package lemonade mix
2-1/2 cups sugar
1 teaspoon cloves
2 teaspoons cinnamon

Mix all ingredients. Use 2 teaspoonfuls to one cup hot water.
Dovie Lucy, McLoud, Okla.

NEW ENGLAND SWEET CIDER PUNCH

3 oranges
1 lemon
1/4 cup maraschino cherries
1 quart cider

Extract juices from oranges and lemon; add to cider together with cherries. Chill thoroughly before serving.

Lucy Dowd, Sequim, WA

FRUIT SMASH PUNCH
Makes 1 gallon

2 cups hot water
1 package raspberry gelatin
1 package cherry gelatin
6 cups cold water

1-1/2 cups lime or lemon juice
5 cups fresh or frozen orange juice
1/2 to 1 cup sugar
5 or 6 ripe bananas
1 quart chilled ginger ale

Make gelatin in usual manner; add cold water and fruit juices; stir in sugar. Just before serving, mash or whip bananas until smooth and creamy. Beat into mixture. Add ginger ale, the last minute.

Marcella Swigert, Monroe City, Mo.

PEACH PICK ME UP
Makes 3-1/2 cups

2 containers (8-ounce each) peach yogurt
6 ounces frozen apple juice concentrate
1/2 teaspoon almond extract
3 ice cubes

Place all ingredients in blender container; cover. Blend on high speed until ice is reduced to small pieces and mixture is well combined. Serve immediately in tall chilled glasses.

Mrs. Peggy Fowler Revels, Woodruff, SC

CHOCOLATE TOFU NUTRITIONAL SHAKE
Serves 4

3 cups milk
1 cup Silken Tofu, drained
2 bananas, broken into chunks
4 tablespoons instant cocoa mix powder
2 tablespoon honey
1 tablespoon wheat germ

Combine ingredients in blender, 1/2 at a time; whirl until smooth and creamy. Serve cold. Wonderful as a complete protein breakfast drink or for snack any time.

Any fresh fruit in season such as berries, cantaloupe or papaya can be substituted for the chocolate flavor.

Pour into tall glasses, sprinkle with nutmeg.

Hyacinth Rizzo, Snyder, NY

Cakes
TO BAKE

CARROT ALMOND CAKE
Makes 1 cake

4 eggs
1 cup oil
1 cup honey
1 cup white flour
1 1/2 cups whole-wheat flour
2 teaspoons baking powder
1/2 teaspoon baking soda
1/2 teaspoon salt
1 teaspoon vanilla extract
1 1/2 cups shredded carrots
1 cup chopped almonds
1/2 cup raisins

Beat eggs with oil and honey. Mix together dry ingredients; stir into egg mixture, beating well. Add vanilla extract, carrots, almonds and raisins.

Pour batter into well-greased tube pan and bake in a preheated 350-degree oven for about 1 hour.

Jean Baker, Chula Vista, Calif.

ALL-TOGETHER CAKE AND FROSTING

1 (8-ounce) package cream cheese
1/2 cup shortening
1 teaspoon vanilla
6 cups confectioners' sugar
1/3 cup warm milk
2/3 cup cocoa
1 teaspoon instant coffee
1/4 cup melted shortening
3 eggs, beaten
3/4 cup milk
2-1/4 cups flour
3 teaspoons baking powder
1 teaspoon salt

Combine first 7 ingredients and mix well. Divide mixture in half, reserving one half for frosting. To remaining half, beat in shortening, eggs, and milk alternately with the dry ingredients. Grease and flour 2 (8-inch) cake pans and pour in cake mixture, dividing evenly. Bake at 350 degrees for 25-30 minutes. When cool, frost with the reserved frosting.

Agnes Ward, Erie, Pa.

CANTALOUPE CAKE

3/4 cup oil
1 3/4 cups sugar
3 eggs
2 cups self-rising flour
1 teaspoon cinnamon
1 teaspoon baking soda
1 cup fresh cantaloupe, diced
1 cup fresh apples, diced
1 cup white raisins

Combine oil, sugar and eggs; beat until smooth. Add flour, cinnamon and baking soda; mix until smooth.

Fold in cantaloupe, apple and raisins. Spread mixture into a greased 9x13-inch pan. Bake in a 375-degree oven for 20 minutes. Lower temperature to 325 degrees and bake 10 more minutes; cool and frost.

Frosting:
Frost with 7 1/2-ounce box of Jiffy Frosting Mix. Add 1/2 teaspoon vanilla to the prepared mix. (Follow directions according to box.)

Phoeba McKinley, Springfield, Ohio

GERMAN CHOCOLATE CAKE

1 package sweet cooking chocolate
1/2 cup boiling water
2 cups sugar
1 cup shortening
4 eggs, separated
2-1/2 cups flour
1 teaspoon baking soda
1/2 teaspoon salt
1 cup buttermilk
1 teaspoon vanilla
Frosting (recipe follows)

Dissolve chocolate in boiling water. Cream sugar and shortening until light and fluffy. Add egg yolks, one at a time, beat well. Sift dry ingredients together and add alternately with buttermilk. Add chocolate and vanilla. Fold in 4 stiffly-beaten egg whites. Place in 12x8-inch pan. Bake at 350 degrees for 35 minutes or until tested done.

Frosting:
1 stick butter
1/2 cup evaporated milk
3 beaten egg yolks
1 cup sugar
1/2 teaspoon salt
1 cup coconut
1 teaspoon vanilla

Combine butter, evaporated milk, egg yolks, sugar and salt in a saucepan. Cook until mixture thickens; stirring constantly. Add coconut and vanilla; mix well. Cool and spread on cake.

Agnes Ward, Erie, Pa.

"500" CAKE

1/2 cup butter
1 cup sugar
2 eggs
1/2 cup sour cream
1 cup mashed bananas
2 cups flour
1/2 teaspoon salt
1 teaspoon baking soda
1 teaspoon baking powder
1/2 cup chopped dates
1/2 cup chopped nuts
1 teaspoon vanilla

Cream butter and sugar. Add eggs. Add sour cream and mashed bananas alternately with sifted dry ingredients. Fold in nuts and dates which have been dusted with a little of the flour. Add vanilla. Pour into greased cake pans or cupcake tins. Bake at 350 degrees for 30 minutes.
Note: Buttermilk may be used instead of sour cream.

Leah Maria Daub, Milwaukee, Wis.

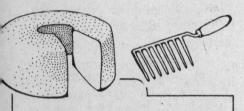

SOUR CREAM CAKE

1/2 cup chopped pecans
1/2 cup sugar
1 teaspoon cinnamon
4 eggs
1 package yellow cake mix
1 package instant vanilla pudding mix
1/2 cup oil
1 cup sour cream

Combine pecans, sugar, and cinnamon; set aside. Combine remaining ingredients; beat for 4 minutes. Spoon half the batter into well-greased and floured bundt or spring pan. Sprinkle half of the pecan mixture over batter, then add remaining batter and remaining pecan mixture over top. Bake in a preheated 350-degree oven for 1 hour. Cake may be glazed with thin icing or dusted with confectioners' sugar.

Leota M. Baxter, Ingalls, Kan.

APPLE CAKE WITH TOPPING

3 cups flour
2 cups sugar
1-1/2 teaspoons soda
1 teaspoon salt
3/4 cup cooking oil
2 eggs, beaten
1 teaspoon vanilla
1 cup chopped walnuts
3 cups chopped apples (unpeeled)

Mix oil, sugar, and eggs. Add dry ingredients and vanilla by hand. Add nuts and apples. Bake at 350 degrees for 1 hour in a well-greased tube or bundt pan. Remove from oven and pour topping over cake. Return cake to oven and bake 15 minutes more. Slide knife around cake to loosen.

Topping:
1 cup light brown sugar
1 stick butter or margarine
1/4 cup orange juice

Cook over low heat for 3 minutes after the mixture starts boiling. Pour over cake as directed above.

Trenda Leigh, Richmond, Va.

POPPY SEED CAKE
Serves 10-12

1 (18-1/2–ounce) package yellow cake mix
1 (3-3/4-ounce) package instant vanilla pudding mix
4 eggs
1 cup sour cream
1/2 cup (1 stick) melted butter
1/2 cup cream sherry
1/3 cup poppy seeds

Preheat oven to 350 degrees. Grease bundt cake pan and flour lightly, shaking out excess. Combine all ingredients in large bowl and beat 5 minutes with electric mixer. Pour batter into pan. Bake until tester in center comes out clean, about 1 hour. Let cool completely in pan. Invert onto platter and serve. Garnish each serving with sliced fruit.

Frances Falk, W. Palm Beach, Fla.

ORANGE PEANUT–BUTTER CAKE
Serves 12

2 oranges
1 (18-ounce) package yellow cake mix with pudding
1-1/4 cups water
3 eggs
1/2 cup peanut butter
1 teaspoon ground cinnamon
1/3 cup packed brown sugar

Grate peeling from oranges; reserve. Peel oranges and cut into bite–size pieces; drain well. In large bowl, combine cake mix, water, eggs, peanut butter, and cinnamon; mix according to package directions. Stir in orange peel and pieces. Pour batter into greased and floured 13x9x2-inch cake pan. Sprinkle brown sugar over top of batter. Bake at 350 degrees for 35-40 minutes or until done. Serve warm or cool.

Kit Rollins, Cedarburg, Wis.

PRALINE CHEESECAKE
Serves 12

Crust:
1-1/2 cups graham cracker crumbs
6 tablespoons butter, melted
1/4 cup sugar
2 tablespoons pecans, finely chopped

Filling:
1-1/2 pounds cream cheese
1 cup dark brown sugar
2 tablespoons flour
3 eggs
1/2 teaspoon vanilla
1/4 cup pecans, finely chopped

Combine all crust ingredients. Press on bottom and up sides of 9-inch springform pan.

For filling beat together cheese and sugar until creamy. Add flour, then eggs. Blend in vanilla and pecans. Pour into crust. Bake at 350 degrees for 50 minutes. Allow to cool. Chill in refrigerator before serving.

Lisa Varner, Baton Rouge, La.

PEACHES AND CREAM CHEESECAKE

1-1/2 cups flour
1 teaspoon salt
2 eggs
1 cup milk
2 teaspoons baking powder
2 small packages regular vanilla
   pudding
1 (20-ounce) can drained peaches,
   reserve juice
2 (8-ounce) packages cream
   cheese
1 cup sugar
6 tablespoons peach juice
1 teaspoon cinnamon
2 tablespoons sugar

Combine first six ingredients and beat 2 minutes at medium speed. Pour into greased 9x13-inch pan. Arrange peaches over top of batter. Combine cheese, sugar, and peach juice; beat for 2 minutes. Spoon over peaches. Mix sugar and cinnamon together and sprinkle over the top. Bake at 350 degrees for 30-35 minutes.

Kit Rollins, Cedarburg, Wis.

BLUEBERRY SNACK-CAKE
Serves 9

1/4 cup butter or margarine
1 cup sugar
1 egg
1-1/2 cups flour
2 teaspoons baking powder
1/2 cup milk
1/2 teaspoon almond flavoring
1 cup fresh or frozen blueberries

Topping:
1/2 teaspoon cinnamon
2 tablespoons sugar
2 tablespoons melted butter

Cream butter and sugar; add egg and beat well. Mix flour and baking powder together and add to creamed mixture alternately with milk mixed with almond flavoring. Beat until smooth. Fold in blueberries. Pour into greased 8x8x2-inch pan. Mix together

cinnamon, sugar and melted butter; sprinkle over top. Bake at 350 degrees for 25-30 minutes, or until it tests done.

GERMAN CHOCOLATE UPSIDE-DOWN CAKE

1 cup coconut
1 cup chopped pecans
1 oackage German Chocolate
   cake mix

Mix these two ingredients and put into a greased 9x13-inch pan. Mix 1 package German chocolate cake mix according to directions and pour on top of coconut pecan mixture.

In saucepan put 1 stick margarine and 1 (8-ounce) package cream cheese, softened. Heat until mixture is warm enough to stir in 1-pound box confectioners' sugar. Spoon over top of cake mix. Bake at 350 degrees for 35-40 minutes. Do not cut until cooled.

Hazel C. Jackson, Glade Spring, Va.

RASPBERRY CREAM COFFEE CAKE
Serves 8-10

1 (3-ounce) package cream
   cheese
1/4 cup butter or margarine
2 cups packaged biscuit mix
1/4 cup milk
1/2 cup raspberry preserves
1 cup sifted confectioners' sugar
1 to 2 tablespoons milk
1/2 teaspoon vanilla

In medium mixing bowl cut the cream cheese and butter into biscuit mix until crumbly. Stir in 1/4 cup milk. Turn onto a lightly floured surface. Knead 8 to 10 strokes. On waxed paper, roll dough to a 12x8-inch rectangle. Invert onto a greased baking sheet. Remove paper.

Spread preserves down center of dough. Make 2-1/2-inch long cuts at 1-inch intervals on long sides. Fold strips over the filling. Bake in a 375 degree oven about 20 minutes or until golden brown. Let coffee cake cool 5 minutes before frosting.

In small mixing bowl stir together sugar, the 1 to 2 tablespoons milk, and vanilla. Drizzle over slightly cooled coffee cake. Serve warm.

EASIEST CHERRY CAKE
Serves 12

1 (14-ounce) can crushed pineapple
2 (20-ounce) cans cherry pie
   filling
1 box white or yellow cake mix
Nuts, coconut, or whipped
   topping
1 1/4 sticks margarine

Spray 9x13-inch cake pan with non-stick spray or grease with shortening. Spread crushed pineapple in pan. Sprinkle cake mix over pineapple and cherry pie filling. Add 1/2 cups nuts or coconut on top. Dot with margarine. Bake at 350 degrees for 1 hour or until golden brown. Top with whipped topping, if desired.

STRAWBERRY CAKE

1 box white cake mix
1 box strawberry gelatin
1 cup strawberries, mashed
1 cup Crisco oil
4 eggs, beaten
1/2 cup sweet milk
1/2 cup coconut
1/2 cup nuts, finely chopped

Combine all ingredients; beat. Bake at 300 degrees until cake springs back when touched.

Frosting:
1 (1-pound) box powdered sugar
1 stick margarine, melted (8 tablespoons)
1/4 cup mashed drained strawberries
1/4 cup coconut

ZUCCHINI PINEAPPLE CAKE

3 eggs
2 cups sugar
2 teaspoons vanilla
1 cup cooking oil
2 cups zucchini, peeled and grated
3 cups flour
1 teaspoon baking powder
1/2 cup raisins
1 teaspoon salt
1 teaspoon nuts
1 cup crushed pineapple, drained

Beat eggs until fluffy; add sugar, vanilla, oil, and zucchini. Blend well. Add dry ingredients and mix well. Stir in pineapple, raisins, and nuts.

Bake in one large greased and floured loaf pan or two small loaf pans. Bake in 325-degree oven for 1 hour. Cool in pan on wire rack. When cool wrap in foil to store.

Mrs. L. Mayer, Richmond, VA.

HAZELNUT CHEESECAKE

1-1/2 pounds cream cheese, at room temperature
1 cup sugar
3 eggs
1 cup hazelnuts, finely chopped
1 teaspoon vanilla extract
1 cup heavy cream
2 tablespoons rum
Bread crumbs

Preheat oven to 375 degrees. In bowl of electric mixer, combine cream cheese, sugar, eggs, hazelnuts, vanilla extract, heavy cream, and rum. Butter a 10x3-inch deep layer-cake or springform pan and coat with bread crumbs. Pour batter into pan. Put pan with the cheesecake batter into a deep pan. Fill outside pan with water until water reaches halfway up sides of cheesecake pan. Bake for 45 minutes. Cool and serve.

Irene Donner, Jamestown, N.Y.

ELEGANT APPLE CHEESECAKE

2 (8-ounce) packages cream cheese, softened
1 (16-ounce) carton cream-style cottage cheese
1-1/2 cups sugar
4 eggs
3 tablespoons cornstarch
1-1/2 tablespoons lemon juice
1 tablespoon vanilla
1/4 pound butter, melted and cooled
2 cups dairy sour cream
1 (21-ounce) can apple pie filling

Lightly butter a 9-inch springform pan. In a large mixing bowl, combine cheeses; beat until light and fluffy. Add sugar; blend well. Add eggs, one at a time, beating well after each addition. Add cornstarch, lemon juice, vanilla, and butter; blend until smooth. Blend in sour cream. Pour batter into prepared pan. Bake at 325 degrees for 1 hour and 10 minutes, or until center is set. Turn oven off. Let cheesecake stand in oven, with the door closed, for 2 hours. Cool completely. Chill 6 hours. Spoon apple pie filling over the top.

Gwen Campbell, Sterling, Va.

APRICOT NECTAR CAKE

1 (46-ounce) can apricot nectar
7 tablespoons cornstarch
1-1/2 cups sugar
1 large angel food cake

Combine the first three ingredients and cook over medium heat until mixture becomes clear and bubbly. Watch closely, stirring constantly. Take off heat and pour over a large angel food cake, which has been torn into small pieces and placed in a greased 9x13 glass baking dish. Cover and allow it to chill 24 hours in refrigerator. Serve with a scoop of whipped topping. This is a quick and easy cake that is absolutely delicious!!

Denise Winchell, Pleasant Hill, Ill.

CRANBERRY CAKE

3 cups sifted flour
1-1/2 cups sugar
1 teaspoon soda
1 teaspoon salt
1 cup mayonnaise
1 cup chopped nuts
3/4 cup whole cranberry sauce
2 tablespoons orange peel
1/3 cup orange juice

Sift dry ingredients. Add remaining ingredients. Pour into greased 9x13-inch pan. Bake at 350 degrees for 45 minutes.

Icing:
2 tablespoons butter
2 cups sifted confectioners' sugar
1/4 cup whole cranberry sauce

Combine ingredients and spread on hot cake.

Sharon McClatchey, Muskogee, Okla.

ORANGE HONEY CAKE

2 cups sifted cake flour
3-1/2 teaspoons baking powder
3/4 teaspoon salt
1/2 cup butter or shortening
1/2 cup sugar
2/3 cup honey
2 egg yolks
1/2 cup orange juice
2 egg whites, stiffly beaten

Sift flour; measure; add baking powder and salt; sift 3 times. Cream butter thoroughly; add sugar gradually; cream until light and fluffy. Add honey; blend. Add egg yolks and beat thoroughly. Add flour alternately with orange juice, a small amount at a time, beating well after each addition until smooth. Fold in egg whites. Bake in 2 greased 9-inch layer pans in 350-degree oven for 30-35 minutes.

Agnes Ward, Erie, Pa.

CHUNKY CHOCOLATE CUPCAKES

Makes 1 dozen

1 cup sifted flour
1 cup sugar
1-1/2 teaspoons baking powder
1/2 teaspoon salt
2 eggs
1/4 cup cooking oil
1 teaspoon vanilla
1/4 cup milk
1-1/2 ounces unsweetened chocolate, chopped
Creamy Orange Frosting (recipe follows)

Sift together flour, sugar, baking powder and salt into bowl. Combine eggs, oil, vanilla, and milk in small bowl. Beat well. Combine egg mixture with dry ingredients; beat until blended. Stir in chocolate. Spoon batter into paper-lined 2-1/2-inch muffin-pan cups, filling two-thirds full. Bake in 400-degree oven 20-25 minutes or until cupcakes test done. Remove from pans, and cool on racks. Frost with Creamy Orange Frosting.

Creamy Orange Frosting:
Combine 2-1/2 cups sifted confectioners' sugar, 3 tablespoons soft butter or margarine, 1 teaspoon grated orange rind, and 2 tablespoons orange juice. Beat until smooth.

Barbara Beauregard-Smith, South Australia

LEMON-BLUEBERRY CAKE

1 (17-ounce) package lemon cake mix
1 cup sour cream or plain yogurt
4 eggs
1 can blueberries in heavy syrup

Mix cake mix, eggs, and sour cream together in large mixing bowl. Mix first on low speed of electric mixer and then on high speed until smooth and creamy. Drain blueberries; rinse, then drain again. Fold blueberries into cake mixture. Pour

into greased and floured tube or bundt pan and bake in preheated 350–degree oven for 35-45 minutes until top springs back when lightly touched. Bake 15 minutes more before removing from oven. When cool, sprinkle with powdered sugar. Serve with a sauce, if desired.

Agnes Ward, Erie, Pa.

WALNUT POUND CAKE

3-1/2 cups flour
1 pound margarine or butter, softened
1/4 teaspoon salt
1 pound confectioners' sugar
6 eggs, unbeaten
1 teaspoon vanilla
1 teaspoon fresh lemon juice
1-1/2 cups walnuts, chopped

Cream butter and sugar until soft. Add salt, vanilla, juice, flour, and eggs. Beat at medium speed for a full 10 minutes until mixture is light and creamy.

Grease a round 10-inch tube pan. Add nuts to batter and blend well. Pour batter into pan. Bake at 350 degrees for 1-1/2 hours. Cake will crack and should be lightly brown. Freezes well.

Vivian Nikanow, Chicago, Ill.

GLAZED FRESH APPLE CAKE

2 cups sugar
1 cup butter or margarine
1 teaspoon soda
1/2 teaspoon salt
3 cups diced apples
1/2 cup chopped nuts
1/2 cup raisins
3 cups flour
3 eggs, well beaten
1-1/2 teaspoons vanilla
1 teaspoon cinnamon

Cream sugar and oil. Add eggs and beat well. Add dry ingredients and vanilla; beat. Add by hand apples,

nuts, and raisins. Bake in tube pan at 350 degrees for 1 hour and 20 minutes.

Glaze:
1/2 stick margarine
1/2 cup brown sugar
2 tablespoons milk

Combine all ingredients in small saucepan and cook over medium heat 3 minutes. Cool and drizzle over warm cake.

Mrs. P. B. Brothers, Richmond, Va.

CRANBERRY-SAUCE CAKE

3 cups flour
2 teaspoons baking soda
1 cup mayonnaise
1 (16-ounce) can whole cranberry sauce, reserving 1/4 cup
1/2 cup orange juice
1 tablespoon grated orange rind
1 cup sugar
1 teaspoon salt
1 cup chopped nuts

Grease 9-inch tube pan. Line bottom with waxed paper. Mix dry ingredients into large bowl. Add other ingredients, except 1/4 cup reserved cranberry sauce, and mix well. Bake in 350-degree oven for 1-1/4 hours. Remove from pan and cool completely before icing.

Icing:
Mix 3 tablespoons soft butter with 2 cups confectioners' sugar and 1/4 cup reserved cranberry sauce. Beat until creamy and spread on cake.

LEMON CRACKLE CAKE

20 soda crackers (2" squares)
3/4 cup brown sugar
1 cup flour
1 teaspoon baking soda
1/2 cup butter or oleo
1 cup coconut

Crush crackers in bowl; add brown sugar, flour and soda. Work in butter; add coconut. Pat 3/4 of mixture into greased and floured 8 or 9-inch baking pan. Carefully spread on filling; cover with rest of crumb mixture. Bake at 350 degrees for 30 to 35 minutes or until slightly brown.

Lemon Filling:

1 cup sugar
2 tablespoons cornstarch
1 cup cold water
2 eggs, beaten
Juice of 2 lemons or 1/2 cup lemon juice
1/4 cup butter
1 teaspoons vanilla

In sauce pan, combine sugar and cornstarch. Gradually stir in water. Add remaining ingredients. Cook over medium heat until thickened. Cool before adding to cake.

Mrs. Stanley M. Lewis, Sussex, WI

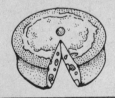

ORANGE - KISS ME CAKE

Serves 12

1-6 ounce can (3/4 cup) frozen orange juice concentrate, (thawed)
2 cups flour
1 cup sugar
1 teaspoon baking soda
1 teaspoon salt
1/2 cup shortening
1/2 cup milk
2 eggs
1 cup raisins
1/3 cup chopped walnuts

Grease and flour bottom of 13 x 9 inch pan. Combine 1/2 cup orange juice concentrate with remaining ingredients in large mixer bowl. Blend at lowest speed of mixer for 30 seconds. Beat 3 minutes at medium speed. Pour into pan. Bake at 350 degrees for 40-45 minutes. Drizzle remaining orange juice concentrate over warm cake; sprinkle with sugar-nut topping (recipe follows).

Sugar-Nut Topping:

1/3 cup sugar
1/4 cup chopped walnuts
1 teaspoon cinnamon

Combine all ingredients in small bowl.

Barbara Nowakowski, N. Tonawanda, NY

CREAM CHEESE TOPPED PINEAPPLE CAKE

2 eggs
2 cups sugar
2 cups all-purpose flour
1 (20-ounce) can crushed pineapple packed in own juice, undrained
1/2 cup chopped pecans
2 teaspoons baking soda
1 teaspoon vanilla

Preheat oven to 350 degrees. Lightly grease 9 x 13-inch baking pan. Beat eggs in large bowl until light and fluffy. Add sugar and beat until thick. Stir in flour, pineapple, pecans, baking soda, and vanilla; mix thoroughly. Pour into pan and bake until tester inserted in center comes out clean. Bake 40-45 minutes. Let cake cool in pan on rack.

Cream Cheese Frosting:

2 cups powdered sugar
1 (8-ounce) cream cheese (room temperature)
1/4 cup (1/2 stick) butter (room temperature)
1 teaspoon vanilla
Additional chopped pecans for garnish

Combine powdered sugar, cream cheese, butter, and vanilla; mix until fluffy. Spread over cooled cake and sprinkle with chopped nuts. Cut into squares to serve.

This is a quick and easy cake to make and is delicious!

Lois Conway, Coloma, WI

PINEAPPLE UPSIDE DOWN CAKE

1/2 cup packed brown sugar
1/4 cup butter
1 - can sliced pineapple (drained - reserve 1 tablespoon juice)
Maraschino cherries, halved
1 - 16 ounce container frozen pancake batter, thawed
1/4 cup granulated sugar

Heat oven to 350 degrees. Melt butter and put in glass pie plate. Add brown sugar and stir till smooth. Cut pineapple slices in half and arrange pineapple and cherries on sugar mixture in a decorative manner. Open top of pancake batter container completely. Add granulated sugar and reserve pineapple juice. Stir well. Pour over pineapple. Bake 30-35 minutes until golden brown and toothpick inserted in center comes out clean. Cool 5 minutes. Loosen edges of cake with small knife. Invert cake on serving platter.

This is a delicious and unusual way to make an upside-down cake. If pineapple is arranged pinwheel fashion, with a half-cherry in each curve, you get a lot more fruit on your cake.

Helen Weissinger, Levittown, PA

MISSISSIPPI MUD CAKE

2 cups sugar
1 cup soft margarine
4 eggs
1-1/2 cups flour
1/3 cup cocoa
2 teaspoons vanilla
1/4 teaspoon salt
1 cup chopped nuts
1 bag small marshmallows

Mix sugar, margarine, and eggs until well blended. Add dry ingredients to above mixture; add vanilla and chopped nuts. Grease and flour an oblong pan, bake at 300 degrees for 30 minutes. Remove from oven and spread marshmallows on top; return to oven for 10 minutes or until marshmallows have melted (watch closely).

Icing:
1 stick margarine
1 box powdered sugar
1/2 cup evaporated milk
1/3 cup cocoa
1 teaspoon vanilla
1 cup chopped nuts

Mix all ingredients together; spread on cake when cool.

Marie Mitchell, Conroe, TX

ALMOND JOY CAKE

2 cups flour
2 cups sugar
1 teaspoon soda
1 stick margarine
3 tablespoons cocoa
1/2 cup shortening
1 cup water
2 beaten eggs
1 teaspoon vanilla
1/2 cup buttermilk

Combine sugar, flour, and soda. Boil together margarine, cocoa, shortening, and water. Pour over flour mixture. Add eggs, buttermilk, and vanilla; mix. Bake in greased and floured 13 x 9-inch pan. Cool.

Filling:
1 can evaporated milk
1 jar marshmallow creme
1 cup sugar
2 cans Angel Flake coconut

Heat milk, marshmallow creme, and sugar until creme and sugar melt. Stir in coconut. Pour over cake.

Icing:
3 tablespoons cocoa
1 stick margarine
6 tablespoons milk
1 package confectioners' sugar
1 cup toasted, whole almonds
1 teaspoon vanilla

Boil cocoa, margarine, and milk. Pour over sugar and stir until smooth. Add almonds and vanilla. Spread over filling.

Suzanne Dawson, Cypress, TX

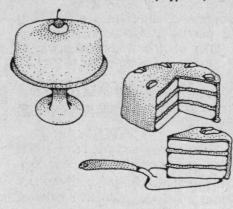

KAHLUA CHEESE CAKE
Serves 12-14

Chocolate crumb crust (recipe follows)
1-1/2 cups semi-sweet chocolate pieces
1/4 cup Kahlua
2 tablespoons butter
2 large eggs, beaten
1/3 cup granulated sugar
1/4 teaspoon salt
1 cup sour cream
2 (8-ounce) packages cream cheese, softened, cut in pieces
Whipped cream and chocolate leaves (optional)

Prepare chocolate crumb crust. Preheat oven to 350 degrees. In small saucepan, over medium heat, melt chocolate with Kahlua and butter; stir until smooth. Set aside. In bowl, combine eggs, sugar, and salt. Add sour cream; blend well. Add cream cheese to egg mixture; beat until smooth. Gradually blend in chocolate mixture. Turn into prepared crust. Bake 40 minutes or until filling is barely set in center. Remove from oven and let stand at room temperature for 1 hour. Then refrigerate several hours or overnight. Garnish, if desired.

Chocolate Crumb Crust: Combine 1-1/3 cups chocolate wafer crumbs, 1/4 cup softened butter, and 1 tablespoon granulated sugar. Press firmly into bottom of 9-inch spring form pan.

Mae Gianocca, Half Moon Bay, Calif.

ZUCCHINI FRUITCAKE

2 eggs
1 cup cooking oil
2 cups sugar
1 teaspoon vanilla
3 cups flour
1 teaspoon baking soda
1 teaspoon salt
1/2 teaspoon baking powder
3 teaspoons cinnamon
1-1/2 teaspoons nutmeg
2 teaspoons allspice
3 cups grated zucchini
1 cup walnuts
1 cup light raisins
1 cup mixed candied fruit
1/2 cup currants

Beat eggs with oil; stir in sugar and vanilla. Sift together flour, soda, salt, baking powder, cinnamon, nutmeg, and allspice. Add to egg-sugar mixture. Stir in zucchini, nuts, raisins, candied fruit, and currants. Turn into two greased 9 x 5-inch loaf pans. Bake in 350-degree oven for one hour and 20 minutes or until done. Cool in pan on rack for 15 minutes, then turn out onto wire rack to complete cooling. When cool, wrap in foil and store in airtight container.

Mrs. P. B. Brothers, Richmond, VA

CHOCOLATE CHERRY UPSIDE-DOWN CAKE

2-1/4 cups flour
1-1/2 cups sugar
3/4 cup cocoa
1-1/2 teaspoons baking soda
3/4 teaspoon salt
1-1/2 cups water
1/2 cup cooking oil
1/4 cup vinegar
1-1/2 teaspoons vanilla
1 can cherry pie filling

Spread pie filling in a greased 9x13-inch pan. In a large bowl mix flour, sugar, cocoa, soda, and salt. In another bowl, mix water, oil, vinegar, and vanilla. Add liquid mixture to dry mixture and stir just to moisten. Pour batter over cherries. Bake 350 degrees for 35 minutes. Cool 10 minutes in the pan. Invert on large platter. Serve with ice cream or whipped topping.

Helen Keillor, Berwyn,
Alta Toh OEH, Canada

CHOCOLATE CHIP CAKE

2 cups all purpose flour
1 cup packed brown sugar
1/2 cup granulated sugar
3 teaspoons baking powder
1 teaspoon salt
1/2 teaspoon baking soda
1/2 cup shortening
1-1/4 cups milk
3 eggs
1/2 cup semi-sweet chocolate chips finely chopped or
1/2 cup miniature semi-sweet chocolate chips
1-1/2 teaspoons vanilla

Heat oven to 350 degrees. Grease and flour oblong pan, 13 x 9 x 2 inches or 2 round layer pans, 8 or 9 inch x 1-1/2 inches. Beat all ingredients in large mixer bowl on low speed, scraping bowl constantly, 30 seconds. Beat on high speed, scraping bowl occasionally, 3 minutes.

Pour into pans. Bake in a 350 degree oven for 40-50 minutes. Bake until wooden pick inserted in center comes out clean. While cake is cooling, prepare Chocolate Butter Frosting.

CHOCOLATE ECLAIR CAKE

Serves 15

1 cup flour
1 stick (1/2 cup) butter or margarine
1/4 teaspoon salt
1 cup water
4 eggs (best at room temperature)
2 packages instant French vanilla pudding
2-1/2 cups cold milk
8 ounces cream cheese, softened
12 ounces (large container) Cool Whip or other whipped topping
3 ounces chocolate chips (1/2 of 6-ounce bag)
2 tablespoons butter or margarine
1 cup confectioners' sugar
3 to 4 tablespoons milk

Bring water and butter to a boil until all butter is melted. All at once add flour and salt; beat until mixture forms a ball that leaves the sides of saucepan; cool slightly. Add eggs one at a time, beating thoroughly after each addition. Spread pastry mixture into ungreased jelly roll pan (15 x 10 x 1-inch). Bake at 400 degrees for 35 minutes. Remove from oven; pierce bubbles with fork while hot. Cool completely.

Mix instant pudding with milk; add softened cream cheese, beat together thoroughly. Spread whipped topping over pudding mixture. Melt chocolate chips and butter over low heat, mix to add confectioners' sugar and milk, alternately until thin glaze forms. Pour or drizzle chocolate glaze over whipped topping. Refrigerate at least 1 hour or longer. Cut into squares to serve.

CHOCOLATE SUNDAE CAKE

1 package devil's food cake mix
1 cup brown sugar
1/3 cup cocoa
2 cups water
2 cups miniature marshmallows
1 cup pecans, chopped

Combine brown sugar, cocoa, and water. Mix well. Pour into a 13x9-inch pan. Place marshmallows evenly on top.

Make cake batter following package directions. Pour into pan. Top with nuts. Bake at 350 degrees for 30 minutes. Cool in pan on wire rack. Cut into bars or squares to serve.

Mrs. P. B. Brothers, Richmond, Va.

COOKIES 'N CREAM CAKE

1 package white cake mix
1-1/4 cups water
1/3 cup oil
3 egg whites
1 cup crushed, creme-filled chocolate sandwich cookies
10 whole cookies

Frosting:

3 cups powdered sugar
3/4 cup shortening
1 teaspoon vanilla
2 egg whites

Heat oven to 350 degrees. Grease and flour 2 round cake pans. In large bowl, combine all cake ingredients, except cookies. Mix at low speed until moistened. Beat 2 minutes at high speed. Stir in crushed creme-filled chocolate cookies. Bake at 350 degrees for 25-35 minutes or until it tests done. Cool layers.

In small bowl combine 1/2 cup of the powdered sugar, shortening, vanilla, and egg whites. Blend well. Beat in remaining sugar until frosting is smooth. Fill and frost cake. Arrange whole cookies on end and on top of frosted cake.

Suzanne Dawson, Cypress, TX

BANANA CAKE

8 servings

1/2 cup butter or margarine
1-3/4 cups sugar
2 eggs
1 cup sour cream
2-1/2 cups cake flour
2 large, well-ripened bananas, mashed
1 teaspoon baking powder
1 teaspoon salt
1 teaspoon soda
1 teaspoon vanilla

Topping:
1-1/4 cups firmly-packed brown sugar
1/4 cup butter or margarine, softened
1/2 cup chopped nuts

Cream together the shortening and sugar until light. Beat in eggs, one at a time, until thoroughly blended, then add the mashed bananas and blend well.

Sift together cake flour, baking powder, salt, and soda. Fold flour mixture into shortening, sugar, egg, banana mixture alternately with the sour cream; beginning and ending with dry ingredients. Pour batter into a greased and floured rectangular pan 12 x 8 x 12 inches. Spread topping which has been mixed into crumbs, over top. Bake at 325 degrees, 45-50 minutes, or until cake tests done. DO NOT OVERBAKE. Cool on wire rack in pan. Cut in squares to serve.

P.B. Brothers, Richmond, VA

BANANA CRUNCH CAKE

5 tablespoons oleo, melted
1 package coconut-pecan frosting mix
1 cup rolled oats
1 cup sour cream
2 eggs
2 large bananas
1 package cake mix (white or yellow)

Preheat oven to 350 degrees. Grease and flour 10-inch tube pan. In large bowl, mix frosting mix, oats and melted oleo. Set aside.

In another bowl, blend next three ingredients until smooth. Blend in cake mix. Pour 1/3 of batter (2 cups) into prepared pan. Sprinkle 1-1/4 cups crumb mixture over batter. Repeat twice with batter and crumbs, ending with crumb mixture. The last crumb mixture will only be 1/2 cup on top. Bake 50 to 60 minutes until toothpick inserted in center comes out clean. Cool upright in pan 15 minutes. Remove from pan and turn cake so crumb mixture is on top.

Louise Walker, Dallas, TX

BLUEBERRY PICNIC CAKE

Serves 8

1 egg
2/3 cup sugar
2 cups cake flour, sifted
2 teaspoons baking powder
1/4 teaspoon cinnamon
1/4 teaspoon cloves
1/4 teaspoon salt
1/3 cup milk
3 tablespoons butter or margarine, melted
1-1/4 teaspoons vanilla extract
1 cup fresh blueberries
2 tablespoons sugar

In a mixing bowl, beat egg; gradually add sugar; beat until light and fluffy. Sift together flour, baking powder, spices, and salt. Add to egg mixture, alternating with the milk; mix thoroughly. Add melted butter and vanilla; gently fold in blueberries. Pour cake batter into a lightly greased 11 x 7 x 1-1/2-inch baking dish; smooth top. Sprinkle top with 2 tablespoons sugar. Bake at 350 degrees for 30-35 minutes. Cool cake and leave in pan; cover and carry to picnic.

Gwen Campbell, Sterling, VA

COCONUT DATE CAKE

1/2 cup sugar
2 eggs
1 teaspoon salt
1/4 cup oil
2 teaspoons baking powder
1/2 cup milk
2 cups flour
1 cup chopped nuts
1 box chopped dates
1/2 teaspoon almond extract
1 teaspoon cinnamon

Mix sugar and eggs. Add other ingredients as listed; mix well. Grease and flour tube cake pan. Bake in a 350 degree oven for approximately 30-35 minutes. Serve with whipped topping. Also delicious served with canned fruit.

Verda Earp, Chouteau, OK

CARROT CAKE

2 cups sifted flour
2 cups sugar
2 teaspoons baking powder
1 teaspoon soda
1 teaspoon salt
2 teaspoons cinnamon
1/2 teaspoon nutmeg
1-1/4 cups oil
4 eggs
3 cups shredded carrots

Preheat oven to 350 degrees. Grease and flour a 10-inch tube pan. Mix flour, sugar, baking powder, soda, salt, cinnamon and nutmeg thoroughly in mixer bowl. Add carrots and eggs. Beat 3 minutes at medium speed on mixer. Pour batter into pan. Bake 1 hour or until cake surface springs back when touched lightly. Cool 10 minutes in pan. Remove from pan and complete cooling on rack.

Glaze:
3-ounce package cream cheese
1-2/3 cups confectioners' sugar
1/8 teaspoon salt
1 teaspoon vanilla

Beat cream cheese, confectioners' sugar, salt and vanilla together until creamy. Spread on cooled cake.

Eva Tilley, Seal Beach, CA

CHOCOLATE ANGEL FOOD CAKE

1/4 cup cocoa
1 cup cake flour
1-3/4 cups sugar
1-1/2 cups egg whites
3/4 teaspoon salt
1-1/2 teaspoons cream of tartar
1 teaspoon vanilla
1/4 teaspoon almond extract

Sift cocoa, cake flour, and 3/4 cup sugar together four times. Beat egg whites and salt until foamy. Sprinkle cream of tartar over egg whites; continue beating until stiff, but not dry. *Fold* in remaining sugar, one tablespoon at a time. Add vanilla and almond extract. *Fold* in dry ingredients, a little at a time. Pour into ungreased 10 inch tube pan. Bake 60-70 minutes at 325 degrees. Frost, if desired, although it is delicious plain.

Mrs. Melvin Habiger, Spearville, Kan.

OLD-FASHIONED TRIPLE FUDGE CAKE

1 package devil's food cake mix
1/2 cup chopped nuts
1/2 cup semi-sweet chocolate pieces
1 (12 ounce) jar thick fudge ice cream topping
Ice cream, whipped topping, or whipped cream

Mix cake as directed on package. Stir in nuts; spread batter in a greased and floured 13 x 9 x 2 inch pan. Sprinkle chocolate pieces evenly over batter; bake as directed on package. Immediately after baking, poke deep holes through top of hot cake (still in pan), space holes about 1 inch apart. Spoon fudge topping evenly over cake. Topping will melt into holes. Serve when completely cool. Top with ice cream or whipped cream.

Pauline Dean, Uxbridge, Mass.

OREO COOKIE CAKE

1 pound oreo cookies
1 cup melted margarine
8 ounce soft cream cheese
2 - 8 ounce containers whipped topping
1 cup powdered sugar
1 large package instant chocolate pudding

Crush cookies and (set aside 1/2 cup). Mix crumbs with butter, and press into 9 ix 13 pan. Refrigerate 1 hour. Mix cream cheese, sugar, 1 carton whipped topping. Spread over cookie crust. Refrigerate 1 hour. Prepare pudding mix by directions on package. Spread over cheese mixture. Refrigerate 1 hour. Top with whipped topping, sprinkle with rest of cookie crumbs. Garnish with maraschino cherries.

Lowela C. McDaniel, Roanoke, VA

TURTLE CAKE

1 package German chocolate cake mix
1 (14-ounce) package caramels
1/2 cup evaporated milk
6 tablespoons margarine
1 cup chopped pecans
1 cup chocolate chips

Prepare cake mix according to directions. Pour 1/2 batter into greased and floured 9 x 13 inch pan. Set other batter aside. Bake at 350 degrees for 18 minutes. Melt caramels and milk together, then stir in pecans. Sprinkle baked part of cake with chocolate chips, and pour caramel mix over that. Pour remaining batter over top. Return pan to oven and bake 20 minutes. Cut into squares to serve.

Cheryl Santefort, Thornton, IL

BUTTERMILK COFFEE CAKE
9 Servings

2 cups sifted flour

1 cup sugar
1/2 teaspoon ground cinnamon
1/4 teaspoon baking powder
1/4 teaspoon salt
1/2 cup butter or margarine
1 teaspoon ground cinnamon
1/2 teaspoon baking soda
3/4 cup buttermilk
1 teaspoon vanilla

Sift together flour, sugar, 1/2 teaspoon cinnamon, baking powder and salt into bowl. Cut in butter with pastry blender or two knives until mixture is crumbly. Reserve 1/2 cup crumb mixture. Combine reserved crumbs with 1 teaspoon cinnamon; set aside. Dissolve baking soda in buttermilk. Add buttermilk mixture and vanilla to remaining crumb mixture, stirring just enough to moisten. Spread batter in greased 8 inch square pan. Sprinkle with reserved crumbs. Bake in 375 degree oven 35 minutes or until done. Cut into squares and serve warm. If you love cinnamon you will love this coffee cake.

Barbara Beauregard-Smith, Northfield, Australia

BLUEBERRY COFFEE CAKE

2 cups flour
1 cup sugar
3 teaspoons baking powder
1/4 teaspoon salt
1/2 cup butter or margarine
2 eggs, beaten
1 cup milk
1-1/2 cups blueberries
1/2 cup coconut
1/2 cup chopped nuts

Mix flour, sugar, baking powder, and salt; cut in butter until mixture resembles cornmeal. Combine beaten eggs and milk; stir in dry ingredients. Stir only until dry mixture is well moistened. Do not overmix! Fold in blueberries. Grease a 9 x 12-inch pan and pour cake batter into pan. Sprinkle with coconut and chopped nuts. Bake in a 350 degree oven for 25-30 minutes. "Great for breakfast."

Agnes Ward, Erie, PA

QUICK COFFEE-CHOCOLATE CAKE

1 package yellow cake mix
1/2 cup brewed coffee
1 teaspoon flavoring

Prepare cake mix according to package directions, using coffee as part of the liquid and add vanilla. Bake according to package directions.

Topping:
3 tablespoons butter or margarine, room temperature
1/2 box confectioners' sugar
1 square unsweetened chocolate, room temperature
Brewed coffee
1 teaspoon vanilla flavoring
1 teaspoon chocolate flavoring (optional)

In a saucepan, brown the butter or margarine. Add chocolate and stir until melted. Pour over confectioners' sugar in bowl and mix, adding enough coffee until spreading consistency. Add flavoring and spread on cake.

Alice McNamara, Eucha, OK

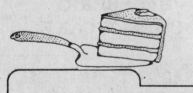

SNICKERDOODLE COFFEE CAKE

1 cup flour
1 cup sugar
1 teaspoon baking powder
1/2 teaspoon salt
1 tablespoon ground cinnamon
1/2 cup milk
1/4 cup melted margarine
1 egg

Mix together the flour, sugar, baking powder, salt, cinnamon, milk, margarine and egg. Pour into a greased and floured 8 or 9 inch square pan. Sprinkle top heavily with sugar (this gives a crusty top). Bake at 400 degrees for 25 minutes. Best when served warm.

Karen Krugman, Tampa, FL

ORANGE BUTTERSCOTCH COFFEE CAKE

Batter:
1/2 cup butter or margarine
1 cup granulated sugar
1 egg
1 teaspoon vanilla
1-1/2 cups sifted all-purpose flour
1-1/2 teaspoons baking powder
1/2 teaspoon cinnamon
1/2 teaspoon salt
1 cup milk
3/4 cup uncooked oats

Topping:
1/4 cup firmly packed brown sugar
1 tablespoon all-purpose flour
1 tablespoon butter or margarine, melted
2 teaspoons grated orange peel

Beat together butter and sugar until light and fluffy; add egg and vanilla; blend well. Sift together flour, baking powder, cinnamon and salt; add to creamed mixture alternately with milk; stir in oats. Pour batter into greased and floured 8 inch square baking pan. Combine all topping ingredients and sprinkle evenly over batter. Bake in preheated 350 degree oven for 40 to 45 minutes. Cool in pan 15 minutes before serving.

ALMOND POUND CAKE

3 cups sugar
2 sticks (1/2 pound) butter or margarine
1/2 cup shortening
5 large eggs
1/4 teaspoon salt
3 cups flour
1 small can evaporated milk (3/4 cup) plus water to make 1 cup liquid
2 teaspoons almond extract

Cream sugar and shortening. Add eggs and salt, cream well. Add remaining ingredients. Pour into a very lightly greased 12 cup bundt pan. Put into cold oven; set temperature at 320 degrees. Bake 1 hour and 30 minutes. Cool 15 minutes and remove from pan.

Leah M. Daub, Milwaukee, WIS

CHERRY NUT BROWNIE CAKE

1/2 cup maraschino cherries
3/4 cup flour, spooned lightly into cup
1/2 teaspoon baking powder
1/4 teaspoon salt
1/2 cup butter or margarine, softened
1 cup sugar
2 large eggs
2 envelopes Choc-bake (or 2 squares unsweetened chocolate, melted)
1 teaspoon vanilla
1/2 cup chopped walnuts or pecans

Quarter cherries with scissors; place on paper towel to drain; set aside. Measure flour, baking powder and salt into small bowl; whisk to blend; set aside.

In large bowl, beat butter or margarine briefly; beat in sugar. Beat in eggs one at a time; beat in chocolate and vanilla. By hand or on lowest mixer speed, beat in dry ingredients. Stir in cherries and nuts. Spread in greased and floured or foil-lined 8-inch squares pan. Bake at 350 degrees until firm in center, about 35 minutes. Cool on rack. Ice as directed below. Freeze leftovers in serving size units.

Chocolate Icing:
Looks and tastes like fudge icing.
2 tablespoons cocoa
2 tablespoons water
2 tablespoons butter or margarine
1 teaspoon maraschino cherry juice
1-1/8 cups unsifted confectioners' sugar (1/8 cup is 2 tablespoons)

Measure cocoa, water, butter and cherry juice into medium saucepan. Heat, stirring, just until smooth. Remove from heat; whisk in sugar. Icing should be just thin enough to pour. Add a little more sugar if necessary. Pour over cool cake; spread to edges. Allow icing to set before cutting cake.

PINEAPPLE BANANA CAKE

3 cups sifted all-purpose flour
1 teaspoon baking soda
1 teaspoon cinnamon
1 teaspoon salt
2 cups sugar
1-1/2 teaspoons vanilla
3 eggs
2 cups diced ripe bananas

Measure the dry ingredients and sift together. Dice the bananas and measure the quantity. Add bananas to the dry ingredients along with oil, eggs, vanilla, crushed pineapple, and juice. Stir to blend, but DO NOT BEAT. Pour into a greased 9-inch tube pan. Bake at 350 degrees for 1 hour and 15 minutes. Set aside to cool without removing from pan.

This cake is served without any kind of frosting. This is a real moist cake, keeps well, and is delicious.

Judy Smith, Indianapolis, IN

PETER'S PUMPKIN CAKE

1/2 cup shortening
1 cup brown sugar
1/2 cup white sugar
1 egg
3/4 cup cooked or canned pumpkin
2 cups flour
3 teaspoons baking powder
1/2 teaspoon cinnamon
1/2 teaspoon nutmeg
1/2 teaspoon ginger
1/2 teaspoon salt
2/3 cup chopped nuts
1/2 teaspoon soda
1/2 cup sour milk

Cream shortening and sugars together. Beat egg and add to the pumpkin. Mix with creamed sugar and shortening. Sift flour, baking powder, spices, and salt together. Mix nuts in flour mixture. Add soda to sour milk; add to creamed mixture. Bake in greased, floured loaf pan in 350 degree oven for 45 minutes.

Agnes Ward, Erie, Pa.

PUMPKIN FIG CAKE

Filling:
1 (8 ounce) package dried figs finely chopped. (about 1 cup)
1/2 cup toasted almonds, chopped
1/2 cup sugar
1/4 cup water
2 tablespoons lemon juice
1/2 teaspoon grated lemon peel
1/2 teaspoon nutmeg

Cake:
1/2 cup butter or margarine
1 cup brown sugar, firmly packed
3 large eggs
1/2 cup white sugar
2-1/2 cups all-purpose flour
1 teaspoon baking powder
1 teaspoon soda
1/2 teaspoon nutmeg
1 teaspoon salt
1 cup canned pumpkin
1/2 cup dairy sour cream
1 teaspoon grated lemon peel
1 teaspoon vanilla
1/2 cup toasted almonds, chopped

Combine filling ingredients in small saucepan. Simmer over medium-low heat until liquid is absorbed, about 10 minutes. Cool.

To make cake, cream together butter and sugars in large mixing bowl. Add eggs, one at a time, beating well after each addition. In a smaller bowl, stir together flour, baking soda, nutmeg, baking powder, and salt. Add to butter-sugar mixture, alternately with pumpkin. Stir in sour cream, lemon peel, and vanilla.

Sprinkle the bottom of a well-greased 12-cup bundt pan with almonds. Spoon half cake batter over nuts. Distribute fig filling evenly over batter. Top filling with remaining batter. Bake in a 350 degree oven for about 50 minutes, until cake tests done. Cool in pan on wire rack, 15 minutes. Turn cake out of pan and cool thoroughly on wire rack.

Mrs. P. B. Brothers, Richmond, Va.

PUMPKIN PIE CAKE

Crust:
1 box (2-layer size) white or yellow cake mix (reserve 1 cup)
1/2 cup margarine, very soft
1 egg

Mix together and press into 13x9-inch baking pan.

Filling:
1 large can (1 pound, 13 ounces) pumpkin
3 eggs
2/3 cup evaporated milk
2 teaspoons cinnamon
1 cup sugar

Mix ingredients together and pour over crust.

Topping:
1 cup reserved cake mix
1/2 cup sugar
1/4 cup margarine, softened
1 cup chopped walnuts or pecans (optional)

Mix cake mix, sugar, and margarine together until crumbly. Sprinkle over filling. Sprinkle nuts on top (optional). Bake at 350 degrees for 1 hour and 15 minutes. Serve warm with whipped topping.

Ruby Goreoski, Albany, Ore.

YELLOW SQUASH CAKE

1 box yellow cake mix
1 (3-1/2 ounce) package vanilla instant pudding
1/4 cup oil
4 eggs
3 cups yellow squash (grated)
1/2 teaspoon salt
1 teaspoon cinnamon
1/4 teaspoon nutmeg
1/4 teaspoon allspice
1 cup walnuts (chopped)

Mix all ingredients together for 4 minutes. Bake in 2 loaf pans or a greased and floured angel food cake pan. Bake at 350 degrees for 55 minutes or until toothpick comes out clean. Frost with your favorite frosting, if desired.

Helen Taugher, Micholson, Pa.

Casseroles
CREATIVE

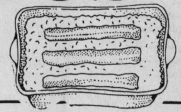

NO-FUSS SHORTCUT PAELLA
Serves 6

2 cups cooked chicken, cut into 1-inch pieces
1-1/2 cups chicken broth
10 ounces shrimp, shelled
1 (8-1/2-ounce) can peas, drained
2 cups rice
1 (3-ounce) can mushrooms, sliced and drained
1 envelope onion soup mix
1 teaspoon paprika

Combine chicken, chicken broth, shrimp, peas, rice, mushrooms, onion soup mix and paprika. Pour into 3-quart casserole; bake at 350 degrees, covered, for 1-1/4 hours until rice is tender.

Gwen Campbell, Sterling, Va.

MARDI GRAS MAGIC
Serves 6

1 pound red beans
1 pound smoked sausage, cut into bite-size pieces (kielbasa is fine)
1-2 stalks celery, chopped
1 onion, chopped
1 garlic clove, crushed
1 teaspoon sugar
1 teaspoon salt
1 bay leaf
8-10 cups water
1-1/2 cups uncooked rice (white, wild, or brown rice)

Rinse beans. In a large pot combine beans, sausage, celery, onion, garlic, sugar, salt, bay leaf, and 8-10 cups water. Bring to boil and stir frequently so mixture does not stick.

Reduce heat to low and cook, covered, until beans are tender, 1-1/2-2 hours. Add uncooked rice and cook until tender, about 15-20 minutes.

Ruby Walsh, West Chicago, Ill.

MACARONI HOT DISH
Serves 6

2 cups warm, cooked macaroni
1-1/2 cups grated cheese
1-1/2 cups bread crumbs
1 green pepper, diced
3 eggs, beaten
1 onion, diced
2 tablespoons margarine, melted
Pepper and salt to taste
1-1/2 cups milk
1 can mushroom soup

Mix all ingredients, except mushroom soup, and place in pan set in hot water. Bake at 350 degrees for 45 minutes. Cut in squares and then pour over undiluted mushroom soup which has been heated.

Suzan L. Wiener, Spring Hill, Fla.

HEARTY CASSEROLE
Serves 6–8

1 (11-ounce) can cheddar cheese soup
1 (1-pound) can julienne carrots, drained (reserve 1/3 cup liquid)
3/4 teaspoon crushed rosemary
1/4 teaspoon pepper
1 (9-1/4-ounce) can tuna, drained and flaked
1 (15-ounce) can macaroni and cheese
1/4 cup minced parsley
1 (3-1/2-ounce) can french-fried onion rings

Heat oven to 375 degrees. Mix soup with reserved liquid from carrots. Stir in rosemary and pepper. Spread tuna in oblong baking dish, 11-1/2 x 7-1/2 x 1-1/2-inch. Layer with macaroni and cheese, carrots and parsley. Pour cheese soup mixture over layers. Bake, uncovered, for 30–35 minutes, or until bubbly. Top with onion rings and bake 5 minutes longer.

Suzan L. Wiener, Spring Hill, Fla.

GRITS CASSEROLE
Serves 10-12

1 pound sausage
1/2 cup chopped green peppers
1 cup chopped onion
1 cup chopped celery
1 cup grits, uncooked
4 cups water
1 teaspoon salt
1 can cream of chicken soup
1 cup grated cheese

Preheat oven to 375 degrees. Brown sausage. Add peppers, onion, celery, and sauté. Cook grits in 4 cups water with 1 teaspoon salt. Combine cooked grits with sausage, peppers, onion, and celery. Pour mixture into 2-quart buttered casserole. Spread soup on top and sprinkle with cheese. Bake 30 minutes.

Renee Wells, Columbia, S.C.

PIZZA RICE PIE
Serves 4-5

2-2/3 cups cooked rice
1/3 cup minced onion
2 eggs, beaten
2 tablespoons melted butter or
    margarine
1 (8-ounce) can tomato sauce with
    cheese
1/4 teaspoon oregano
1/4 teaspoon basil
1 cup shredded mozzarella cheese
1 (4-1/2-ounce) package sliced
    pepperoni or salami
1/2 cup sliced stuffed olives

Mix together rice, onion, eggs, and melted butter. Line a 12-inch pizza pan with rice mixture and bake 12 minutes at 350 degrees, or until set. Spread tomato sauce with cheese over rice crust. Sprinkle with spices and cheese. Top with pepperoni and olives. Bake at 350 degrees for 20-25 minutes. After removing from oven, allow to stand a few minutes before serving.

Sharon McClatchey, Muskogee, Okla.

SAUCY PIZZA SURPRISE
Serves 6

3 cups cooked rice
2 cups (8 ounces)
    cheese, shredded
½ teaspoon basil
2 eggs, beaten
2 (8-ounce) cans tomato
    sauce
½ teaspoon oregano
½ teaspoon garlic powder

Combine rice, eggs and 1 cup cheese. Press firmly into 2 (9-inch) pans. Spread evenly. Bake at 450 degrees for 20 minutes. Combine tomato sauce and seasonings. Spread evenly over rice crust. Top with remaining cheese. Bake 10 minutes longer. *Note:* Other ingredients, such as cooked sausage, green pepper, mushrooms, etc., may be added before baking.

This pizza is great. A good way to use leftover rice, which makes a crust like deep-dish.

Leota L. Arnold, Vincennes, Ind.

CHICKEN-BROCCOLI BAKE
Serves 4–5

1 (10-ounce) package broccoli cuts
2 cups chopped, cooked chicken
4 ounces medium noodles
1 cup sour cream
1 (10 3/4-ounce) can cream of
    chicken soup
2 tablespoons chopped pimiento
1 tablespoon minced onion
1 teaspoon salt
1/2 teaspoon Worcestershire sauce
1 tablespoon melted butter
1/2 cup soft bread crumbs
1 cup grated Swiss cheese

Prepare broccoli as directed on package; drain. Cook noodles and drain. Combine chicken, sour cream, soup, pimiento, onion, salt and Worcestershire sauce. Add butter to bread crumbs and mix well. Place noodles in greased, shallow 2-quart baking dish. Sprinkle with 1/3 of the cheese. Add broccoli. Sprinkle with 1/2 of the remaining cheese. Pour on the chicken mixture. Sprinkle with rest of cheese, and then with bread crumbs. Bake at 350 degrees for 1 hour.

Pauline Dean, Uxbridge, Mass.

BEEFY CASSEROLE
Serves 4

1 large eggplant
1 medium onion, chopped
2 tablespoons butter
1 pound ground beef
Salt and pepper to taste
1 bay leaf

Peel eggplant and cut into slices 1 or 1 1/2 inches thick. Cook in boiling, salted water for 10–15 minutes, or just until tender. Drain. Sauté onion in butter until soft; add beef and seasonings. Cook until meat is nicely browned. Place slices of eggplant in a greased baking dish. Remove bay leaf and add meat/onion mixture to eggplant. Cover with thin slices of cheese. Bake at 400 degrees for 20 minutes, or until cheese is melted.

Leota Baxter, Ingalls, Kan.

TOWN AND COUNTRY CASSEROLE

1 package French's Real Cheese
    Scalloped Potatoes
1 pound smoked kielbasa or Polish
    sausage, cut in 1/4-inch slices
1 cup thinly sliced carrots
1 tablespoon freeze-dried chives
1 cup soft bread crumbs
1 tablespoon butter or margarine
1 tablespoon parsley flakes

Follow microwave method on package, except *increase* water to 3 cups and add carrots; microwave, covered, for 15 minutes. Add seasoning mix, milk, sausage, and chives. Microwave, covered, for 3-5 minutes. Combine crumbs, butter and parsley flakes; sprinkle casserole with crumb mixture; microwave, uncovered, for 5-7 minutes.

CORNED BEEF QUICHE

1 (9-inch) pie shell, unbaked
1 (15-ounce) can corned beef hash
1 small onion, finely shredded
1 cup Swiss cheese, shredded
2 teaspoons flour
1/4 teaspoon salt
Dash allspice
2 eggs, slightly beaten
1-1/4 cups milk

Pre-bake pie shell at 375 degrees for 7 minutes; remove from oven; set aside. Reduce oven temperature to 325 degrees. Crumble corned beef hash into pie shell; sprinkle onion over meat; top with Swiss cheese. Combine remaining ingredients; pour over hash and cheese. Bake 35-40 minutes, or until set. Cool 20 minutes before serving.

Gwen Campbell, Sterling, Va.

PORK CHOP CASSEROLE
Serves 4

6 pork chops
1 teaspoon salt
1/8 teaspoon pepper
4 medium apples, peeled and sliced
1 cup water
4 medium sweet potatoes, peeled and sliced
1 teaspoon Worcestershire sauce
1 medium onion, chopped

Wipe chops; brown them in a little fat in frying pan. Place chops in a large casserole; sprinkle with half the salt and pepper. Place apples and sweet potatoes in layers on chops and sprinkle with remaining salt and pepper. Sauté onion in the same frying pan where chops were browned. Add water and Worcestershire sauce. Mix and pour over chops, apples and potatoes. Cover and bake 1-1/2 hours in a moderate 375-degree oven.

Lucy Dowd, Sequim, Wash.

LEMON DILLED BEEF

2 1/2 pounds stewing beef
1/2 cup butter
2 1/2 cups chopped celery
1 1/2 cups chopped onion
1 cup chopped green pepper
1/3 cup lemon juice
2 cups beef stock
3 cloves garlic, finely chopped
1 1/2 teaspoons dill weed
Salt to taste
1 1/2 cups sour cream
3 tablespoons butter, softened
3 tablespoons flour
1 medium package noodles

Lightly brown beef in butter. Add vegetables, liquid and seasoning. Cover and simmer on low for 2 hours. Add sour cream and simmer, uncovered, for 30 minutes. Combine flour and butter; add by spoonfuls to bubbling mixture. Simmer 10 minutes and serve on prepared noodles.

Patricia Anderson, Fremont, Neb.

DELI REUBEN CASSEROLE
Serves 6.

3 cups sauerkraut, drained
1-1/2 cups tomatoes, drained
2 tablespoons Thousand Island dressing
2 tablespoons butter or margarine
3 packages corned beef, shredded
1 (10-ounce) can refrigerated flaky biscuits
3 rye crackers, crushed
1/4 teaspoon caraway seeds

Spread sauerkraut in a 13x9x2-inch baking dish; arrange tomatoes on top; spread with dressing; dot with butter. Place shredded corned beef and cheese over all. Separate each biscuit into halves; arrange over casserole. Sprinkle with the rye crackers and caraway seeds. Bake at 350 degrees, 12 minutes, or until biscuits are flaky and golden.

Gwen Campbell, Sterling, Va.

HAM & NOODLE BAKE

2 cups cooked ham, cubed
1/4 cup onion, chopped
1/8 teaspoon thyme leaves, crushed
2 tablespoons margarine
1 (10-3/4-ounce) can cream of chicken soup
3/4 cup water
2 cups cooked noodles (5 ounces)
1 cup canned, cut green beans, drained
1/2 cup shredded cheddar cheese

In saucepan, brown ham, cook onion with thyme in margarine until tender. Stir in remaining ingredients, except cheese. Pour into 2-quart casserole. Bake at 350 degrees for 30 minutes. Top with cheese; bake until cheese melts, 8 minutes longer. If refrigerated before cooking, bake 45 minutes longer.

This is made quickly and is nice for a company dinner.

Mrs. Albert Foley, Lemoyne, Pa.

CHICKEN AND BROCCOLI RICE CASSEROLE
Serves 6

1/2 cup chopped onions
1/2 cup sliced mushrooms
1 tablespoon butter
2 cups hot, cooked rice
2 cups cubed chicken breast
2 cups chopped, fresh broccoli (steamed) *or*
1 (10-ounce) package frozen broccoli, thawed
1 (10-3/4-ounce) can cream of mushroom soup, condensed
1/2 cup (2 ounces) shredded cheddar cheese

Simmer onions and mushrooms in large skillet with butter until tender. Stir in rice, chicken, broccoli, and soup. Pour into buttered 1-1/2-quart baking dish. Top with cheese. Bake at 350 degrees for 20-25 minutes.

My husband is fussy about casseroles, but he *loves* this one.

Dorothy Sorenson, Muskego, Wis.

CHICKEN CASSEROLE SUPREME

3   cups cooked chicken, deboned
1   (6-ounce) package Uncle Ben's rice, cooked
1   can cream of celery soup, undiluted
1   can cream of chicken soup, undiluted
1   can French-style green beans, drained
1   medium jar pimientos, sliced
1   cup mayonnaise
1   small can water chestnuts. sliced
Salt and pepper to taste

Mix all ingredients together and pour into 3-quart casserole. Bake 25–30 minutes at 350 degrees.

Mrs. A. Curtis, Rector, Ark.

LAZY BEEF CASSEROLE
Serves 4

1 pound lean beef chuck, cut into 1-1/2-inch cubes
1/2 cup red wine
1 (10-1/2-ounce) can consomme, undiluted
1/4 cup all-purpose flour
Freshly ground black pepper, to taste
1 medium onion, chopped
1/4 cup fine dry bread crumbs
1/4 teaspoon rosemary

Put meat in a casserole with the wine, consomme, pepper, rosemary, and onion. Mix flour and bread crumbs and stir into the liquid. Cover and bake at 300 degrees, about 3 hours. Serve with rice or noodles. (206 calories per serving)

Ronnie J. Heroux, Uxbridge, Mass.

EASY BEEF GOULASH
Serves 4

1 to 2 tablespoons vegetable oil
1 pound ground beef (chuck)
3 cups uncooked medium egg noodles
2 cups water
1 (8-ounce) can tomato sauce
1 envelope dry onion soup mix

Heat oil in a medium-size skillet over medium heat. Add ground beef and cook until lightly browned, stirring occasionally with a fork to break up meat. Drain off any excess fat. Sprinkle uncooked noodles over meat. Combine water, tomato sauce, and onion soup mix. Pour over noodles in skillet. Do not stir. Cover and bring to a boil. Reduce heat to moderately low and simmer about 30 minutes, or until noodles are tender. Stir and serve.
Note: You may have to add a small amount of water if the noodles seem to be sticking. This is very easy and quick for those hectic days.

Doris L. Rayman, Somerset, Pa.

GERMAN POTATO CASSEROLE

6 medium-size potatoes, peeled and sliced
1 pound hot pork sausage, cooked and drained
8 ounces sour cream
2 teaspoons dry onion soup mix
2 teaspoons lemon juice
1 can cream of mushroom soup
2 teaspoons Dijon mustard
1 can sauerkraut, washed and drained
1 cup buttered bread crumbs
Salt and pepper to taste

Peel, wash, and slice potatoes. Boil in salted water until tender. Mix sour cream, dry onion soup mix, mushroom soup, lemon juice, and mustard. Heat sauerkraut in 2 tablespoons sausage drippings. Alternate layers of potatoes, cream mixture, and sauerkraut. Put bread crumbs on top and bake in 350-degree oven until hot and bubbly, about 20-25 minutes.

Ruby Walsh, West Chicago, Ill.

INDIAN CASSEROLE

1 can hominy, drained
1 pound ground beef
1/2 cup chopped onion
1/2 cup chopped green pepper
1-3/4 cups canned tomatoes
1/2 teaspoon salt
1/4 teaspoon pepper
1 cup grated cheese

Brown beef, salt, onions, and green pepper. Add tomatoes and hominy. Pour into buttered casserole and bake at 350 degrees for 40 minutes. Remove from oven and sprinkle cheese on top. Return to oven and bake 15 minutes.
Note: I tried this recipe and cooked it in an electric skillet. I cooked it on low until thick, then placed slices of cheese over the top and put lid of skillet on until cheese melted. I served it with French bread and a cottage cheese and peach salad.

Corena J. Bennington, Whitestown, Ind.

MOCK OYSTER CASSEROLE
Serves 6

1 large eggplant
1 cup cracker crumbs (approx. 25 soda crackers, crushed)
2 eggs
1/2 cup milk
3 tablespoons butter
1/4 cup chopped celery
1/4 cup chopped green pepper
1/4 cup chopped onion
1 (11 ounce) can mushroom soup
Tabasco sauce to taste

Peel eggplant and cut into cubes. Boil eggplant for 3 minutes in salt water; set aside. Place 1/3 of the crushed crumbs in a buttered 2 quart casserole dish; add 1/2 the eggplant. Repeat layering the cracker crumbs and eggplant. Beat eggs slightly, add 1/2 cup milk, mushroom soup, peppers, onions, celery and Tabasco sauce, mixing well. Pour slowly over eggplant mixture. Dot with butter. Cover and bake at 375 degrees for 30 minutes. Uncover and add more milk if needed. Bake 15 minutes more uncovered, until golden brown.

Rose McBride, Kent, OH

RICE OLÉ
Serves 3-4

2 slices bacon
1/3 cup chopped onion
1/4 cup finely chopped green pepper
1-1/2 cups water
2 envelopes Lipton Tomato Cup-a-Soup
1 cup uncooked instant rice
1/2 teaspoon garlic salt

In skillet cook bacon until crisp; drain, reserving 2 tablespoons drippings. Crumble bacon; set aside. Add onion and green pepper to skillet; cook until tender. Add water and bring to boil. Stir in Cup-a-Soup, uncooked rice, garlic salt, and crumbled bacon; cover and remove from heat. Let stand for 5 minutes.

Agnes Ward, Erie, Pa.

YELLOW SQUASH CASSEROLE

6-8 Servings

2 pounds yellow squash, sliced (6 cups)
1/4 cup chopped onion
1 can cream of chicken soup
1 cup sour cream
1 cup shredded carrots
1 (8-ounce) package herb-seasoned stuffing mix
1/2 cup melted margarine

Cook squash and onion in boiling, salted water for 5 minutes; drain. Mix soup and sour cream. Stir in the carrots; fold in squash and onion. Combine stuffing mix and margarine. Spread half stuffing mixture in lightly buttered 12 x 7-1/2-inch baking dish; spoon vegetable mixture over stuffing. Sprinkle remaining stuffing mixture over vegetables. Bake in preheated 350 degree oven for 25-30 minutes, until heated thoroughly.

Iona Hodges, Springdale, Ark.

PINTO BEAN CASSEROLE

Serves 4-6

1 to 1-1/2 pounds ground beef
1/2 cup chopped onion
1/2 cup chopped green pepper
1 clove garlic, minced
1 (15-ounce) can tomato sauce
2 teaspoons chili powder
1 teaspoon salt
1 cup cooked rice
1 (15-ounce) can pinto beans
1-1/2 cups grated Cheddar cheese

Brown beef, onion, green pepper, and garlic. Blend in tomato sauce, chili powder, and salt. In greased 2-quart casserole, layer part of meat sauce, beans, half of cheese, and remainder of meat sauce. Top with other half cheese. Bake 350 degrees for 15-20 minutes. Let stand a few minutes before serving.

Rolls or garlic toast and salad with this casserole make a complete meal.

Mrs. Hobert Howell, Waco, TX

YAM AND CRANBERRY CASSEROLE

Serves 8

1 (40 ounce) can yams, drained
3 cups fresh, whole cranberries
1-1/2 cups sugar
1 small orange, sliced
1/2 cup pecan halves
1/4 cup orange juice or brandy
3/4 teaspoon cinnamon
1/4 teaspoon nutmeg
1/4 teaspoon mace

Combine cranberries, sugar, orange slices, pecans, orange juice, and spices in 2-quart casserole. Bake uncovered at 375 degrees for 30 minutes. Stir yams into cranberry mixture. Bake until heated through—about 15 minutes.

Nice to serve with your holiday turkey.

Helen Weissinger, Levittown, Pa.

CABBAGE CASSEROLE

1 medium onion, chopped
3 tablespoons butter
1/2 pound ground beef
1 teaspoon salt
1/8 teaspoon pepper
6 cups chopped cabbage
1 can tomato soup

Sauté meat and onion. Place 3 cups cabbage in 2 quart casserole; cover with meat mixture; top with remaining cabbage. Pour soup over top. Bake 350 degrees for 1 hour.

Sandy Marqueling, Fort Wayne, Ind.

GREEN TOMATO CASSEROLE

4 large green tomatoes, sliced
Salt and pepper to taste
3/4 cup Cheddar cheese, grated
1 tablespoon butter

Preheat oven to 400 degrees. Butter casserole dish. Lay 1/3 of tomato slices on bottom. Sprinkle with salt and pepper and 1/4 cup of cheese. Repeat with remaining slices. Top with 1/2 cup of cheese and dot with butter. Bake covered 40 to 60 minutes. Brown under broiler if desired.

This is a simple way to use green tomatoes and it tastes great.

Lillian Smith, Montreal, Canada

ROUND-UP BEAN CASSEROLE

1 pound ground beef
1 can red (kidney) beans
1 can butter beans
1 can pork and beans
1/2 cup catsup
3/4 cup brown sugar
1 teaspoon mustard
2 tablespoons vinegar
Chopped onion and bell pepper (optional)

Brown beef; season with salt and pepper. (Add onion and bell pepper at this time.) Combine with remaining ingredients. Put into casserole dish. Bake about 1 hour at 350 degrees.

This is also good cooked in a slow pot. It is simple to prepare, and with a salad makes a quick meal.

Mavis McBride, Conway, AR

SPINACH CASSEROLE

1 package frozen spinach
1 (8 ounce) package cream cheese
1 can cream of mushroom soup
1 can French onion rings
6 tablespoons butter or margarine
Cracker crumbs

Cook spinach according to package directions. Heat soup and cream cheese to soften. Mix with spinach; add onion rings. Pour into casserole. Melt butter; add enough cracker crumbs to absorb butter. Spread buttered crumbs on top and bake at 350 degrees for 20 minutes.

G. G. Crabtree, Lansing, MI

MACARONI LOAF

2 cups cooked macaroni
1/2 cup bread crumbs
1/2 cup grated cheese
3 tablespoons butter
1/2 tablespoon chopped parsley
1/2 tablespoon chopped onion
1/2 teaspoon salt
1/2 cup milk
1 egg, beaten

Place a layer of cooked macaroni into a greased baking dish. Sprinkle bread crumbs, grated cheese, parsley, onions, salt, and butter between each layer. Repeat until all ingredients are used. Pour egg and milk over mixture. Bake in 350 degree oven for 30 minutes or until it is set.

Joy B. Shamway, Freeport, IL

ORIENTAL RICE CASSEROLE

6-8 servings

1 pound ground beef
1 cup chopped celery
1 cup chopped onions
4 ounce can mushrooms
8 ounce can water chestnuts, sliced
8 ounce can bamboo shoots, drained
1/3 cup soy sauce
1 can cream of mushroom soup
2 beef bouillon cubes
2 cups hot water
3/4 cup rice

Brown beef, celery and onions. Drain off excess fat. Mix in mushrooms, water chestnuts, bamboo shoots and soy sauce. Dissolve bouillon cubes in hot water, stir in mushroom soup. Add to beef mixture. Stir in rice, place in 13 x 9 inch baking pan. Bake uncovered for 1 hour in a 350 degree oven. Delicious!

Sharon Crider, Evansville, WI

TOSTADO CASSEROLE
Serves 6

1 pound ground beef
15-ounce can (2 cups) tomato sauce
1 envelope taco seasoning mix
2-1/2 cups corn chips
15-1/2 - ounce can refried beans
2 ounces (1/2 cup) shredded Cheddar cheese

In skillet, brown ground beef. Add 1-1/2 cups of tomato sauce and seasoning mix, stirring to mix well. Line bottom of 11 x 8 x 2-inch baking dish with 2 cups corn chips. Crush remaining corn chips; set aside. Spoon meat mixture over corn chips in baking dish. Combine remaining tomato sauce and refried beans; spread over ground beef mixture. Bake at 375 degrees for 25 minutes. Sprinkle with shredded cheese and crushed corn chips. Bake 5 minutes more.

Sharon Sisson, Longview, WA

POT LUCK CASSEROLE

8 ounces noodles
1-1/2 pounds hamburger
1 onion, chopped
1 teaspoon salt
Pepper
2 (8 ounce) packages cream cheese
1 cup cottage cheese
1/4 cup sour cream
1/3 cup chopped green pepper
1/3 cup chopped green onion

Cook noodles. Simmer hamburger, onion, salt, pepper and tomato sauce. Cream in blender the cottage cheese, cream cheese and sour cream. Add chopped peppers and green onions. Layer noodles, meat and cheese sauce. Top with grated cheese and bake at 350 degrees for 30-40 minutes.

Fay Duman, Eugene, OR

HAMBURGER CASSEROLE
Serves 4

1 pound lean ground beef
1 (26 1/4 ounce) can of Franco-American Spaghetti
1 medium onion, chopped
1 medium green pepper, chopped

Saute onions and green pepper in 2 tablespoons margarine until nearly done, remove from pan and drain. Saute ground beef until brown; drain grease. Add spaghetti from can. Slightly chop while mixing. Add peppers and onions. Mix well. Pour into 1-1/2 quart casserole. Bake 375 degrees for 30-45 minutes.

Optional additions:
Mushrooms, sliced
Black and or green olives, sliced
1 small can green beans

Serve with Parmesan cheese, garlic bread and tossed salad.

Mrs. Joseph Erhardt, Lake Worth, FL

HAMBURGER MACARONI CASSEROLE

2 cups macaroni
1 pound ground beef
1 can condensed tomato soup
1 can condensed mushroom soup
1 medium green pepper
1/4 cup colby cheese, cubed
1/4 cup chopped pimiento, optional
1 (3-ounce) can French fried (Durkee) onions

Cook macaroni; drain. Brown the ground beef; drain. Add soups, green pepper, pimiento, macaroni, and the ground beef. Place half the mixture in a greased 2-quart casserole. Sprinkle with half the cheese and onions. Top with remaining macaroni mixture and cheese. Bake at 350 degrees for 25 minutes. Sprinkle with remaining onions, bake 5 additional minutes.

Connie Lawhun, Brunswick, OH

CREAMY CHIPPED BEEF CASSEROLE

2 packages chipped beef
1/2 package (16-ounce) frozen hash brown's (thawed)
1 can cream of mushroom soup
1 cup evaporated milk
2 tablespoon Crisco
1 can Durkee French fried onion rings

Snip beef in bite size pieces. Brown in Crisco until edges curl; drain. Mix milk and soup. Add beef, hash brown's and 1/2 can onion rings. Place in 2-quart casserole dish; bake covered for 30 minutes in 350 degree oven. Remove lid; crumble remainder of onion rings over top. return to oven for 5 to 10 minutes.
NOTE: Also good with hamburger or leftover ham.

Audria Moylan, Keokuk, IA

REUBEN CASSEROLE

5 cups herb seasoned croutons
1 cup hot water
1 (8-ounce) package Swiss cheese (sliced), set aside 2 slices
6-9 slices of canned corn beef
1/2 cup melted margarine
2 cups sauerkraut (drained)
1 teaspoon caraway seeds (if desired)

In a large bowl, put in croutons and margarine; toss gently. Add hot water, sauerkraut, and caraway seeds. Set aside 1 cup of mixture. Grease casserole dish. Layer crouton mixture, corn beef, and cheese slices. End up with the 1 cup of crouton mixture. Cover and bake in a 350 degree oven for 20 minutes. Top with the 2 cheese slices and bake uncovered 10 minutes until cheese melts.

Edna Mae Seelos, Niles, IL

DRESSING CASSEROLE

Serves 12

2 cups diced celery
1 clove garlic
12 cups toasted bread cubes
4 cups cubed corn bread
1/2 teaspoon pepper
4 cups turkey or chicken broth
1-1/2 cups chopped onion
1/2 cup butter
1 tablespoon sage
2 tablespoons salt
1 (13 ounce) can evaporated milk
2 eggs, slightly beaten

Cook celery, onion, and garlic in butter until light brown. Crumble bread cubes and corn bread in large bowl. Add sage, salt, and pepper. Stir celery mixture into bread cubes. Add evaporated milk, broth, and eggs. Mix well. Pour into greased 9 x 13" pan. Bake at 325 degrees for 35 to 40 minutes.

This is a good way to use up leftover corn bread. Recipe can easily be cut in half and baked in an 8 x 8" pan for smaller families. Bouillon may be substituted for the broth.

Terry Knower, Holmen, WI

NIGHT BEFORE CASSEROLE

Serves 10

2 cups macaroni, cooked
2 cups chicken, turkey, *or* tuna (if using chicken or turkey, it should be cooked)
2 cans mushroom soup
1/2 pound American cheese, cut into fine pieces
3 eggs, hard-cooked, cut into small pieces
2 cups milk
Chopped pimiento and green pepper to taste

Mix all ingredients together and refrigerate overnight or for at least 6-12 hours. Remove from refrigerator and bake for 1 hour in 350 degree oven.

Diantha Susan Hibbard, Rochester, NY

PENNYWISE CASSEROLE

1 pound lean stewing beef, cut into 1" cubes
(Lamb or pork can also be used for this recipe)
Salt and pepper
1/3 cup vegetable oil
2 medium onions, sliced
2 teaspoons honey
1/2 teaspoon ground cinnamon
1/2 teaspoon ground nutmeg
1/2 teaspoon parsley
1/2 teaspoon basil
8 ounce can tomatoes
4 slices wheat (or white) bread, buttered and quartered

Lightly salt and pepper beef. In skillet over moderate heat, fry beef cubes until browned. Transfer meat to ovenproof dish. In the same skillet, fry onions for 5 minutes until soft, but not browned. Stir in remaining ingredients (except bread); bring to a boil. Pour over meat; cover. Bake in a 350 degree oven for 1 hour. Taste and adjust seasonings, if necessary. Arrange bread slices neatly on top; return to oven for 30 minutes (or until the bread is golden and crisp).

Gwen Campbell, Sterling, VA

MEXICAN COMBO

1 pound ground beef
1 medium onion, diced
1 medium green pepper, diced
2 tablespoons chili powder
1-1/2 cups hot water
1/2 pound sharp cheese, diced
1 can red kidney beans
Salt & pepper to taste

Brown ground beef, onion, and pepper in a large skillet, using fork to break up meat. Mix chili powder and hot water; pour over meat mixture. Simmer 5 to 10 minutes. Add cheese, beans with juice, salt, and pepper. Simmer until cheese melts. Be careful not to let it burn.

Kathy Rankins, Woodford, VA

DYNASTY CASSEROLE
Serves 4-6

1 (8-ounce) can water chestnuts, sliced
1 (3-ounce) can chow mein noodles
1 carrot sliced
1 can bean sprouts, drained
1 can cream of mushroom soup
1 cup half-and-half cream
1 cup chopped celery (cut on the diagonal)
Dash of hot–pepper sauce and black pepper
2 tablespoons soy sauce
1-1/2 cups cooked chicken chunks or strips
1/4 cup minced green onion
3/4 cup chopped cashew nuts
Hot cooked rice

Preheat oven to 350 degrees and set aside 1/2 cup of crisp chow mein noodles. Mix all other ingredients (except rice) in a large buttered 2-quart casserole or long baking dish. Bake, uncovered, for about 30 minutes. Sprinkle remaining chow mein noodles on top of casserole and bake 10 minutes longer. Serve casserole over hot cooked rice. Pass the soy sauce at the table.

Donna Holter, West Middlesex, Pa.

BAKED BEANS WITH SAUSAGE
Serves 6

1/4 cup molasses
2 tablespoons prepared mustard
2 tablespoons vinegar
2 teaspoons Worcestershire sauce
1/4 teaspoon Tabasco sauce
2 (1-pound) cans baked beans
1 (20-ounce) can apple slices
1 pound pork sausage links, cooked

Mix all ingredients, except sausages, and place in a bean pot. Bake at 350 degrees for 40 minutes. Top with hot sausages and serve.

This is a complete meal with French or garlic bread and a crisp salad.

Mrs. H.W. Walker, Richmond, Va.

CHILI RELLENOS CASSEROLE

16 ounces Ortega whole green chilies
12 ounces Cheddar cheese, grated
12 ounces Monterey Jack cheese, grated
2 eggs, separated
2 egg whites
3 tablespoons flour
12 ounces evaporated milk
14 ounces Ortega green chili salsa

Remove seeds from chilies; flatten and drain. In a greased 9x9-inch pan, layer half the chilies and top with Cheddar cheese. Cover with rest of chilies and top with Monterey Jack cheese. Mix egg yolks, flour, and milk. Whip the 4 egg whites until stiff, then fold into yolk mixture. Pour the whole mixture over chilies and cheese. Bake in a 325 degree oven for 45 minutes. Pour green chili salsa over the top and return to oven for 30 minutes. After baking, allow to sit for 10 minutes. Cut into squares.

Mrs. S. R. Burt, Winnemucca, Nev.

SHRIMP CASSEROLE
Serves 4-5

1 can condensed mushroom soup
1/2 cup milk
2 tablespoons minced parsley
1 tablespoon instant minced onion
1/2 teaspoon salt
2-3 dashes Tabasco sauce
2-1/2 cups cooked rice
2 cups cooked shrimp
1 cup corn flakes
2 tablespoons melted butter
2 tablespoons toasted slivered almonds (optional)

Combine soup, milk, parsley, onions and seasonings. Add rice and shrimp; mix thoroughly. Pour into greased 10x6x2-inch baking dish. Slightly crush corn flakes; combine with melted butter and almonds; sprinkle over top of casserole. Bake at 375 degrees for about 20 minutes or until bubbly.

Agnes Ward, Erie, Pa.

BACON MACARONI 'N CHEESE
Serves 4-6

3/4 pound bacon, diced
1 cup onions, chopped
1 quart milk
2 teaspoons celery salt
1/2 teaspoon pepper
1/4 teaspoon Tabasco sauce
2 cups elbow macaroni
1 cup cheese, grated
1/2 cup pimiento, chopped

In large skillet, cook bacon and onion over low heat for 15 minutes. Drain drippings. Add milk, celery salt, pepper, and Tabasco. Heat to boiling; gradually add macaroni, so that milk continues to boil. Simmer, uncovered, for 20 minutes, stirring often. Add cheese and pimiento; stir until cheese melts. Serve hot.

Agnes Ward, Erie, Pa.

QUICK CHILI-RICE DINNER
Serves 4

3/4 pound ground beef
1/3 cup chopped onion
1 tablespoon chili powder
1/2 teaspoon dry mustard
1 (10-ounce) package whole-kernel corn
1 cup diced green pepper
1 (15-ounce) can tomato sauce
1/2 cup water
1 cup Minute Rice
1/2 cup shredded cheddar cheese

Brown beef and onion in skillet. Add spices, corn, green pepper, tomato sauce, and water. Cover and bring to a full boil, stirring occasionally. Stir in rice; reduce heat; cover and simmer for 5 minutes. Sprinkle with cheese.

Good for when time is limited; takes only 20 minutes to prepare.

Mrs. George Franks, Millerton, Pa.

VEGETABLE CASSEROLE

1 can French-style green beans, drained
1/2 cup chopped celery
1/2 cup chopped green pepper
1/2 cup sour cream
1 can white shoepeg corn, drained
1/2 cup chopped onion
1/4 cup grated sharp cheese
1-1/2 cups crushed cheese crackers
1 can cream of mushroom soup
1/4 cup margarine
1/2 cup sliced almonds

Mix drained beans, corn, celery, green pepper, and onion. Alternate one layer vegetables with a layer of soup, grated cheese, then sour cream. Bake 25 minutes at 350 degrees.

Melt margarine and stir in crackers and almonds. Spread this on top of casserole and cook for 10 more minutes.

Connie Matthes, Florence, SC

CORN AND SAUSAGE CASSEROLE

1 pound sausage
1/4 cup bell pepper, chopped
1 can whole kernel corn, drained
1 large can evaporated milk
2 tablespoons flour
1/4 teaspoons salt
1-1/2 cups grated cheese

Brown sausage and pepper until sausage is cooked. Drain and save 2 tablespoons sausage drippings. Add sausage to casserole dish with corn. Blend sausage drippings with flour in skillet over medium heat. Add milk and salt; simmer 2-3 minutes until thickened, stirring constantly. Pour over sausage and corn mixture; stir together. Top with grated cheese. Bake in a 350 degree oven for 25-30 minutes until bubbly.

Mary M. West, Columbia, IN

SPAGHETTI RING

1/2 pound spaghetti
2 cups hot milk
1/4 cup butter
2 cups shredded Cheddar cheese
2 cups soft bread crumbs
2 eggs, well beaten
2 tablespoons minced onions
2 tablespoons minced parsley
2 tablespoons minced pimento
1 teaspoon salt
1/4 teaspoon pepper

Cook and drain spaghetti. Combine remaining ingredients. Mix thoroughly. Pour into well-greased 10-inch ring mold. Set in pan of hot water 1-inch deep. Bake at 350 degrees until set, about 30 minutes. Unmold on hot platter. Fill center with choice of creamed chicken, creamed seafood or any combination of creamed vegetables.

Hyacinth Rizzo, Snyder, NY

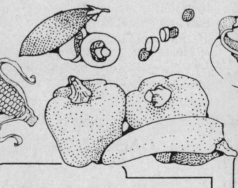

HASH BROWN POTATO CASSEROLE

1 (32-ounce) package frozen hash brown potatoes
1/2 cup melted margarine
8 ounces shredded Cheddar cheese
1 cup onions, chopped
1 pint sour cream
1 can cream of chicken soup
1 teaspoon salt
1/2 teaspoon garlic salt
1 cup corn flakes
1/4 cup melted margarine

Partially defrost hash browns. Mix potatoes, 1/2 cup margarine, cheese, onions, sour cream, soup, and spices. Put into greased 9 x 13-inch dish. Sprinkle corn flakes on top of potatoes; pour the 1/4 cup margarine over corn flakes. Bake uncovered in 350 degree oven for 1 hour and 15 minutes.

Edna Mae Seelos, Niles, Ill.

LAZY DAY LIMA BEAN CASSEROLE

2 cups grated American cheese
2/3 cup undiluted evaporated milk
1/2 teaspoon prepared mustard
2 cups cooked, large lima beans
2 medium tomatoes
Salt and pepper to taste

Combine cheese, milk and mustard. Cook and stir over hot water until cheese melts and sauce is smooth. Put lima beans into ovenproof casserole. Cover with 3/4 of sauce. Top casserole with tomato slices, salt and pepper and the remaining sauce. Bake in a 375 degree oven for 25 minutes or until lightly browned and bubbly on top.

Mrs. Gwen Campbell, Sterling, VA

SKILLET MACARONI AND CHEESE

Serves 6 to 8

1/4 cup butter or margarine
1 cup chopped onion
1 tablespoon all-purpose flour
1-1/2 teaspoons salt
1/4 teaspoon oregano
7 or 8 ounce package elbow macaroni
3-1/2 cups milk
2 cups shredded Cheddar cheese

Melt butter in skillet; add onion and saute until tender. Stir in flour, salt and oregano; add macaroni and milk. Cover and bring to boil; reduce heat and simmer 15 minutes or until macaroni is tender, stirring occasionally. Add cheese and stir until cheese is melted (do not boil).

Barbara Beauregard-Smith, South Australia

STEAK AND POTATO CASSEROLE

2-1/2 pounds round steak, 1/2 - 3/4 inch thick
1/4 cup flour
4 teaspoons salt
1/2 teaspoon pepper
1/4 cup oil
3-1/2 cups water
8 medium carrots, thinly sliced diagonally
8 medium potatoes, thinly sliced
1-3/8-ounce envelope onion soup mix
Chopped parsley for garnish

Preheat oven to 325 degrees. Cut meat into 6 - 8 serving pieces, trimming fat and bone. On wooden board or waxed paper, using meat mallet or edge of heavy saucer, pound mixture of flour, salt and pepper into meat.

In heavy skillet over medium heat, brown meat well on both sides in hot oil. Do not crowd pieces. Arrange browned meat in 3-quart casserole. Place carrots and potato slices on top. Sprinkle with onion soup mix and pour over 3-1/2 cups water. Bake, covered 2 hours or until tender. Skim excess fat. If you wish, thicken with 2 tablespoons flour mixed with 1 tablespoon butter; form into balls and drop into casserole. Return to oven 10 minutes. Sprinkle with parsley and serve.

Eleanor V. Craycraft, Santa Monica, CA

CHINESE TUNA CASSEROLE
Serves 4

14 ounce can Chinese vegetables, drained
10 3/4 ounce can cream of mushroom soup
9 1/4 ounce can tuna fish, drained and flaked
3/4 cup celery, thinly sliced
1 tablespoon soy sauce
1/4 teaspoon pepper
3 ounce can Chinese noodles

Preheat oven to 350 degrees. Mix all ingredients, except noodles, in ungreased 1-1/2 quart casserole. Sprinkle with noodles. Bake uncovered until contents are bubbly and noodles golden brown, about 40 to 45 minutes. Serve with hot rolls and salad.   **Judy M. Sax, San Antonio, TX**

SHRIMP AND ASPARAGUS CASSEROLE
Serves 6 to 8

1 cup rice, cooked
1 pound fresh asparagus, cut up and cooked, (or 1 package frozen cut-up asparagus, cooked)
3 cans (4-1/2 ounces each) shrimp
2 tablespoons butter
2 tablespoons flour
1-1/4 cups milk
1/2 pound sharp Cheddar cheese, grated
Salt and paprika

Heat oven to 350 degrees (moderate). Spread rice in buttered baking dish, 11-1/2 x 7-1/2 x 1-1/2". Spread asparagus over rice. Cover with shrimp. Melt butter, stir in flour; cook over low heat, stirring until mixture is smooth, bubbly. Remove from heat. Stir in milk and cheese. Bring to boil; boil 1 minute, stirring constantly. Season to taste with salt and paprika. Pour sauce over shrimp in baking dish. Sprinkle with paprika. Bake 20 minutes.

CHICKEN AND HAM CASSEROLE

7 slices white meat of chicken, uniform size
3 slices boiled ham, cut same size
1/2 small Bermuda onion, finely minced
1/4 cup butter
1/2 cup sliced mushrooms
1 teaspoon paprika
1 teaspoon salt
1/4 teaspoon nutmeg
3/4 cup cream
3-4 tablespoons grated Parmesan cheese

Cook the onion in butter for 5 minutes, stirring constantly and do not let it brown. Add the sliced mushrooms and seasonings and let simmer for 15 minutes. Turn the mixture into an oblong baking dish and arrange chicken and ham on the top. Add enough hot cream to cover the meat. Let simmer in a hot 400 degree oven for 10 minutes. Cover with Parmesan cheese; let remain in oven until cheese is browned.

Agnes Ward, Erie, PA

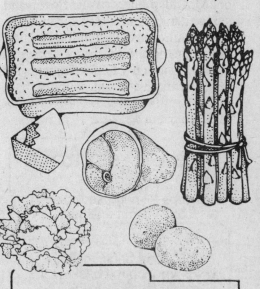

"SOUPER" CHICKEN CASSEROLE

2 cups diced, cooked chicken
1 (16-ounce) bag frozen broccoli, carrots, and cauliflower (thawed and drained)
1 can cream of mushroom soup
1 cup shredded Swiss cheese
1/3 cup sour cream
1/4 teaspoon pepper
1 can French fried onions

Combine all ingredients *except* the cheese and onions. Add one-half of the cheese, and one-half of the onions. Pour into casserole; bake uncovered, in a 350 degree oven for 30 minutes. Top with remaining onions and cheese; bake uncovered 5 minutes longer.

Debbie Vlahoric, Mesa, AZ

TOMATO, BURGER 'N' BEANS
Serves 5

1 pound ground chuck
1 cup water
1 (1 1/2-ounce) package sloppy joe mix
1 (6-ounce) can tomato paste
2 (16-ounce) cans French-style green beans, drained
1 small can mushrooms, drained
1/2 cup shredded cheddar cheese

Brown ground chuck in large skillet; drain off all fat. Stir in sloppy joe seasoning; mix in water until thickened. Add tomato paste. Cover and simmer for 10 minutes. Stir in beans and mushrooms. Turn into a 2-quart casserole; top with cheese. Bake in preheated oven of 350 degrees for 20–30 minutes, or until bubbly.

Hazel Wagener, Carrollton, Ill.

PIZZA CASSEROLE

3 cups all-purpose flour
3 cups instant mashed potatoes
1¼ cups milk
1 cup margarine, melted
1 pound ground beef
1 pound bulk sausage
1 large onion, chopped
1 (8-ounce) can tomato sauce
1 (6-ounce) can pitted ripe olives, drained
1 (6-ounce) can tomato paste
½ package sloppy joe seasoning mix
¼ teaspoon garlic powder
1¼ cups shredded mozzarella cheese

For crust, combine flour, potatoes, milk and margarine. Set aside. For filling, in a 12-inch skillet, cook beef, sausage and onion until onion is tender and meat is no longer pink. Drain off fat. Stir in tomato sauce, olives, tomato paste, seasoning mix and garlic powder.

Press half of crust into 13 x 9 x 2-inch baking pan. Spread filling over crust. Sprinkle with cheese. Roll remaining crust and put on top of filling. Bake at 425 degrees for 30–35 minutes, or until crust is golden. Let stand 5 minutes.

Mrs. A. Curtis, Rector, Ark.

AMISH-STYLE YUM-A-SETTA
Serves 6–8

2 pounds hamburger
Salt and pepper to taste
2 tablespoons brown sugar
¼ cup chopped onion
1 (10¾-ounce) can tomato soup, undiluted
1 (10¾-ounce) can chicken soup, undiluted
1 (16-ounce) package egg noodles
1 (8-ounce) package processed cheese, such as Kraft or Velveeta

Brown hamburger with salt, pepper, brown sugar and onion. Add tomato soup. Cook egg noodles according to package; drain. Add cream of chicken soup. Layer hamburger mixture and noodle mixture in 9 x 12-inch casserole with processed cheese between layers. Bake at 350 degrees for 30 minutes.

This is a great recipe to make for a potluck dinner, for a reunion, or to use up staples around the house. Can easily be made the day before.

Mary C. Canfield, Cuyahoga Falls, Ohio

COUNTRY PIE

Crust:
1 (8-ounce) can tomato sauce (reserve 1/2 cup for filling)
1/2 cup bread crumbs
1/2 teaspoon salt
1/4 cup chopped green pepper
1/4 cup chopped onion
1 pound ground beef
1/8 teaspoon pepper
1/8 teaspoon oregano

Combine these ingredients and mix well. Pat meat mixture into bottom of a greased 9-inch pie plate. Set aside.

Filling:
1-1/3 cups Minute Rice
1-1/2 (8-ounce) cans tomato sauce (plus the reserved 1/2 cup from previous measure)
1-1/2 cups grated cheddar cheese
1 cup water
1/2 teaspoon salt

Combine rice, sauce, salt, water and 1 cup cheese. Spoon rice mixture into meat shell. Cover with foil and bake at 350 degrees for 40 minutes. Uncover and sprinkle remaining cheese on top of pie. Return to oven and bake, uncovered, for 10–15 minutes longer.

Carol Nodoline, Easten, Pa.

FRENCH TUNA BAKE
Serves 4

1 medium eggplant, sliced
1 tomato, peeled and sliced
1 green pepper, cut in strips
1 zucchini, sliced
1 onion, sliced
¼ cup minced fresh parsley
2 tablespoons fresh lemon juice
½ teaspoon salt
⅛ teaspoon black pepper
½ teaspoon dried leaf thyme
2 (6½–7-ounce) cans water-packed tuna, drained
1 cup shredded, low-fat mozzarella cheese

Layer eggplant, tomato, pepper strips, zucchini and onion in buttered (low-calorie margarine) casserole dish. Sprinkle with parsley, lemon juice, salt, pepper and thyme. Bake, uncovered, in preheated 375-degree oven for 45 minutes. Stir in tuna; sprinkle with cheese. Return to oven and bake 15 minutes longer. Aromatic, too! (193 calories per serving)

Judie Betz, Eureka, Calif.

SUNSHINE TORTILLA PIE
Serves 7

1½ pounds ground beef
1 onion, chopped
1 green pepper, chopped
½ cup flour
½ teaspoon salt
1¼ teaspoons chili powder
1 (16-ounce) can tomato sauce
1 cup water
½ cup pimiento-stuffed olives, chopped
12 tortillas
3½ cups sharp cheddar cheese, grated
6 hard-cooked eggs, divided

Sauté meat; add onion and green pepper; cook 5 minutes. Sprinkle vegetables and meat with flour, salt and chili powder. Stir in tomato sauce, water and olives; simmer 5 minutes. In ovenproof dish alternate layers of tortillas, cheese, 3 sliced eggs and sauce over all. Finely chop or sieve remaining 3 eggs; sprinkle on top of sauce.

Gwen Campbell, Sterling, Va.

QUICK AND EASY MACARONI AND CHEESE

1 (7-ounce) package Creamettes macaroni (2 cups)
1 pound lean ground beef
½ cup chopped onion
½ cup sliced celery
2 (8-ounce) cans Hunt's tomato sauce with mushrooms
1 teaspoon salt
¼ teaspoon pepper
1 (8-ounce) package shredded cheddar cheese (2 cups)

Cook macaroni as directed on package; drain. Brown ground beef, onion and celery in skillet. Pour off excess fat. Stir in tomato sauce with mushrooms, salt and pepper. Combine meat mixture with Creamettes macaroni. Pour into a 2-quart casserole and stir in a portion of the cheese; sprinkle top with additional cheese. Bake at 350 degrees for about 25 minutes, or until cheese melts.

Very good with a lettuce salad and Italian bread.

Pat Blanchetta, Coal City, Ill.

MEXICALI CASSEROLE
Serves 8

1/2 cup chopped onion
1 tablespoon shortening, melted
1 (16-ounce) can tomatoes, chopped and drained
1 (17-ounce) can whole-kernel corn, drained
2 (15-ounce) cans chili with beans
1 (8-ounce) package corn muffin mix
1 cup (4 ounces) shredded cheddar cheese

Heat oven to 350 degrees. In skillet, cook onion in shortening for 10 minutes. Add tomatoes, corn and chili; mix until well-blended. Pour into 12 x 8-inch baking dish. Prepare corn muffin mix according to package directions; stir cheese into batter. Spoon batter mixture around edge of baking dish. Bake 30 minutes. This is great with jalapeño pepper cheese, as well as with cheddar cheese.

Leota Baxter, Ingalls, Kan.

LASAGNA-STYLE CASSEROLE
Serves 6

6 ounces large bow-tie pasta (2-1/4 cups)
1 pound ground beef or pork
1 (15-ounce) can pizza sauce
1 teaspoon minced dry onion
1/2 teaspoon dry basil, crushed
1 egg, beaten
1 cup ricotta cheese or cottage cheese
1/4 cup grated Parmesan cheese
1 cup shredded mozzarella cheese

Cook pasta until tender; drain. Fry meat until browned; drain off fat. Add pizza sauce, onion, and basil to meat and mix well. In a bowl, combine egg and cottage cheese or ricotta. In a greased 12x9-1/2x2-inch baking dish, layer half of the pasta.

Spoon cheese mixture over pasta. Sprinkle with Parmesan cheese. Layer remaining pasta, meat, and mozzarella cheese. Bake, covered, at 425 degrees for 15 minutes. Uncover and bake 5-8 minutes longer, or until heated through.

Vickie Vogt, Kewaskum, Wis.

MANDARIN ORANGE CASHEW CASSEROLE
Serves 5

1 pound ground beef
1/4 cup celery, cut diagonally
1/2 cup green onion, cut diagonally in 1-inch pieces
1/4 cup green pepper, chopped
1 1/2 teaspoons garlic, minced
1 cup water
1/4 teaspoon toasted sesame oil
2 tablespoons cornstarch
1 teaspoon sugar
1/4 teaspoon 5-Spice Powder
1/4 teaspoon ginger root, minced
1/4 cup soy sauce
2 tablespoons water
1 (16-ounce) can chop suey vegetables, drained
1 (10-ounce) package frozen peas
1 (3-ounce) can chow mein noodles
1 cup cashew halves

In a skillet cook beef, celery, green onion, green pepper, garlic; drain. Add the water and sesame oil; bring to a boil. Combine cornstarch, sugar, 5-Spice Powder, ginger root, soy sauce and water. Add to beef mixture in skillet; cook until thickened and bubbly. Stir in the drained chop suey vegetables; add frozen peas. Turn into 2-quart casserole; bake, covered, at 375 degrees for 1 1/2 hours; uncover and bake 10 minutes more.

To serve: Sprinkle each individual serving with chow mein noodles; scatter the cashew halves over top surface.

Gwen Campbell, Sterling, Va.

SPINACH NOODLE CASSEROLE

serves 10-12

1 pound package noodles
2 (10-ounce) packages frozen
  chopped spinach
1 pound fresh mushrooms, sliced
1/2 onion, chopped
2-4 tablespoons margarine
1 (10-ounce) can cream of chicken
  soup
1 (10-ounce) can cream of mushroom soup
1 cup sour cream
2 tablespoons Worcestershire
  sauce
2 tablespoons margarine
Salt & pepper to taste

Cook noodles and drain. Cook spinach and drain well. Sauté mushrooms and onion in margarine. Mix together all ingredients, except 2 tablespoons margarine. Place in large greased casserole. Dot with margarine. Bake at 350 degrees for 30 minutes or until bubbly.

Note: Recipe may be halved. Omit either can of soup. For a variation you may add 1 (7-ounce) can tuna or 1 pound ground beef, cooked and drained, before baking.

Mrs. George Franks, Millerton, Pa.

MACARONI AND SAUSAGE BAKE

Serves 6

1 pound bulk pork sausage
1/2 cup chopped onion
1 cup elbow macaroni
1 (10-1/2 ounce) can cream of
  celery soup
2/3 cup milk
3 beaten eggs
1-1/2 cups shredded processed
  American cheese

Cook macaroni according to package directions. Cook sausage and onion until browned. Drain off excess fat. Combine sausage mixture, macaroni, soup, milk, eggs, and cheese. Place in 2-quart casserole. Bake at 350 degrees for 40-45 minutes.

Sharon M. Crider, Evansville, Wis.

BROCCOLI CASSEROLE

Serves 8

1/4 cup chopped onion
6 tablespoons butter or margarine
1/2 cup water
2 tablespoons flour
8 ounces processed cheese spread
2 packages frozen chopped broccoli,
  thawed and drained
3 eggs, well beaten
1/2 cup cracker crumbs

Sauté onion in 4 tablespoons butter until soft; stir in flour and add water. Cook over low heat, stirring, until mixture thickens and comes to a boil. Blend in cheese. Combine sauce and broccoli. Add eggs; mix gently until blended. Turn into a 1-1/2 quart casserole; cover with crumbs and dot with remaining butter. Bake at 325 degrees for 30 minutes.

Agnes Ward, Erie, PA

TURNIP CASSEROLE

Serves 4

1 1/2 lbs. turnips, peeled and
  thinly sliced
2 tablespoons butter
1 onion, thinly sliced
2/3 cup chopped celery
2 tablespoons flour
1 cup milk
1/2 cup grated sharp cheese
Salt and pepper to taste
3 tbsps. bread crumbs

Cook turnips in boiling, salted water to cover until just tender. Drain. Saute in butter the oinion, green pepper, and celery until tender. Sprinkle with flour and cook 1 minute. Add milk and stir until thickened. Stir in cheese, salt and pepper. Combine cheese sauce with turnips, place in baking dish and top with curmbs. Brown under broiler. May be prepared ahead and place-dunder broiler just before serving.

Marcella Swigert, Monroe City, MO

YELLOW SQUASH CASSEROLE

2 pounds yellow squash
1 large onion
1 can cream of chicken soup
1 jar pimientos (optional)
1 cup sour cream
1 teaspoon salt
1/4 teaspoon pepper
1 stick margarine
1 (8-ounce) package Pepperidge
  Farms herbal dressing

Boil squash until tender; drain and mash. Chop onion; sauté in a half stick margarine until tender. Add soup, chopped pimiento, sour cream, salt, and pepper. Melt the remaining margarine and add to dressing crumbs. Put half of dressing in bottom of baking dish. Mix all ingredients together. Pour on dressing. Spread remaining half of the dressing on top. Bake at 350 degrees for approximately 1 hour.

Mildred Beckham, Edgar, FL

PARSNIP CASSEROLE

2 pounds parsnips
2 tablespoons butter
1/4 teaspoon fresh or dried rosemary
2 tablespoons flour
1/4 cup grated Parmesan cheese
2 cups light cream or half-and-half
1/2 cup cracker crumbs
1/4 cup melted butter

Peel parsnips. Cook in boiling, salted water until tender. Drain; cut each in half lengthwise, or slice in rounds, if parsnips are large. Arrange half the parsnips in bottom of greased 1-1/2 quart baking dish. Dot with half the butter; sprinkle with half the rosemary, flour, and cheese. Drizzle with half the cream. Repeat layers. Mix cracker crumbs with melted butter; sprinkle over casserole. Bake, uncovered, in 400 degree oven for 20 minutes.

Diantha Hibbard, Rochester, NY

Classic
COOKIES

SOUR CREAM COOKIES

2 cups sugar
1 cup lard
1 cup sour cream
3 eggs, beaten
1/2 teaspoon salt
1 teaspoon baking soda
1 teaspoon vanilla or lemon flavoring
Enough flour to make a soft dough (2 cups or more as needed)

Combine dry ingredients (except sugar). Beat together sugar and lard; add beaten eggs and sour cream; mix well. Add flavoring. Combine dry ingredients with creamed mixture, blending well. Roll out on a floured surface and cut with cookie cutters. Bake in preheated 400-degree oven until golden brown, about 12 minutes.

Margaret Kudlacik, Rockford, Ill.

NO-BAKE LEMON GRAHAM SQUARES

Whole graham crackers
1 cup margarine
1/2 cup milk
1 cup sugar
1 egg, slightly beaten
1 cup coconut
1 cup chopped nuts
1 cup graham cracker crumbs

Cover bottom of 9x13-inch pan with whole crackers. Heat to boiling the margarine, milk, sugar, and egg. Add coconut, nuts, and graham cracker crumbs. Spread over the graham crackers in the pan. Chill. Frost with Lemon Icing.

Lemon Icing:
2 cups confectioners' sugar
1 stick margarine
2 tablespoons lemon or to taste

Cut into 1-inch squares. Prepare to have recipe handy when this is served. The recipe is *always* requested. Freezes well, too.

Marjorie McDowell, West Salem, Ill.

RAISIN CRISSCROSS COOKIES
Makes 3 dozen

1/2 cup shortening (part butter *or* margarine)
3/4 cup sugar
1 egg
1/2 teaspoon lemon extract
1 3/4 cups all-purpose flour
3/4 teaspoon cream of tartar
3/4 teaspoon soda
1/4 teaspoon salt
1 cup raisins

Preheat oven to 400 degrees. Mix thoroughly shortening, sugar, egg and extract. Measure flour and sift. Blend flour, cream of tartar, soda and salt. Stir into shortening mixture. Stir in raisins. Roll into 1-inch balls. Place about 3 inches apart on ungreased baking sheet. Flatten with fork dipped in flour, making a crisscross pattern. Bake 8–10 minutes.

Delicious lemon-flavored raisin cookies … children love them!

Marcella Swigert, Monroe City, Mo.

CRISPY CHOCOLATE CARAMEL BARS
Makes 36

Crust:
1¼ cups all-purpose flour
½ cup margarine *or* butter
½ cup confectioners' sugar

Filling:
1 (14-ounce) package vanilla caramels
⅓ cup half-and-half *or* evaporated milk
¼ cup margarine *or* butter

Topping:
1 (6-ounce) package (1 cup) semisweet chocolate chips
3 tablespoons shortening
¾ cup crisp rice cereal

Heat oven to 350 degrees. Lightly spoon flour into measuring cup. In medium bowl, combine flour and confectioners' sugar. Using pastry blender or fork, cut in ½ cup margarine until crumbly. Lightly press mixture in ungreased 13 x 9-inch pan. Bake at 350 degrees for 10–12 minutes, or until light brown. Meanwhile, in heavy saucepan melt caramels, half-and-half and ¼ cup margarine over low heat, stirring constantly. Spread over baked crust. In medium saucepan over low heat, melt chocolate chips and shortening, stirring constantly. Stir in cereal. Carefully spread over filling. Cool completely; cut into bars.

Grace Moser, Goshen, Ind.

PEANUT BUTTER ORANGE DATE COOKIES

Makes 6 dozen

3/4 cup butter *or* margarine
1 cup peanut butter, plain or chunky
  style
1 cup granulated sugar
1 cup firmly packed brown sugar
2 eggs
1 1/2 teaspoons grated orange peel
1 teaspoon real vanilla
1 1/2 cups whole-wheat flour
1 cup all-purpose flour
1 teaspoon baking powder
1 teaspoon baking soda
1/2 teaspoon salt
1 cup finely chopped dates

Preheat oven to 350 degrees. Cream butter or margarine; add peanut butter and sugars; beat until light and fluffy. Beat in eggs, orange peel and vanilla. Stir together whole-wheat flour, all-purpose flour, baking powder, baking soda and salt. Sift flour mixture into butter mixture to form a soft dough. Stir in dates. Refrigerate dough for several hours or overnight. Shape dough into walnut-size balls. Place on cookie sheets. Flatten with tines of fork. Bake in 350-degree oven for 10–12 minutes, or until lightly browned. Cool in pan on wire rack; remove from pan and complete cooling. Store in airtight container when cool.

Trenda Leigh, Richmond, Va.

APRICOT-COCONUT BALLS

Makes 5 dozen

2 (6-ounce) packages dried
   apricots, ground
1 cup shredded coconut
⅔ cup sweetened condensed
   milk
   Confectioners' sugar

Combine apricots and coconut; stir to mix. Add condensed milk and mix well. Shape into 1-inch balls and coat with confectioners' sugar.

Mrs. Bruce Fowler, Woodruff, S.C.

GUMDROP JEWELS

Makes 5–6 dozen

1   cup (2 sticks) butter
1   cup firmly packed light
     brown sugar
1   egg
1   teaspoon vanilla extract
1½   cups all-purpose flour
½   teaspoon *each* baking
     soda, baking powder, salt
1   cup quick oats, uncooked
1   cup cut-up gumdrops
½   cup chopped nuts

Preheat oven to 350 degrees. Cream butter. Gradually add sugar and continue beating until blended. Beat in egg and vanilla. Combine flour, soda, baking powder and salt. Gradually add to creamed mixture. Stir in oats, gumdrops and nuts. Drop by rounded teaspoonfuls onto unbuttered cookie sheets. Bake 12–14 minutes. Remove to wire rack to cool.

APPLE BARS

2-1/2 cups flour
1 tablespoon sugar
1 teaspoon salt
1 cup margarine
1 egg yolk and milk to make 2/3 cup

Combine ingredients to make dough. Roll out half of dough; place in 15x10-inch jelly roll pan.

5 cups sliced apples
1 cup sugar
1 teaspoon cinnamon
1 or 2 tablespoons flour
1 egg white

Combine remaining ingredients, except egg white. Put on crust; roll out rest of dough; place on top of apples. Beat the egg white until stiff; spread on top crust. Bake at 400 degrees for 40 minutes. While hot, drizzle glaze over top.

Glaze:
1 cup confectioners' sugar
2 tablespoons milk

Elaine Dodd, Pasco, Wash.

PINEAPPLE-COCONUT COOKIES

Makes 3½ dozen

½   cup sugar
¼   cup brown sugar
¼   cup margarine
¼   cup shortening
1   egg
1   teaspoon vanilla
1¼   cups flour
¾   teaspoon salt
½   teaspoon soda
¼   teaspoon ginger
1   cup coconut
½   cup crushed pineapple, well-
     drained
½   cup chopped nuts

Cream first 6 ingredients together until light and fluffy. Stir dry ingredients together and beat into creamy mixture. Stir in coconut, pineapple and nuts. Drop teaspoonfuls 2 inches apart on a greased cookie sheet. Bake at 375 degrees for 8–10 minutes. Let stand 30 seconds on sheet after removing from oven, then cool on wire racks.

Mrs. A.C. Yoder, Meherrin, Va.

BANANA OATMEAL DROPS

Makes 4 dozen

¾   cup shortening
1   cup sugar
1   egg
1   medium-size banana, mashed
½   teaspoon lemon juice
1½   cups sifted flour
½   teaspoon soda
1   teaspoon salt
¾   teaspoon cinnamon
¼   teaspoon nutmeg
1½   cups quick-cooking oats
½   cup chopped walnuts

Cream together shortening and sugar until light and fluffy. Beat in egg. Stir in banana and lemon juice. Sift together flour, soda, salt, cinnamon and nutmeg. Stir into creamed mixture. Mix in oats and walnuts. Drop from a teaspoon onto greased baking sheets, about 2 inches apart. Bake in a moderate oven of 350 degrees for 12–15 minutes, or until edges turn golden.

Marcella Swigart, Monroe City, Mo.

BRAZIL NUT MELTS

1 cup flour
1/3 cup sugar
1 egg
3 tablespoons orange juice or milk
Confectioners' sugar
1/2 teaspoon salt
1/2 cup shortening
1 teaspoon grated orange peel
3/4 cup chopped Brazil nuts

In large bowl, combine all ingredients except confectioners' sugar. Blend well. Drop by rounded teaspoonsful onto ungreased cookie sheets. Bake at 350 degrees for 10 to 12 minutes.

While still hot, roll in confectioners' sugar.

Mrs. Raymond Weeks, Columbus, Ohio

ORANGE COCONUT REFRIGERATOR COOKIES

Makes 11 dozen

½ cup (1 stick) butter
½ cup firmly packed light brown sugar
¾ cup granulated sugar
1 egg
2 teaspoons grated orange peel
1 teaspoon vanilla extract
1¾ cups all-purpose flour
2 teaspoons baking powder
¼ teaspoon salt
⅓ cup flaked coconut

Cream butter. Add sugars and continue beating until blended. Beat in egg, orange peel and vanilla. Combine flour, baking powder and salt; add to creamed mixture. Blend in coconut. On floured surface form into rolls 1½ inches in diameter. Wrap in waxed paper. Chill several hours. Preheat oven to 400 degrees. Cut rolls into ⅛-inch slices and place on buttered cookie sheets. Bake 5–6 minutes. Remove to wire rack to cool.
Note: The rolls can be placed in wrapping and refrigerated up to 1 week or frozen up to 3 months. If frozen unthaw and bake as directed.

APPLE TREASURE COOKIES

Makes 5–6 dozen

1 cup shortening
1½ cups firmly packed light brown sugar
¼ cup molasses
3 eggs, unbeaten
3½ cups sifted all-purpose flour
½ teaspoon salt
1 teaspoon baking powder
3 teaspoons cinnamon
½ teaspoon nutmeg
½ teaspoon cloves
1 cup roasted peanuts, chopped
1 cup finely chopped apples

Cream shortening with brown sugar until light and fluffy. Add molasses. Add eggs, 1 at a time. In separate bowl sift flour, salt, spices and baking powder; add to sugar-molasses mixture; mix lightly. Stir in peanuts and apples. Drop by spoonfuls onto greased baking sheets. Bake at 350 degrees for 12–15 minutes.

Peggy Fowler, Woodruff, S.C.

GRAHAM CRACKER BARS

Makes 3 dozen

1-1/2 cups graham cracker crumbs
1/4 cup sugar
1/3 cup margarine, melted
1 (8-ounce) package cream cheese, softened
1/2 cup sugar
1 egg
3/4 cup flaked coconut
3/4 cup chopped nuts
1 (6-ounce) package semisweet chocolate pieces

Combine crumbs, sugar, and margarine. Press onto bottom of 13x9-inch baking pan. Bake at 350 degrees for 5 minutes.

Combine cream cheese, sugar, and egg, mixing until well-blended. Spread over crust. Sprinkle with remaining ingredients; press lightly into surface. Bake at 350 degrees for 25-30 minutes, or until lightly browned. Cool and cut into bars.

Ruby Walsh, West Chicago, Ill.

CALIFORNIA TRAIL BARS

Makes 3 dozen

1 cup light corn syrup
1/2 cup packed brown sugar
1/4 teaspoon salt
1-1/2 cups chunk-style peanut butter
1 teaspoon vanilla
1 cup non-fat dry milk
1 cup granola cereal (crush large lumps)
1 cup whole-bran cereal
1 cup raisins
1 (6-ounce) package semisweet chocolate pieces

Line 9x13-inch pan with waxed paper. In heavy saucepan combine syrup, sugar, and salt; bring to boil. Remove from heat; stir in peanut butter and vanilla. Stir in remaining ingredients, except chocolate; cool slightly. Add chocolate; press into prepared pan. Refrigerate 30 minutes; cut into bars. Store in refrigerator.

Sarah Lane, Philadelphia, Pa.

HAWAIIAN OATMEAL COOKIES

Makes 3 dozen

1 cup flour
1 teaspoon baking powder
1 teaspoon baking soda
¾ teaspoon salt
½ cup shortening
½ cup granulated sugar
½ cup brown sugar, packed
1 egg
½ teaspoon vanilla
1 cup rolled oats
1 cup shredded coconut

Sift together flour, baking powder, baking soda and salt; set aside. Cream shortening and sugars until light and fluffy; add egg; mix well. Add vanilla, then flour mixture. Add oats and coconut; mix until well-blended. Shape into small walnut-size balls; place on ungreased cookie sheets. Bake at 350 degrees about 12–15 minutes, or until golden.

Margaret Russo, Winsted, Conn.

CORNFLAKE MACAROONS
Makes 2½ dozen

3 egg whites
1 cup sugar
¼ teaspoon almond extract
¼ teaspoon vanilla extract
1½ cups flaked coconut
3 cups cornflakes

Beat egg whites until stiff but not dry; gradually add sugar. Add flavorings; fold in coconut and cornflakes. Drop by teaspoonfuls onto well-greased cookie sheets. Bake at 300 degrees for about 20 minutes. Remove from cookie sheet as soon as removed from oven.

Sandra Russell, Gainesville, Fla.

FROSTED CHOCOLATE CHIP BARS

2½ cups (1 pound) brown sugar
3 eggs
⅔ cup shortening, melted
2¾ cups flour
2½ teaspoons baking powder
½ teaspoon salt
1 cup salted nuts
1 (6-ounce) package chocolate chips

Cream sugar and eggs, 1 at a time, beating well after each 1. Add melted shortening, then sifted dry ingredients. Mix well. Add nuts and chocolate chips. Batter will be thick. Grease a 10 x 15½ x ¾-inch pan. Bake at 350 degrees for 25–30 minutes. Frost with recipe which follows. Cut when cool.

Frosting:
Confectioners' sugar (enough for spreading consistency desired)
2 tablespoons butter, melted
3 tablespoons milk
2 tablespoons cocoa

Blend butter, milk and cocoa; add confectioners' sugar to spreading consistency. Add ½ teaspoon vanilla.

Ilene Ongman, Klamath Falls, Ore.

COCOA BROWNIES
Makes 48-60 bars

1 cup flour
1 cup sugar
1/2 teaspoon salt
1/3 cup cocoa
1 cup (2 sticks) butter or margarine
3 eggs
1 1/2 teaspoons vanilla
1/2 cup chopped nuts
1 box fudge frosting mix

Mix and sift flour, sugar, salt and cocoa into bowl. Work softened butter into dry ingredients. Beat in eggs one at a time; add vanilla, ceasing to beat when blended. Stir in nuts. Turn into greased and floured 9x13x2-inch pan. Level batter with a flat blade to depth of 3/4 inch. Bake in a preheated 325-degree oven for 20 minutes, or until brownies test done.

Cool and frost with prepared frosting mix. Cut into bars.

Mrs. Shirley E. Churchill, Mattawan, Mich.

CREAM CHEESE CHOCOLATE CHIP COOKIES
Makes 4 dozen

1 cup margarine
1 cup sugar
1 (3-ounce) package cream cheese
2 eggs
1 teaspoon vanilla
½ teaspoon lemon extract
2½ cups flour
1 teaspoon baking powder
½ teaspoon baking soda
1 cup coarsely chopped pecans or walnuts
1 cup semisweet chocolate pieces

Cream margarine, then add sugar, beating until smooth and fluffy. Add cream cheese; blend in eggs, vanilla, and lemon extract. Mix flour, baking powder and baking soda together; stir into cream cheese mixture. Add nuts and chocolate pieces. Drop by teaspoon on lightly greased cookie sheet. Bake at 350 degrees for 12–15 minutes.

D. Villines, Clinton, Mo.

CHOCO DATE BALLS
Makes 3½ dozen

½ cup chunky peanut butter
¼ cup cocoa or carob powder
2 teaspoons vanilla
2 cups uncooked oat cereal
¼ cup butter or margarine
⅔ cup mild-flavored honey
1 cup finely snipped dates

In a small mixing bowl, blend peanut butter, cocoa or carob powder and vanilla, using 2 forks. Mix in oats. In a small saucepan bring butter and honey to a boil; stir 1 minute. Remove from heat and add dates. Blend into oat mixture. Shape into bite-size balls. Chill until firm. When firm, store in refrigerator in plastic bags. Best when served chilled.

Peggy Fowler Revels, Woodruff, S.C.

BANANA DROP COOKIES
Makes 4 dozen

2 ripe medium bananas, peeled
1 cup butter, softened
1 cup granulated sugar
½ cup brown sugar, packed
2 eggs
1 teaspoon vanilla extract
2 cups flour
1 teaspoon ground cinnamon (optional)
½ teaspoon baking soda
½ teaspoon salt
1 cup peanut butter chips
1 cup chopped walnuts
1 cup raisins

Purée or mash bananas to yield 1 cup; cream together butter and sugars. Beat in bananas, eggs and vanilla; combine flour, cinnamon, soda and salt. Gradually beat dry ingredients into banana mixture. Fold in peanut butter chips, nuts and raisins. Drop by tablespoonfuls onto greased cookie sheets. Bake in a 375-degree oven for 12 minutes until golden brown. Remove to wire rack to cool.

Peggy Fowler Revels, Woodruff, S.C.

HUNKER DUNKER COOKIES

2 cups butter or margarine
2 cups brown sugar
2 cups granulated sugar
4 eggs
2 teaspoons vanilla
2 teaspoons salt
2 teaspoons baking soda
4 cups flour
2 cups oatmeal
2 cups Rice Krispies

Cream butter and sugars together; add eggs and vanilla. Sift dry ingredients together and add to butter mixture. Stir in oatmeal and Rice Krispies. Bake at 350 degrees for 10 minutes.

This recipe is my family's favorite. I sometimes add chocolate chips for variation.

Sharon Sisson, Longview, Wash.

CITRUS SUGAR COOKIES
Makes 5 dozen

½ cup butter *or* margarine
1 cup sugar, divided
2 eggs
1 tablespoon frozen orange juice concentrate, thawed and undiluted
3 tablespoons grated orange rind, divided
2 cups flour
2 teaspoons baking powder

Cream butter and ½ cup sugar until light and fluffy. Add eggs, 1 at a time, beating well after each addition. Blend in orange juice and 1 tablespoon grated orange rind. Combine flour and baking powder; blend into creamed mixture. Wrap dough in waxed paper and refrigerate for 3 hours. Roll out on lightly floured surface to ¼-inch thickness. Cut with a 2-inch cookie cutter. Place on greased cookie sheet. Combine ½ cup sugar and 2 tablespoons grated orange rind; sprinkle mixture over cookies. Bake at 375 degrees for 8–10 minutes.

Barbara Beauregard-Smith, Northfield, South Australia

ICED PEANUT BUTTER COOKIES

½ cup margarine
½ cup sugar
½ cup brown sugar
2 eggs
⅓ cup peanut butter
½ teaspoon baking soda
¼ teaspoon salt
½ teaspoon vanilla
1 cup flour
1 cup rolled oats
1 cup chocolate chips

Mix together margarine, sugar and brown sugar. Blend in eggs, peanut butter, baking soda, vanilla, flour, salt and rolled oats. Spread in a greased 13 x 9 x 2-inch pan and bake at 350 degrees for 20 minutes. As soon as the pan is removed from the oven, sprinkle chocolate bits on the top. Return to oven for a few minutes to melt the chocolate; remove again, spreading chocolate evenly; allow to cool.

Icing:
¼ cup peanut butter
½ cup confectioners' sugar
Milk (2–4 teaspoons)

Combine peanut butter and confectioners' sugar. Moisten with milk until consistency to spread. Ice cooled cookies.

Amelia M. Brown, Pittsburgh, Pa.

OATMEAL FUDGE COOKIES

½ cup milk
½ cup vegetable shortening
6 tablespoons cocoa
¼ teaspoon salt
2 cups sugar
1 teaspoon vanilla
3 cups quick-cooking oatmeal

In saucepan place all ingredients, except oatmeal. Heat and bring to boil, and boil for 1 minute, stirring constantly. Remove from heat and stir in oatmeal. Drop by spoonfuls onto waxed paper. Chill to firm.

Mrs. Thurman White, Troy, N.Y.

BUTTERSCOTCH BARS

1 cup sugar
2 eggs
½ cup butter
2½ cups graham cracker crumbs
1½ cups marshmallows (cut up)
1 cup butterscotch chips
3 tablespoons peanut butter

In saucepan, bring sugar, eggs and butter to a boil, stirring constantly. Remove from heat and cool. Stir in cracker crumbs and marshmallows; press into 9 x 13-inch pan. Melt 1 cup butterscotch chips with peanut butter over hot water. Spread on top of crumbs. Cool. Cut into bars.

Mrs. E.J. Kuchenbecker, Prairie du Chien, Wis.

ORANGE COOKIES
Makes 2-1/2 dozen

1-1/3 cups flour
1/2 teaspoon baking powder
1/4 teaspoon baking soda
1/2 cup sugar
3 tablespoons shortening
3 tablespoons margarine
1 egg
1/3 cup buttermilk
1 teaspoon finely shredded orange peel
2 tablespoons orange juice
Orange Frosting (recipe follows)

Stir together flour, baking powder, and soda; set aside. Beat together sugar, shortening, and margarine. Add egg; beat until fluffy. Beat in buttermilk, orange peel, and orange juice. Add dry ingredients and beat until combined. Drop by teaspoonfuls onto ungreased cookie sheets. Bake at 350 degrees for 10-13 minutes. Cool, then frost.

Orange Frosting:
Beat together 2 cups confectioners' sugar, 3 teaspoons shredded orange peel, and 3 tablespoons orange juice to make a spreadable, thick frosting.

Denise Garcia, Salina, Kans.

RASPBERRY MERINGUE KISSES

3 egg whites
¾ cup sugar
3½ tablespoons raspberry gelatin
1 cup miniature chocolate bits
¼ teaspoon salt
1 teaspoon vinegar

Beat egg whites with salt until foamy. Add raspberry gelatin and sugar gradually. Beat until stiff peaks form and sugar is dissolved. Mix in vinegar and fold in chocolate bits. Drop by teaspoon onto ungreased cookie sheets covered with brown paper. Bake at 250 degrees for 20 minutes. Turn oven off and leave in oven 20 minutes longer.

Note: Too hot an oven may cause the cookies to lose some of their pink coloring, so set temperature at 225–250 degrees according to how your oven heats. For more color, add a few drops of red food coloring.

Wanda J. Harrison, Fremont, Wis.

PECAN BARS

1 stick margarine
1 1/4 cups white flour
2 beaten eggs
1 cup light brown sugar
1/2 cup chopped pecans
1/2 cup shredded coconut
1/2 cup chopped and drained maraschino cherries
1 tablespoon Grape Nuts cereal
2 tablespoons white flour
1/2 teaspoon baking powder
1 teaspoon almond extract

In large mixer bowl, make a crumb mixture of margarine and flour. Pat down firmly into non-stick 9x13-inch pan. Bake for 10 minutes in 350 degree oven. Remove from oven.

Mix together all other ingredients and spread over prepared base. Return to oven and bake at 350 degrees for 20 minutes. Cool in pan, then cut into bars with sharp knife.

Pearle M. Goodwin, South Ryegate, Vt.

CARAMEL-COATED COOKIES
Makes 28–30

Ingredients:
½ cup butter
1 teaspoon vanilla
½ cup confectioners' sugar
½ cup brown sugar, packed firmly
1 egg
2 cups flour

Coating:
36 caramels
6 ounces evaporated milk
Coarsely chopped pecans and shredded coconut

For the dough:
Cream butter with vanilla until soft. Add confectioners' sugar and brown sugar; blend well. Add egg; beat until blended. Mix in flour; blend well; form dough into 1-inch balls. Bake on ungreased cookie sheet in preheated 350-degree oven for 15–18 minutes.

For the coating:
In top of double boiler over simmering water, melt the caramels with evaporated milk, stirring until smooth. Dip cookies, 1 at a time, into caramel mixture; roll lightly into coconut; then roll into nuts. Place each into a small paper liner.

Marie Fusaro, Manasquan, N.J.

SESAME MACAROONS
Makes 3 dozen

½ cup sesame seeds
¼ teaspoon cream of tartar
¼ cup egg whites (about 2)
¼ cup sugar
½ teaspoon almond extract

Toast sesame seeds in 350-degree oven for 15 minutes, or until golden brown. Pulverize seeds in blender. Add cream of tartar to egg whites; beat until stiff. Gradually add sugar, beating well after each addition. Fold in sesame seeds and almond extract. Drop by teaspoonfuls onto lightly greased baking sheet. Bake in 250-degree oven for 30 minutes. Remove at once from baking sheet.

Agnes Ward, Erie, Pa.

SPECIAL SUGAR COOKIES

1/2 cup powdered sugar
1/2 cup white sugar
1 stick butter, softened
1/2 cup vegetable oil
1/2 teaspoon vanilla
2 cups all-purpose flour, plus 2 tablespoons
1 egg, beaten
1/2 teaspoon soda
1/2 teaspoon salt
1/2 teaspoon cream of tartar

Cream two sugars, butter and oil; add beaten egg; beat until fluffy. Sift dry ingredients, add to first mixture. Drop by teaspoonsful onto cookie sheet. Dip a glass bottom into sugar and press cookies down lightly.

Bake at 375 degrees for 10 minutes.

Mrs. Pearl L. Stevenson, Lafayette, Ind.

BANANA DROP COOKIES
Makes 4 dozen

2 ripe bananas, peeled
1 cup butter, softened
1 cup sugar
½ cup brown sugar, packed
2 eggs
1 teaspoon vanilla extract
2 cups flour
1 teaspoon ground cinnamon, optional
1 teaspoon baking soda
½ teaspoon salt
1 cup peanut butter chips
1 cup chopped walnuts
1 cup raisins

Preheat oven to 375 degrees. Mash bananas. Cream together butter and sugars. Beat in bananas, eggs and vanilla. In separate bowl, combine flour, cinnamon, soda and salt. Gradually beat dry ingredients into banana mixture. Fold in peanut butter chips, nuts and raisins. Drop by tablespoonfuls onto greased cookie sheets; bake 12 minutes, or until golden brown. Remove to wire rack to cool.

Kit Rollins, Cedarburg, Wis.

ANGEL FOOD COOKIES
Makes 4 dozen

1 cup shortening
1/2 cup brown sugar
1/2 cup white sugar
1 egg, beaten
1/4 teaspoon salt
1 teaspoon vanilla flavoring
2 cups flour
1 teaspoon baking soda
1 teaspoon cream of tartar
1 cup Angel Flake coconut

Mix shortening and sugars until creamy. Add egg, then sifted dry ingredients. Stir in flavoring and coconut. Roll dough into small balls. Bake on greased baking sheet for 12-15 minutes at 350 degrees.

Ralph Spencer, Guage, Ky.

JUMBO PEANUT BUTTER APPLE COOKIES
Makes 1½ dozen

1 cup sifted flour
1 cup sifted whole-wheat flour
2 teaspoons baking soda
1 teaspoon cinnamon
¾ teaspoon salt
⅓ cup butter, softened
⅔ cup chunk-style peanut butter
¼ cup sugar
1¾ cups brown sugar
2 eggs
1 teaspoon vanilla
1 cup rolled oats
1 cup peeled, diced apples
½ cup raisins

Mix and sift first 5 ingredients. Cream butter, peanut butter and sugars. Add eggs and vanilla; mix. Add sifted dry ingredients to creamed mixture and mix well. Stir in oats, apples and raisins. Using about ¼ cup of dough for each, shape into balls. Place on ungreased cookie sheet and flatten slightly. Bake in a 350-degree oven for about 12–15 minutes. Let stand on cookie sheet 1 minute before removing to wire cooling rack.

Melba Bellefeuille, Libertyville, Ill.

BUTTERMILK CHOCOLATE CHIP COOKIES
Makes 7 dozen

1 cup shortening
1 cup sugar
1 cup brown sugar, firmly packed
2 eggs
1½ teaspoons vanilla
3 cups sifted flour
1 teaspoon baking soda
½ cup buttermilk
1 (6-ounce) package semisweet chocolate pieces
1 cup chopped pecans

Cream together shortening and sugars until light and fluffy. Beat in eggs, 1 at a time. Blend in vanilla. Sift together flour and baking soda. Add dry ingredients alternately with buttermilk to creamed mixture; mix well. Stir in chocolate pieces and pecans. Drop by teaspoonfuls about 2 inches apart on greased baking sheets. Bake in 350-degree oven for 12–15 minutes, or until done. Remove from baking sheets; cool on racks.

These are my favorite chocolate chip cookies. They are so fabulous!!

Barbara Beauregard-Smith, Northfield, South Australia

ROCKY ROAD S'MORES BARS

½ cup margarine
½ cup packed brown sugar
1 cup flour
½ cup graham cracker crumbs
2 cups miniature marshmallows
1 (6-ounce) package semisweet chocolate pieces
½ cup chopped walnuts (optional)

Beat margarine and brown sugar until light and fluffy. Add combined flour and crumbs; mix well. Press onto bottom of greased 9-inch square pan. Sprinkle with remaining ingredients. Bake at 375 degrees for 15–20 minutes, or until golden brown. Cool; cut into bars.

Loriann Johnson, Gobles, Mich.

BUTTERSCOTCH DATE BARS

1/2 cup margarine
2 cups packed brown sugar
3 eggs
2 teaspoons vanilla
2 cups flour
2 teaspoons baking powder
1 teaspoon salt
1 cup chopped nuts
1 cup chopped dates

Cream margarine and sugar until light and fluffy. Blend in eggs and vanilla. Add combined dry ingredients; mix well. Stir in nuts and dates. Pour into greased 13x9-inch baking pan. Bake at 350 degrees for 30-35 minutes, or until wooden pick inserted in center comes out clean. Cool; cut into bars.

Allie Fields, Pensacola, Fla.

CHERRY PINEAPPLE BARS
Makes 24 bars

1 cup butter
2 cups sifted all-purpose flour
2 egg yolks, beaten
3 tablespoons chopped candied orange peel
2 tablespoons cornstarch
1 cup firmly packed brown sugar
½ teaspoon salt
1 cup crushed pineapple, undrained
½ cup granulated sugar
1 cup maraschino cherries

Combine butter, brown sugar, flour and salt; mix until crumbly. Press about ¾ of crumb mixture on bottom of buttered 13 x 9 x 2-inch baking pan. Bake at 350 degrees for 15 minutes. In a saucepan, combine egg yolks, pineapple, orange peel, granulated sugar and cornstarch. Cook over medium heat, stirring constantly, until thickened. Remove from heat; stir in maraschino cherries. Spoon fruit mixture over baked layer. Sprinkle remaining crumbs over top. Bake at 375 degrees for 40 minutes. Cool before cutting.

Sandra Russell, Gainesville, Fla.

RAISIN JUMBO COOKIES

1 cup water
2 cups raisins
1/2 cup (1 stick) margarine
1 cup brown sugar
3 eggs
1 cup granulated sugar
4 cups flour
1 teaspoon baking powder
2 teaspoons salt
1 1/2 teaspoons cinnamon
1/4 teaspoon cloves
1/4 teaspoon nutmeg
1/4 teaspoon allspice

Boil water and raisins for 5 minutes. Set aside and cool. Mix shortening, both sugars, and eggs. Beat well. Combine dry ingredients and add raisins; mix with creamed mixture. Drop by teaspoonsful onto cookie sheets. Bake at 375 degrees for 12-15 minutes.

Mrs. Marie Popovich, Warren, Mich.

ZUCCHINI COOKIES

1 cup grated zucchini
1 cup sugar
1/2 cup shortening *or* margarine
1 egg
2 cups flour
1 teaspoon ground cinnamon
1/2 teaspoon ground nutmeg
3/4 teaspoon baking powder
1/2 teaspoon baking soda
3/4 cup crushed pineapple, drained
1 cup chopped nuts
1 cup raisins

Cream sugar, shortening and egg. Add grated zucchini and crushed pineapple. Stir in dry ingredients; stir in nuts and raisins. On greased cookie sheet, drop by rounded teaspoonfuls. Bake at 375 degrees for 15 minutes, or until no imprint is left when you press top of cookie lightly. These do not brown on top. While still warm, glaze with a thin confectioners' sugar, canned milk and vanilla frosting.

Note: Dough will keep well for a week if covered and refrigerated.

Mrs. S.R. Burt, Imlay, Nev.

OLD-FASHIONED RAISIN BARS

1 cup raisins
1 cup water
1/2 cup shortening
1/2 teaspoon soda
Pinch of salt
2 cups flour
1 cup sugar
1 teaspoon cinnamon
1/2 teaspoon cloves
1/2 cup nuts (optional)

Boil raisins and water; remove from heat; add shortening and soda to melt. Add dry ingredients and nuts. Spread on cookie sheet and bake 20 minutes at 375 degrees. Top with a thin confectioners' sugar icing. Cut into bars.

Mrs. Melvin Habiger, Spearville, Kan.

WHOLE-WHEAT SNICKERDOODLES
Makes 30

1/2 cup margarine
3/4 cup brown sugar, firmly packed
1 egg
1 teaspoon vanilla
1 1/2 cups whole-wheat flour
1/2 teaspoon baking soda
1/2 teaspoon cream of tartar
1/4 teaspoon salt
2 tablespoons sugar
1/2 teaspoon cinnamon

Preheat oven to 375 degrees. In a small mixer bowl beat margarine with electric mixer on medium speed until softened (about 30 seconds). Add brown sugar and beat until fluffy. Add egg and vanilla. Beat well. In a medium bowl stir together flour, baking soda, cream of tartar and salt. With mixer on low speed, gradually add flour mixture to butter mixture, beating until well-mixed. Stir together sugar and cinnamon. Shape dough into 1-inch balls. Roll the balls in sugar-cinnamon mixture. Place about 2 inches apart on ungreased cookie sheet. Flatten slightly with bottom of drinking glass. Bake in 325-degree oven for 8–10 minutes, or until edges are firm. Cool on rack.

Sharon McClatchey, Muskogee, Okla.

BUTTER PECAN TURTLE BARS

Crust:
2 cups flour
1 cup firmly packed brown sugar
1/2 cup butter, softened

In a 3-quart bowl, combine crust ingredients and mix at medium speed for 2-3 minutes or until particles are fine. Pat firmly into ungreased 13x9x2-inch pan. Sprinkle pecans evenly over unbaked crust.

Caramel layer:
2/3 cup butter
1/2 cup firmly packed brown sugar
1 cup pecan halves
1 cup milk chocolate chips

Preheat oven to 350 degrees. Prepare caramel layer by combining brown sugar and butter in a heavy 1-quart saucepan. Cook over medium heat until entire surface of mixture begins to boil. Boil 1/2-1 minute, stirring constantly. Pour caramel evenly over pecans and crust. Bake at center of oven for 18-22 minutes, or until entire caramel layer is bubbly and crust is light golden brown. Remove from oven. Immediately sprinkle with chips. Let chips melt slightly (2-3 minutes) and slightly swirl them as they melt. Leave some whole for a marbled effect. *Do not spread* them. Cool completely and cut into bars.

ETHEL'S FRUIT COOKIES

3 egg whites
1/2 cup sugar
1/2 cup flour
1 pound chopped dates
3 slices candied pineapple, chopped
2 cups pecans, chopped
1 teaspoon vanilla

Beat egg whites until stiff. Gradually add sugar, flour, fruit and nuts. Stir in vanilla. Drop by teaspoonsful onto greased, foil-lined baking sheet. Bake in a 275-degree oven for about 40 minutes.

Jean Baker, Chula Vista, Calif.

MOCHA NUT BUTTERBALLS
Makes 6 dozen

1 cup butter or margarine, softened
1/2 cup granulated sugar
2 teaspoons vanilla
2 teaspoons instant coffee powder
1/4 cup unsweetened cocoa
1 3/4 cups flour
1/2 teaspoon salt
2 cups finely chopped pecans
Confectioners' sugar

Cream first 3 ingredients together until light. Add next 4 ingredients, mixing well. Add nuts. Shape into 1-inch balls and place on greased cookie sheets. Bake in a preheated 325-degree oven for about 15 minutes. Cool on racks. Roll in confectioners' sugar.

These are delicious buttery, nutty cookies!

Mrs. Agnes Ward, Erie, Penn.

JAM SANDWICH COOKIES
Makes 24 filled cookies

½ cup butter
½ cup packed brown sugar
¼ cup honey
1 egg
½ teaspoon vanilla
1¾ cups all-purpose flour
1 teaspoon baking soda
¼ teaspoon salt
Raspberry or other jam

Cream together butter, brown sugar and honey. Beat in egg and vanilla. Combine flour, baking soda and salt. Blend flour mixture into creamed mixture. Chill dough for 30 minutes. Shape dough into small balls (about 1 inch in diameter). Place on lightly greased baking sheets. Flatten balls slightly with bottom of glass dipped in flour. Bake at 350 degrees for 8–10 minutes, or until golden. Cool on baking sheet for few minutes; remove to wire racks to cool completely. When cool, put together in pairs filled with jam. If desired, squeeze filled cookies slightly until jam is visible on edges. Roll edges in coconut. Especially pretty with red jam and coconut.

Donna Bilyk, Alberta, Canada

BLOND BROWNIES

1 cup (2 sticks) butter
1 cup packed brown sugar
4 eggs
1 teaspoon vanilla
1 3/4 cups flour
1/2 teaspoon baking powder
1/2 teaspoon salt
3/4 cup chopped walnuts

Cream butter with brown sugar until fluffy; add eggs, one at a time, beating well after each addition. Sift dry ingredients together. Add to egg mixture, beating until smooth. Stir in nuts.

Bake in preheated 375-degree oven in a greased and floured 9x13-inch pan for about 30 minutes. Cool and cut into squares. Top with spoonsfuls of *Brown Sugar Meringue, Tart Lemon Glaze* (recipes follow), or frost as desired.

Brown Sugar Meringue:

Beat *1 egg white* until frothy. Gradually beat in *1/2 cup packed brown sugar* until stiff peaks form. Top squares of Blond Brownies with spoonsful and broil a few minutes to brown meringue.

Tart Lemon Glaze:

Gradually add *1 tablespoon lemon juice* to *2/3 cup confectioners' sugar*. Mix until smooth. Stir in 1 *teaspoon grated lemon rind*. Drizzle over brownies. Chill before cutting into squares.

Hedi Johnson, Great Falls, Mont.

CARROT RAISIN BROWNIES
Makes about 55

1 1/2 cups light brown sugar, packed
1/2 cup (1 stick) butter
2 eggs
1 teaspoon vanilla
1 1/2 cups flour, unsifted
1/2 teaspoon salt
1/2 teaspoon baking soda
1/2 teaspoon baking powder
1/2 cup finely chopped raisins
1 1/2 cups finely grated carrots
1/2 cup finely chopped walnuts

Preheat oven to 350 degrees. Grease and flour a 9x13-inch pan.

Mix sugar and butter; add eggs and vanilla; beat well. Stir in all dry ingredients; add raisins and carrots. Blend to mix well. Spread into a baking pan; sprinkle with chopped walnuts.

Bake at 350 degrees for 40 minutes or until a toothpick inserted in the center comes out clean. Cool. Cut into 1x2-inch rectangles.

Charlotte Adams, Detroit, Mich.

TRILBIES
Makes 8 dozen

1 cup shortening
1 cup butter *or* margarine, softened
3 cups brown sugar
1 teaspoon vanilla
6 cups all-purpose flour
4 cups rolled oats
1 teaspoon salt
2 teaspoons baking soda
1 cup buttermilk
Date Filling (recipe follows)

Preheat oven to 375 degrees. In a large bowl, cream shortening, butter or margarine, and sugar together; add vanilla.

In a large bowl, sift flour; add oats, salt and baking soda; mix together. Add dry ingredients, alternately, with buttermilk to shortening mixture. Mix thoroughly; chill in refrigerator several hours.

Turn out dough onto a lightly floured board and roll out to ⅛-inch thickness. Cut with round cookie cutter and place 1 inch apart on greased baking sheet. Bake until golden brown, 10–12 minutes. Cool on wire racks.

Date Filling:

2 cups finely chopped dates
1 cup water
1 cup sugar
2 tablespoons flour

In a large saucepan, mix ingredients together and cook over medium heat until thick. Let cool. Spread on half the cookies and top with remaining cookies.

Mrs. H.W. Walker, Richmond, Va.

CRISPY CHOCOLATE CHIP COOKIES

3 sticks margarine
2 cups white sugar
2 eggs
2 teaspoons baking powder (mixed with)
2 teaspoons vinegar
1 teaspoon vanilla flavoring
1 teaspoon almond flavoring
3–3 1/4 cups flour
1 (12-ounce) bag chocolate chips *or* M&M candies

Cream margarine and sugar until fluffy (at least 5 minutes). Add eggs, 1 at a time; beat well. Add baking powder-and-vinegar mixture, then flavorings. Add flour gradually. Fold in chocolate chips.

Chocolate mint chips are very good, or M & M's. I often put 2 or 3 M & M's on top of chocolate chip cookies. Store in refrigerator or freezer. Kids love them!!

Mary Jeanne Maas, Rochester, N.Y.

BLACK WALNUT CHOCOLATE DROP COOKIES

Makes 4 dozen

1-3/4 cups sifted flour
1/2 teaspoon baking soda
1 teaspoon baking powder
1/4 teaspoon salt
1 cup chopped black walnuts
1/2 cup butter
1-1/4 cups brown sugar, sifted and packed
1 egg
2 ounces unsweetened chocolate, melted and cooled
1 teaspoon vanilla extract
1/2 cup milk

Mix and sift flour, soda, baking powder, and salt; add nuts and mix. Cream butter; add sugar gradually and cream until fluffy. Add well-beaten egg and chocolate. Add extract to milk. Add dry mixture alternately with milk to creamed mixture, mixing just enough after each addition to combine ingredients. Drop by

spoonfuls on ungreased baking sheets. Bake in preheated 375-degree oven for about 12 minutes. When cool, spread with Chocolate Frosting.

Chocolate Frosting:
1-1/2 ounces unsweetened chocolate, melted
1 egg yolk
3 tablespoons light cream
1-1/4 cups sifted confectioners' sugar

Combine chocolate, slightly beaten egg yolk, and cream; add sugar and mix well.

Kit Rollins, Cedarburg, Wis.

BANANA BROWNIES

Makes 2 dozen bars

1 cup all-purpose flour
1 cup light brown sugar, firmly packed
1/3 cup margarine
1-1/2 teaspoons baking powder
1 egg, lightly beaten
1 cup coarsely mashed bananas
1 (6-ounce) package semisweet chocolate pieces
2 teaspoons grated lemon rind
Milk, if needed

Preheat oven to 350 degrees. Grease an 8-inch square baking pan. In a large bowl, with a mixer set at low speed, blend flour, sugar, and margarine until mixture resembles coarse cornmeal. Blend in baking powder. Stir in egg and bananas. Gently fold in chocolate pieces and lemon rind (add a little milk, if batter is stiff). Spread mixture in baking pan. Bake 25-30 minutes, or until cake tester or wooden toothpick inserted in center comes out clean. Set pan on wire rack to cool. Cut into 1-1/2-inch squares.

Suzan L. Wiener, Spring Hill, Fla.

CREAM CHEESE LEMON BARS

Makes 24

1 (18½-ounce) package lemon cake mix
½ cup butter *or* margarine
3 eggs, divided

2 cups canned lemon frosting
1 (8-ounce) package cream cheese, softened

Grease 9 x 13-inch pan. Combine cake mix, butter and 1 egg. Stir until moist. Press into pan. Blend frosting into cream cheese. Reserve ½ cup mixture to frost bars. Preheat oven to 350 degrees.

Add remaining eggs to remaining frosting mixture. Beat 3–5 minutes at high speed. Spread over base. Bake about 30 minutes. Cool slightly and frost with reserved frosting. Cut into bars.

Kit Rollins, Cedarburg, Wis.

BRAN BLONDIES

Makes 36 squares

3/4 cup flour, spooned lightly into cup
1/2 teaspoon baking powder
1/4 teaspoon soda
1/4 teaspoon salt
1/2 cup All-bran cereal
1/2 cup chopped walnuts **or** pecans
1 cup semisweet chocolate morsels
1/2 cup (1 stick) margarine
1 cup brown sugar (use part granulated, if desired)
1 large egg
1 teaspoon vanilla

Prepare a 9-inch square baking pan—spray with pan release, or grease and flour. (I foil-line and spray with pan release.)

Preheat oven to 350 degrees.

Into a small bowl measure flour, baking powder, soda, salt, All-bran, nuts, and chocolate morsels; stir together; set aside. In a medium-size saucepan barely melt margarine. Remove from heat; stir in sugar. Add egg and vanilla; whisk or beat with fork to blend well. With a rubber spatula, stir in dry ingredients. Spread in prepared pan. Bake until cake tester comes out dry, about 20 minutes.

Especially good warm, while chocolate is still soft. Freeze extras; warm in microwave oven.

Note: For chocolate bars, combine only 2/3 cup chocolate morsels with dry ingredients. Melt remaining 1/3 cup morsels with margarine. Proceed as directed.

CHOCOLATE PECAN PIE BARS

Makes 36 bars

1-1/4 cups all-purpose flour
1/4 cup sugar
1/2 teaspoon baking powder
1/2 teaspoon cinnamon
1/2 cup margarine
1 cup finely chopped pecans
1/4 cup butter
1 square (1-ounce) semisweet chocolate
3 eggs, beaten
1-1/4 cups packed brown sugar
2 tablespoons water
1 teaspoon vanilla

In mixing bowl, stir together flour, sugar, baking powder and cinnamon. Cut in 1/2 cup margarine until mixture resembles coarse crumbs; stir in pecans. Press into bottom of ungreased 13 x 9-inch pan. Bake in 350 degree oven for 10 minutes. Meanwhile, in a small saucepan, combine 1/4 cup butter and chocolate; heat; stir over low heat until chocolate is melted. In a small mixing bowl, combine eggs, brown sugar, water and vanilla. Stir mixture until well blended; pour over crust. Return to oven. Bake 20 minutes more or until set. Cool on wire rack. Cut into bars.

Patricia Habiger, Spearville, KS

PEANUT BUTTER COOKIES

Makes 100 cookies

3-1/3 cups peanut butter
2-2/3 cups shortening
6 eggs
3/4 teaspoon salt
3/4 teaspoon baking soda
2-1/2 cups brown sugar
3 cups white sugar
4-1/2 cups flour
1 tablespoon vanilla

Cream the sugars, peanut butter,

and shortening all together. Add well beaten eggs and vanilla. Add dry ingredients sifted together. Roll mixture in balls and place on greased sheets. Flatten with fork dipped in granulated sugar. Bake in preheated oven at 375 degrees for 8 or 9 minutes.

This is a large recipe, but it can be adjusted to needs. I usually make the full amount - some to use right away, some to freeze, and some to give away. I am a head cook at our Chichester School and everyone who has eaten these cookies loves them.

Natalie Henshaw, Pittsfield, NH

MOIST OATMEAL COOKIES

Boil gently for 10 minutes:
1 cup water
1 cup sugar
1 cup shortening
1 cup golden raisins
1/2 teaspoon cinnamon
1/2 teaspoon nutmeg
1/2 teaspoon salt

Set aside to cool. Then add:
2 eggs
1 teaspoon vanilla
2 cups flour
1/2 cup nut meats
2 cups oatmeal

Drop by spoonfuls on greased cookie sheet. Bake 10-12 minutes at 350 degrees. Check bottom of cookie—if evenly browned, it's done and not too crispy.

O. Elizabeth Todd, Minneapolis, Minn.

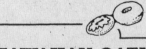

HAWAIIAN OATMEAL COOKIES

Makes 3 dozen

1 cup flour
1 teaspoon baking powder
1 teaspoon baking soda
3/4 teaspoon salt

1/2 cup shortening
1/2 cup granulated sugar
1/2 cup packed brown sugar
1 egg
1/2 teaspoon vanilla
1 cup rolled oats
1 cup shredded coconut

Sift together flour, baking powder, baking soda and salt; set aside. Cream shortening and sugars until light and fluffy; add egg; mix well. Add vanilla, then flour mixture. Add oats and coconut; mix until well blended. Shape into small walnut size balls, place on ungreased cookie sheets. Bake at 350 degrees about 12 to 15 minutes or until golden.

Margaret Russo, Winsted, CT

OATMEAL-CARROT COOKIES

Makes 24 bars

1/2 cup brown sugar
1 tablespoon honey
1/3 cup margarine, melted
1 egg
1-1/2 teaspoon vanilla
3/4 cup shredded carrots
1 cup whole wheat flour
1 teaspoon baking powder
1 teaspoon cinnamon
1/2 teaspoon ground cloves (optional)
1/2 cup oatmeal
1/4 cup wheat germ
1/2 cup raisins

In a small bowl, cream together sugar, honey, margarine, egg and vanilla until light and fluffy. Add carrots and mix well.

In another bowl, thoroughly stir together flour, baking powder, cinnamon, cloves (if used), oatmeal and wheat germ. Stir in the dry ingredients into the creamed mixture; fold in the raisins. Pour mixture into a 9 x 2 x 2 inch pan sprayed with vegetable oil. Bake at 350 degrees for 30 minutes. Let cool in pan on wire rack. Cut into bars or squares.

Let cookies set overnight so flavors can blend.

Trenda Leigh, Richmond, VA

PUMPKIN CANDY COOKIES

Makes 2 dozen

1/2 cup sugar
1/2 cup firmly-packed brown sugar
1 cup margarine or butter, softened
1 teaspoon vanilla
1 egg
1 cup canned or smoothly-mashed, cooked pumpkin
2 cups flour
1 teaspoon baking soda
1/2 teaspoon salt
1-1/2 teaspoons cinnamon
1/2 teaspoon ginger
1 cup candy-coated chocolate-covered peanuts

Heat oven to 350 degrees. In large bowl, beat sugar, brown sugar, and margarine until light and fluffy. Add vanilla, egg, and pumpkin; blend well. Lightly spoon flour into measuring cup; level off. Stir in flour, baking soda, salt, ginger, and cinnamon; mix well. Stir in candy. Drop by rounded tablespoonfuls, 3 inches apart, onto ungreased cookie sheet. Using metal spoon, flatten into 3-inch circles. Bake 14-17 minutes or until edges are light golden brown. Cool 1 minute; remove from cookie sheets.

FRENCH CHOCOLATE MERINGUES

Makes 4 dozen

1 (6 ounce) package (1 cup) semi-sweet chocolate morsels
3 egg whites (room temperature)
1/2 teaspoon vanilla
1 cup sugar
1 cup finely crushed saltines

Preheat oven 350 degrees. Melt chocolate morsels in top of double boiler over hot water (not boiling). Remove from water; let cool 5 minutes. Combine egg whites and vanilla; beat until stiff, but not dry. Add sugar gradually; beat until very stiff.

Fold in crackers and melted chocolate. Drop by teaspoons on greased cookie sheets. Bake in 350 degree oven for about 10 minutes. Remove from cookie sheets; cool on rack.

Mary A. Grills, New London, Conn.

CHOCOLATE CHIPPER CHAMPS

Makes 2-1/2 dozen

1-1/3 cups packed brown sugar
3/4 cup margarine or butter, softened
1 teaspoon vanilla
2 eggs
2-1/4 cups all purpose flour
1 cup M&M's plain chocolate candies
1/2 cup chopped nuts
1 teaspoon baking soda
1/2 teaspoon salt

Mix brown sugar, margarine, vanilla and eggs in large bowl until well blended. Stir in remaining ingredients. Drop dough by rounded tablespoons about 3 inches apart onto lightly greased cookie sheet. Press 3 or 4 additional candies on top of cookie if desired. Bake until light brown, in a 350 degree oven for 10-12 minutes. Cool slightly; remove to wire rack.

CHOCOLATE PUDDING COOKIES

2-1/4 cups unsifted all-purpose flour
1 teaspoon baking soda
1 cup margarine, well-softened
1/4 cup granulated white sugar
3/4 cup brownulated light brown sugar (or regular brown sugar, packed)
1 teaspoon vanilla
1 (4-serving size) package chocolate instant pudding and pie filling, used dry
2 eggs
1 (12 ounce) package chocolate chips
1 cup chopped walnuts

Combine flour and baking soda in medium bowl. In large bowl combine margarine, both sugars, vanilla, and instant pudding powder. Beat until

smooth and creamy. Beat in eggs. Gradually, stir in flour mixture. Stir in chips and nuts. Batter will be very stiff. Mix well, using your hands to combine all ingredients. Cover bowl; refrigerate several hours or overnight for easier handling. Shape into smooth balls by rounded *teaspoonfuls* (make them very small). They may be rolled around in your hands, making sure at least one of the nuts is in each one. Place 2 inches apart on ungreased cookie sheets. Bake at 375 degrees 8-10 minutes. Do not overbake. Cool on rack.

Frosting:

1 stiffly-beaten egg white
2-1/2 cups sifted confectioners' sugar
2 teaspoons hot water
1 teaspoon vanilla

Add 1/2 cup of the sugar to egg whites. Beat thoroughly. Add remaining sugar alternately with hot water until right spreading consistency. Beat in vanilla. If preferred, a simple confectioners' sugar-milk glaze may be substituted, or just a sifting of the sugar.

Hyacinth Rizzo, Snyder, N.Y.

CHOCOLATE HERMITS

1/2 cup butter
2/3 cup sugar
2 eggs
1/4 cup grated chocolate
2 tablespoons hot water
1/2 cup raisins
1/4 teaspoon salt
2 teaspoons baking powder
1-3/4 cups flour
1 teaspoon cinnamon

Cream butter; add sugar, eggs, raisins, and flour into which the baking powder has been sifted. Add chocolate melted in water, salt, and cinnamon. Mix well and drop from spoon onto greased cookie sheet. Put a raisin in middle of each cookie. Bake in 350 degree oven for 8-10 minutes.

Cooking
FOR TWO

PIZZA SAUCE
Makes 1 cup

2 tablespoons oil
1/2 medium onion, chopped (about 1/3 cup)
1/4 cup chopped green pepper
1 (8-ounce) can tomato sauce
2 teaspoons dried oregano
1 teaspoon vinegar
1/8 teaspoon pepper
Pinch sugar

In a medium saucepan or skillet heat oil; add onion; cook until transparent; stir in green pepper; cook just until wilted. Add tomato sauce, oregano (rub in palm of hand to release flavor), vinegar, pepper and sugar. Stir until boiling; reduce heat to low; simmer about 5 minutes to blend flavors.

Timesaver: Chopped onion and green pepper are available frozen.

THE WORLD'S BEST WATERMELON
Serves 2

2 servings of cubed, seeded watermelon
8 fresh mint leaves
2 wedges of fresh lime

Prepare melon—it's easy to cut into cubes if bought in slices. Remove visible seeds with knife tip; pile into dessert dishes. With scissors snip on slivers of fresh mint. Just before serving squeeze lime juice over melon.

BAKED BROWN BREAD
Makes 12 slices

Especially good spread with cream cheese or served with cheddar cheese.

1 cup All-bran cereal
1 cup buttermilk
2 tablespoons molasses
1 cup flour, spooned lightly into cup
1/3 cup sugar
1 teaspoon soda
1/2 teaspoon salt
1/3 cup chopped walnuts

In a medium-size bowl stir together cereal, buttermilk, and molasses. Set aside for cereal to absorb liquid.

Preheat oven to 350 degrees. Prepare 2 (16-ounce) cans (or an 8x4-inch loaf pan). Spray with pan release, or grease and flour.

Into a small bowl measure flour, sugar, soda, and salt. Whisk thoroughly; whisk in nuts. Stir dry ingredients into cereal just until blended. Spoon into cans (or pan).

Bake until cake tester comes out dry, about 40 minutes. Let cool 5 minutes, rolling cans on counter now and then to loosen bread. Turn out onto rack to cool. Store in refrigerator or freeze, sliced, so it can be thawed as needed.

POTATO SALAD FOR TWO
Serves 2

2 cups cold, boiled potatoes, cubed
2 tablespoons French dressing
1 hard-cooked egg, cut up
1/2 cup finely diced celery
1/2 cucumber, finely diced
1/2 teaspoon celery seeds
1/2 cup grated carrots, optional
1/4 cup mayonnaise

Marinate potatoes in French dressing for 2 hours. Add remaining ingredients. Season with salt and pepper. Garnish with parsley or minced pimiento or olives.

Flo Burtnett, Gage, Okla.

SOY BARBECUE SAUCE
Makes 1/2 cup

This unusual sauce combines with either meatballs or hot dogs to make good sandwiches. Don't be put off by the soy sauce. If it's good-quality it will add a delicate flavor. (I also spoon this sauce over baking pork chops, spare ribs, or whole pork tenderloin.)

1/4 cup water
1/4 cup ketchup
1 tablespoon brown sugar
1 tablespoon soy sauce (I use Kikkoman's)
1 clove garlic, split or 1/8 teaspoon garlic powder

Measure water in liquid measuring cup; add ketchup to the 1/2 cup mark. Add brown sugar, soy sauce, garlic clove or powder. Stir to mix well. Simmer in microwave oven about 2 minutes or transfer to a small saucepan; stir over medium heat until boiling; reduce heat; simmer about 2 minutes.

SHORTCAKE
Serves 2

1/2 cup flour, spooned lightly into cup
3/4 teaspoon baking powder
1/8 teaspoon salt
1 tablespoon sugar
2 tablespoons shortening (I use half butter)
3 tablespoons milk (I add a few drops vanilla)

Preheat oven to 425 degrees.

Measure flour, baking powder, salt, and sugar into a small bowl; mix. Add shortening; cut in with pastry blender. When like fine crumbs add milk; mix lightly with fork until it comes together (it will be a sticky ball). Drop into two mounds on a small ungreased baking sheet. Use a fork to gently flatten and shape to a thick 3-inch biscuit. Sprinkle with sugar. Bake until beginning to brown, 10 to 12 minutes. Transfer to cooling rack. Split as soon as cool enough to handle. Serve warm or cold.

To assemble strawberry shortcake spread bottom of biscuit with sweetened whipped cream; spoon on sliced berries; cover with biscuit top, berries, and then remaining whipped cream.

PLUM TORTE
Serves 4

3 large red or 4 purple plums
1/2 cup flour, spooned lightly into cup
1/2 teaspoon baking powder
1/8 teaspoon salt
1/4 cup butter, softened
1/2 cup sugar
1 large egg
1/2 teaspoon vanilla (optional)
Sugar and cinnamon

Spray with pan release or grease and flour an 8-inch pie plate.

Wash plums; cut in half; remove seeds; cut red plums into quarters; leave purple ones in halves. Set aside.

Preheat oven to 350 degrees.

Combine flour, baking powder, and salt. To do this, measure baking powder and salt into one-half cup dry measure; add a spoonful of flour; mix well with spoon; lightly spoon in flour to over fill; scrape to level. Set aside.

Measure butter and sugar into medium mixing bowl; beat about 1 minute. Add egg; beat until light and fluffy, several minutes. Beat in flavoring, if using. On low speed beat in dry ingredients, just until blended in. Spread in prepared pie plate. Arrange plum pieces on top, cut side down. Sprinkle lightly with sugar and cinnamon.

Bake until cake tester comes out dry, 30-35 minutes. Let cool on cake rack 5 minutes; turn out. Turn again so crispy sugar crust is on top. Serve plain or with whipped cream.

Freeze leftovers, cut in serving-size pieces. Reheat to warm before serving.

CHOCOLATE BREAD PUDDING
Two large servings

1 tablespoon butter or margarine
1-1/2 cups loosely packed 1/2-inch bread cubes (use French, Italian or Vienna bread)
Scant 1 cup half-and-half or milk
1 envelope or square (1 oz.) unsweetened chocolate
1 large egg
1/3 cup sugar
1/8 teaspoon salt
1 teaspoon vanilla

Preheat oven to 350 degrees. For this pudding, use a small flat-bottom casserole, or a 6-inch souffle dish. Melt butter in dish while preheating oven. Add bread cubes; toss with a fork to mix; set aside.

In small saucepan, combine half-and-half or milk with chocolate. Whisk over low heat until mixture is hot and thoroughly blended. In a small bowl, combine egg, sugar, salt and vanilla; whisk to blend. Add hot chocolate mixture slowly, while whisking. Pour over bread cubes; mix gently, but thoroughly.

Set dish in pan containing 1/2 inch warm tap water. Bake until a rinsed knife inserted half way to center comes out clean, not milky, 25-30 minutes. Remove dish from hot water; cool about 20 minutes before serving. Serve warm with Hard Sauce or serve cool with whipped cream.

Hard Sauce:
2 tablespoons butter, softened
1/3 cup confectioners' sugar
1-2 teaspoons brandy or dark rum

In a small bowl beat butter and sugar with a fork until light. Gradually beat in brandy or rum until no more liquid can be absorbed. Spoon into two mounds; cover and chill. Set out about 20 minutes before serving on warm bread pudding.

ONION PIE
Serves 2

2 medium onions
3 tablespoons butter or margarine, divided
1/2 cup milk
1 large egg
1 tablespoon Parmesan cheese*
1/2 cup crushed saltine crackers

Preheat oven to 325 degrees. Grease or spray with pan release a 7-inch pie plate. Cut onions in half lengthwise; place cut side down on cutting board and slice thinly. In a small skillet melt 1 tablespoon butter; sauté onions until transparent. Spread in prepared pie plate; set skillet aside.

In pint pitcher measure milk; add egg and cheese; whisk or beat well with a fork. Pour over onions. Bake 15 minutes. Meanwhile, melt remaining 2 tablespoons butter in skillet; add cracker crumbs; toss well; toast lightly over low heat. Sprinkle over pie. Bake just until set, 5-10 minutes longer. Good with any leftover sliced meat. *Use 1/2 cup grated Cheddar cheese instead of Parmesan cheese, if you prefer.

CORN PUDDING
Serves 2

(A soft creamy pudding)

1 large egg
1/4 teaspoon salt
Pinch pepper
1 teaspoon sugar
1 tablespoon flour
1/3 cup milk
1 (8-ounce) can cream-style corn

Preheat oven to 350 degrees.
Grease or spray with pan release a small baking dish (flat-bottomed, if possible; I use a 6-inch soufflé dish). In a small bowl whisk egg to blend. Whisk in salt, pepper, sugar, flour, and milk. When smooth, whisk in corn. Pour into prepared dish. Bake until set—firm when dish is jiggled—35-40 minutes.

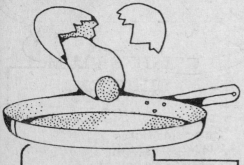

PUFFY FRENCH TOAST
Serves 2

4 slices bread
1/2 cup milk
1 egg
3/4 cup biscuit mix
2 tablespoons sugar
1/2 teaspoon cinnamon
1/2 cup margarine

Melt margarine in skillet on medium heat. With electric mixer, combine milk, egg, biscuit mix, sugar and cinnamon. Cut each slice of bread in half diagonally. Dip in batter; coating completely. Fry four pieces at a time until golden brown and puffy. (About 3 minutes on each side). Sprinkle with confectioners sugar and cinnamon. Serve with warm syrup. (Blueberry syrup is delicious.)
Helen Weissinger, Levittown, PA

GLAZED PARSNIPS
Serves 2

1/2 pound parsnips
1 tablespoon butter or margarine
2 tablespoons brown sugar
Salt and pepper
Pinch nutmeg
1 tablespoon whipping cream
1 tablespoon dry white wine, dry vermouth or sherry

Half-fill a medium saucepan with water; add salt; bring to boiling.
Meanwhile trim top and root ends from parsnips; pare with vegetable peeler. Cut in half lengthwise then crosswise; cut into lengthwise strips to make uniform pieces so they will cook evenly. Drop into boiling water; cover; cook until barely tender, 4 to 5 minutes. Drain; rinse under cold water to stop the cooking; drain well. If done ahead cover and refrigerate; drain again before using.
Melt butter in shallow baking dish in oven with roasting hens. Add parsnips; toss to coat with butter. Sprinkle on brown sugar, salt, pepper, and nutmeg. Dribble on cream and wine. Bake at 350 degrees (with hens) about 20 minutes, stirring once to baste.

THOUSAND ISLAND SALAD
Serves 2

A main–dish salad.

Dressing:
1/4 cup mayonnaise
1-1/2 tablespoons ketchup
1-1/2 teaspoons sweet pickle relish
1/2 green onion

Salad:
Lettuce
1/4 pound ham in bite-size pieces (I add salami if I have it)
3 hard-cooked eggs

Prepare dressing; combine mayonnaise, ketchup, and relish. With scissors, snip in green onion; mix well.
Cover plates with chunks and leaves of lettuce. Top with ham; slice on eggs; spoon on dressing.

CHILI CHEDDAR OMELET
Serves 2

4 eggs
1 tablespoon water
1/4 teaspoon seasoned salt
Butter
1 cup chili
1/4 cup grated Cheddar cheese
1/2 avocado, peeled and sliced

In small bowl, beat eggs, water and seasoned salt together. Pour mixture into well-buttered 10-inch skillet.
Cook omelet over medium heat, letting liquid egg run to edges when eggs are set; slide omelet onto serving plate. Place chili, grated cheese and avocado slices on half of omelet; fold over other half.
Susan L. Wiener, Spring Hill, Fl

CHOCOLATE SAUCE
Serves 2

So good over coffee ice cream!

1/4 cup light cream
1/4 cup sugar
1 square (or envelope) unsweetened chocolate
1 teaspoon butter
1/4 teaspoon vanilla

Measure cream; add sugar to cream in measuring cup; stir to partially dissolve sugar. Set aside.
In a small saucepan combine chocolate and butter. Stir over low heat until melted and smooth. Add cream; stir sauce over medium heat until it thickens, just as it begins to boil. Remove from heat; stir in vanilla. Serve warm or at room temperature.

HOLIDAY CORNISH HENS
Serves 2

Sometimes 22-ounce hens are the smallest available. They are too large for us but the leftover meat makes good sandwiches.

2 Rock Cornish game hens
2 juice oranges
1 large clove garlic
1/4 teaspoon salt
Pinch black pepper
2 tablespoons brown sugar

Line a shallow baking pan with foil. Place two pieces of crushed foil on pan as racks for hens (without racks hens will stick and burn on the bottom due to sugar in the glaze).

Preheat oven to 450 degrees.

Rinse cavity and outside of hens; pat dry with paper towel. Thickly slice one orange; cut slices in half; reserve several center slices for serving decoration. Stuff half of remaining orange slices and half of garlic clove into the cavity of each hen. Place hens breast side up on prepared pan.

Squeeze remaining orange. Combine orange juice (about 1/3 cup), salt, pepper, and brown sugar; stir until sugar dissolves. Brush hens all over with orange sauce. Roast at 450 degrees for 15 minutes, brushing once with sauce. Reduce oven temperature to 350 degrees; roast 50 minutes longer, brushing several times with remaining sauce. Remove orange slices and garlic from cavity. Serve with reserved orange slices on the side.

SWISS VEAL
Serves 2

3/4 pound veal cutlet (or 2 boned and skinned chicken breasts)
3 tablespoons butter
Salt and pepper
Flour
2 thin slices onion, chopped
1/8 teaspoon dried tarragon
1/4 cup dry white wine (use chicken broth if you do not have wine)
1-1/2 teaspoons lemon juice
1/4 cup sour cream

Trim away fat and bone from veal. Cut veal (or chicken) into narrow strips about one inch long. Sprinkle with salt, pepper, and a light dusting of flour.

In a medium skillet heat butter until bubbly. Over medium heat cook meat until evenly brown. Add onions; cook just until soft. Add tarragon and wine; cover; cook on low heat 4 to 5 minutes, until meat tests done with a fork. Drizzle on lemon juice; toss to mix. Stir in sour cream; cook just until sour cream is hot, not boiling.

Serve with buttered noodles.

VEAL IN CREAM
Serves 2

1/2 pound veal scallops (or 2 boned and skinned chicken breasts)
2 tablespoons flour
1/2 teaspoon salt
1/4 teaspoon pepper
1/4 teaspoon paprika
1 tablespoon butter or margarine
1/2 tablespoon cooking oil
1/4 cup whipping cream

Pound veal (or chicken) until very thin according to directions given above.

Mix flour, salt, pepper and paprika; spread on waxed paper or large plate. Coat meat on both sides with mixture; leave on paper in a single layer until needed.

In a large skillet heat butter and oil until bubbly. Add meat, single layer, and cook over medium heat until brown on both sides. Reduce heat to low; cover skillet; cook until tender, 3 to 5 minutes. Add cream; cook uncovered a few minutes until cream has thickened to sauce consistency.

Serve with mashed potatoes or buttered noodles.

LEMON CHICKEN WINGS
Serves 2

3 tablespoons oil
1/2 teaspoon grated lemon peel
1 tablespoon lemon juice
1/2 teaspoon dried oregano leaves
1/2 teaspoon garlic salt
8 chicken wings, tips removed

Measure oil into a medium bowl. Grate lemon peel onto foil; add 1/2 teaspoon to oil; store remaining peel in foil; freeze for later use. Squeeze lemon; add 1 tablespoon juice to oil; chill or freeze remaining juice for another use. Add oregano and garlic salt to oil; whisk until blended. Add chicken wings, toss well; cover and refrigerate up to 24 hours.

Preheat oven to 425 degrees. Place chicken wings, skin-side down, on rack on pan prepared as directed in italics at beginning of this article. Reserve marinade. Bake 20 minutes; brush with marinade, turn; brush other side. Bake until brown and tender, about 30 minutes longer.

CHINESE PLUM CHICKEN
Serves 2

3 red plums, rinsed
2 tablespoons sugar
2 tablespoons orange juice
1/2 teaspoon lemon juice
1/2 teaspoon salt
1 teaspoon flour
1 whole chicken breast, halved

Preheat oven to 350 degrees.

Slice plums into small bowl. Mix in sugar, orange juice, lemon juice, salt, and flour. Spread in center of a square of foil (Use 18-inch heavy-duty foil for this).

Remove skin from chicken and score (make long shallow cuts in a diamond pattern in the flesh). Place cut side down on plum mixture. Fold foil to make a secure package. Place foil package on shallow baking pan (just in case). Bake until fork tender, about 45 minutes. Flip the package over and back, once during baking, to distribute the juices.

To serve, spoon plum sauce over chicken.

Coffee TIME

PEANUT BUTTER SQUARES
Makes 16-24

1 cup graham cracker crumbs
2 cups confectioners' sugar
1/2 cup butter, melted
1 cup peanut butter
1 small bag (6 ounces) semisweet
  chocolate chips, melted

Mix together first four ingredients. Spread in 8- or 9-inch square pan. Spread melted chocolate chips over mixture; refrigerate until set. Cut into squares to serve.

Kim Schluchter, Racine, Wis.

APPLE SCHMARREN

¼ cup flour
2 teaspoons sugar
⅜ teaspoon salt
⅔ cup milk
2 eggs

1 medium tart apple,
  peeled and thinly sliced
1½ teaspoons raisins,
  optional
  Cinnamon and confec-
  tioners' sugar
3 tablespoons butter

Combine first 3 ingredients. Whisk in milk and eggs. Peel the apple; slice into batter. Add raisins; fry batter in the butter. I use an 8-inch non-stick fry pan. It should be nicely browned on all sides, so don't stir too often. Serve with cinnamon and confectioners' sugar sprinkled over the top.

Linda Taylor, Gravois Mills, Mo.

VIENNESE RAISIN NUT COFFEE CAKE
1 large coffee cake

2/3 cup milk
1/2 cup (1 stick) butter or margarine
1/4 teaspoon salt
1/2 cup granulated sugar
1 envelope active dry yeast
1 teaspoon sugar
1/4 cup very warm water
3 eggs
4 teaspoons grated lemon rind
3-1/4 cups sifted all-purpose flour
1 cup golden raisins
1/2 cup sliced blanched almonds
Confectioners' sugar

Stir milk, butter, salt and 1/2 cup sugar in small saucepan over very low heat just until butter is melted. Pour mixture into large bowl, cool to lukewarm.

Sprinkle yeast and 1 teaspoon sugar over very warm water in 1 cup glass measure. (Very warm water should feel comfortably warm when dropped on wrist). Stir in dissolved yeast. Let stand until bubbly, about 10 minutes. Stir eggs, yeast mixture, lemon rind and 2 cups flour into cooled milk mixture. Beat with electric mixer at low speed until blended. Increase speed to medium, beat 3 minutes longer. By hand, beat in remaining flour until batter is smooth, beat 1 minute longer. Stir in raisins. Cover with buttered wax paper and a towel. Let rise in warm place, away from drafts, until doubled in volume, about 50 minutes.

While batter is rising, butter 10-inch bundt pan. Sprinkle bottom and sides evenly with almonds. Stir batter vigorously about 30 seconds. Turn into prepared pan. Cover with buttered wax paper and towel. Let rise in warm place, away from drafts, until almost doubled in volume, about 45 minutes. Bake in preheated oven 350 degrees for 30 minutes or until golden brown and cake sounds hollow when tapped with fingers. Remove from pan to wire rack, cool. Sprinkle lightly with confectioners' sugar.

Leona Teodori, Warren, Mich.

P.D.Q. COFFEE CAKE

1 compressed yeast cake
2-1/2 cups lukewarm milk
1/2 cup shortening (part butter adds
  flavor)
1/2 cup sugar
1 egg
2 teaspoons salt
5 cups flour
1 stick butter or margarine, melted
Cinnamon and sugar mixture

Crumble yeast cake into a bowl and add milk. Stir until dissolved. In separate bowl combine shortening, sugar, egg, and salt. Combine the two mixtures. Add 1 cup of flour at a time to combined yeast mixture; beat after each addition. Beat dough until smooth and blended. Cover bowl and let rise until double. Punch dough down by giving it a stir with a spoon. Divide dough into 3 layer cake pans. Melt 1 stick of butter or margarine. Drizzle on top of cakes. Sprinkle mixture of sugar and cinnamon over cakes. Let rise again. Bake 20 minutes in a 450-degree oven.

Jane Williams, Columbus, Ohio

BANANA DATE COFFEE CAKE
Serves 8-10

1/3 cup mashed bananas
1/2 cup butter, softened
3 large eggs
1 teaspoon vanilla
1-1/4 teaspoons water
3 cups flour
1 teaspoon baking soda
2 teaspoons baking powder
1-1/2 cups chopped dates

Topping:
1/3 cup chopped dates
1/3 cup chopped nuts
1/3 cup flaked coconut

Beat together mashed bananas and butter until creamy. Add eggs, vanilla, and water; beat well. Blend in flour, baking soda, and baking powder, and beat well; stir in 1-1/2 cups chopped dates. Spoon batter into a greased and floured 9x13-inch baking pan. Combine topping ingredients and sprinkle over batter. Bake in a 350-degree oven for 20-25 minutes, or until knife inserted comes out clean. Cool on rack.

Mrs. D. Garms, Anaheim, Calif.

CINNAMON PUFFS

1-1/4 cups scalded milk
1 package yeast
1 cup quick oatmeal
1/2 cup butter
1/4 cup sugar
1-1/2 teaspoons salt
1 egg
3 cups flour

Dissolve yeast in 1/4 cup milk, cooled. Pour 1 cup hot milk over oatmeal, butter, sugar, and salt. Mix; add 1 egg and yeast. Add 2 cups flour and mix. Add 1 cup flour, more or less. (I use 3-1/2 cups flour). Don't make it too stiff. Let rise 1 hour. Knead down. Let rest for 15-20 minutes. Form into 1 large ball. Divide into quarters, then divide each quarter into 8 parts. Form into balls and put on cookie sheet. Let rise. Bake at 350 degrees for 20-25 minutes. Melt 1 cup margarine. Roll balls in melted margarine and in cinnamon-sugar. (1 cup sugar to 2 teaspoons cinnamon) Roll in mixture while they are still warm.

Sharon Crider, Evansville, Wis.

BLUEBERRY COFFEE CAKE
Serves 10-12

2 cups sifted cake flour
1 teaspoon baking powder
1 teaspoon baking soda
1 cup sugar
2 sticks (1/2 pound) margarine
2 eggs
1 cup cultured sour cream
1 teaspoon vanilla
1 can blueberry pie filling

Preheat oven to 375 degrees. Sift flour, baking powder, soda, and sugar together into a large bowl. Cut in margarine as you would for pie crust. Beat together eggs, sour cream, vanilla, and combine with flour mixture, blending well. Spread half the batter in a greased 13x9x2-inch baking pan. Spoon pie filling over batter and spread evenly. Spread remaining batter over blueberry filling. Sprinkle with the following topping:

Blend together as for pie crust 1/4 cup cake flour, 3 tablespoons margarine, and 1/4 cup sugar. Sprinkle over top of batter in pan. Bake in a moderately hot oven of 375 degrees for 40 minutes, or until lightly browned. Serve warm or cold.

Trenda Leigh, Richmond, Va.

PUMPKIN BREAD
Makes 2 loaves

4 cups flour
3 cups sugar
2 teaspoons baking soda
1 1/2 teaspoons salt
1 teaspoon baking powder
1 teaspoon cinnamon
1 teaspoon nutmeg
1/2 teaspoon cloves
1/4 teaspoon ginger
1 can (16 ounces) pumpkin
1 cup oil
4 eggs
2/3 cup water

Preheat oven to 350 degrees. Grease two 9x5x3-inch loaf pans.

Mix dry ingredients well. Beat pumpkin, oil, eggs and water together; add to dry ingredients. Stir just until moistened; do not overmix.

Divide batter between the two prepared pans. Bake at 350 degrees for 1 hour to 1 hour 15 minutes, or until toothpick inserted in center comes out clean. Cool on rack, removing loaves from pans after 10 minutes.

Charlotte Adams, Detroit, Mich.

NO-FRY DOUGHNUTS
Makes 1½–2 dozen

2 packages yeast
1½ cups lukewarm milk
   (scalded then cooled)
½ cup sugar
1 teaspoon nutmeg
2 eggs
4½ cups flour
¼ cup warm water
1 teaspoon salt
¼ teaspoon cinnamon
⅓ cup shortening
¼ cup margarine, melted
   Cinnamon and sugar

In large mixer bowl, dissolve yeast in warm water. Add milk, sugar, salt, spices, eggs, shortening and 2 cups flour. Blend ½ minute on top speed, scraping bowl occasionally. Stir in remaining flour, until smooth, scraping sides of bowl. Cover. Let rise in warm place until double, 50–60 minutes. Turn dough onto well-floured, cloth-covered board; roll around lightly to coat with flour (dough will be soft to handle). Roll dough to about ½-inch thickness. Cut with a 2½-inch doughnut cutter. Place 2 inches apart on baking sheet; brush doughnuts with melted margarine. Cover; let rise until double, about 20 minutes. Heat oven to 425 degrees. Bake 8–10 minutes, or until golden brown. Immediately brush with melted margarine and shake in sugar and cinnamon or use doughnut glaze.

Sharon Crider, Evansville, Wis.

CINNAMON TOAST COFFEE CAKE

Serves 10-12

2 cups flour
1 cup sugar
2 teaspoons baking powder
1 teaspoon salt
1 cup milk
2 tablespoons melted butter
1 teaspoon vanilla
1/4 teaspoon cinnamon
1/4 teaspoon nutmeg
1/2 cup seedless raisins

Topping:
1/2 cup melted butter
1/2 cup sugar
1-1/2 tablespoons cinnamon

Combine dry ingredients; stir in milk, 2 tablespoons butter, and vanilla until batter is smooth. Add raisins. Spread evenly into well-greased and lightly floured 15x10x1-inch jelly roll pan or sheet cake pan. Bake at 350 degrees for 20-25 minutes until lightly browned. While coffee cake is baking, combine 1/2 cup sugar and cinnamon. Remove cake from oven after 10 minutes of baking; drizzle 1/2 cup melted butter evenly over top of hot cake; sprinkle with sugar-cinnamon topping mixture and return to oven. Bake 10-15 minutes more. Serve warm.

Dee L. Getchell, Old Lyme, Conn.

DEARBORN INN SWEET BLUEBERRY MUFFINS

Makes 1 dozen

1 egg
1/2 cup milk
1/4 cup salad oil
1 1/2 cups flour
1/2 cup sugar
2 teaspoons baking powder
1/2 teaspoon salt
1 cup fresh blueberries or canned blueberries, drained

Beat egg in bowl and stir in milk and oil. Combine dry ingredients and quickly mix into liquid mixture just until flour is moistened. Do not over-mix; there will be lumps in the batter. Fold in blueberries. Line muffin tins with 12 paper liners and fill each two-thirds full.

Bake in a preheated 400-degree oven for 20-25 minutes or until muffins are golden brown. Remove from muffin pan immediately.

Note: In place of the blueberries, you can use fresh cherries, or fresh peaches cut into cubes, if you wish.

Harriet Blair, Milwaukee, Wis.

ORANGE MARMA-LADE COFFEE CAKE

Serves 6-8

1 package dry yeast
2 tablespoons water
1/2 cup milk
2 tablespoons sugar
1/2 teaspoon salt
4 tablespoons margarine
1-1/2 cups flour
1 egg
1/2 cup orange marmalade
1/4 cup sugar
1/4 teaspoon cinnamon

Sprinkle yeast in warm water. Heat milk until film forms over surface. Pour into mixing bowl. Add sugar, salt, and margarine. Stir. Beat in 1/2 cup flour into milk mixture. Beat egg slightly. Stir into milk mixture with yeast. Add remaining 1 cup flour and beat briskly. If a little more flour is needed, beat in additional amount. It should not be more than 2 tablespoons extra. Grease a large bowl. Turn dough into it. Turn dough around once to grease its surface. Grease top lightly with softened margarine. Cover bowl. Let stand in warm place about 1 hour, or until doubled in bulk. Grease 9-inch cake pan. Punch dough down in bowl and turn it out into prepared cake pan. Spread dough lightly. Drop spoonfuls of jam on top and swirl it into dough with spoon. Sprinkle top with sugar and cinnamon. Cover pan. Let rise until doubled. Preheat oven to 375 degrees. Bake for 20-30 minutes, until lightly browned around edges. Remove from pan. Let cool slightly. Serve warm or cool.

Sharon Crider, Evansville, Wis.

PEACH (LOW-CHOLESTEROL) COFFEE CAKE

Serves 16

3 cups flour
2 cups sugar
1/4 teaspoon salt
2 teaspoons baking powder
1 cup margarine (2 sticks)
4 egg whites
1/2 cup egg substitute
1 cup skim milk
2 teaspoons vanilla
1 (10-ounce) can sliced peaches, drained

Preheat oven to 300 degrees. Sift together dry ingredients. Cut in margarine. Reserve 1 cup of the mixture to be used as a topping. In separate bowl, blend in egg substitute, milk, and vanilla; add to remaining dry ingredients. Fold in beaten egg whites. Pour into 9-inch tube pan and top with peach slices, then reserved topping. Bake 40-50 minutes.

Ida Bloedow, Madison, Wis

POTATO DOUGHNUTS

1/4 cup sugar
2 eggs
1 cup mashed potatoes
1/2 cup milk
1 tablespoon baking powder
2-1/2 cups flour
1-1/2 tablespoons shortening
1/2 teaspoon salt
1/4 teaspoon nutmeg
Confectioners' sugar
Cinnamon-sugar

Beat mashed potatoes; add melted shortening, beaten eggs, and milk. Sift dry ingredients together and add to liquid. Dough should be soft enough to roll. Separate and roll out to 3/4-inch thickness. Cut with doughnut cutter and cook in deep fat (365 degrees); fry to golden brown. Drain on absorbent paper and dust with powdered sugar or sugar-cinnamon mixture.

Elizabeth Dunn, Harrisonville, NY

CINNAMON RAISIN BATTER BREAD

1 package active dry yeast
1-1/2 cups warm water (105-115 degrees)
2 tablespoons honey
2 tablespoons butter
1 teaspoon salt
3 cups flour, divided
1 tablespoon cinnamon
1 cup raisins

In a large bowl, dissolve yeast in warm water. Stir in honey. Add butter, salt, and 2 cups of the flour. Beat with electric mixer on low speed until blended. Beat 1 minute on high speed. Stir in remaining flour with a wooden spoon. Cover and let rise in a warm place until doubled in size. Punch down by stirring with a heavy spoon. Add cinnamon and raisins. Spoon batter into a loaf pan. Let rise again until batter reaches the top of the pan (not over!). Bake in preheated 350-degree oven for about 40 minutes or until loaf sounds hollow when lightly tapped. Cool on wire rack.

This batter bread is a wonderful treat for breakfast or in the "munchkin's" lunch sack as a peanut-butter-and-jelly sandwich.

Phyliss Dixon, Fairbanks, Alaska

CRANBERRY COFFEE CAKE

1/2 cup margarine
1 cup sugar
2 eggs
1/2 pint sour cream
1 teaspoon baking soda
1 teaspoon baking powder
2 cups flour
1/2 teaspoon salt
3/4 teaspoon almond extract
1 can whole cranberry sauce
1/2 cup broken walnuts

Cream margarine and sugar. Add eggs, mix medium speed. Reduce speed and add dry ingredients, alternating with sour cream. Add almond extract. Grease 9x13-inch pan. Put half batter in pan and spread evenly. Swirl half the can of cranberry sauce over batter in pan. Add rest of batter to pan. Top with remaining cranberry sauce. Sprinkle on nuts. Bake 350 degrees 50 minutes. Frost while warm.

Icing:
3/4 cup powdered sugar
1 tablespoon warm water
1/4 teaspoon almond extract

Mix together. Drizzle over cake.
Sherri Crider, Stoughton, Wis.

HEATH BAR COFFEE CAKE

2 cups flour
1/4 cup brown sugar
1/4 pound butter or margarine
6 chilled Heath candy bars
1 egg
1 cup milk
1 teaspoon vanilla
1 teaspoon baking soda
1-1/2 teaspoons salt
1-1/2 cups nuts, chopped

Grease and flour a 9x13-inch pan. Mix together flour, sugar, soda, salt, and butter to the consistency of pie dough (reserve 1 cup for topping).

Beat together egg, vanilla, and milk; add to first mixture. Pour into prepared pan. Break up Heath bars into small pieces, using a rolling pin. Add Heath bars and chopped nuts to reserved cup of first mixture; sprinkle on top of cake. Bake at 350 degrees for 40 minutes.

Agnes Ward, Erie, Pa.

CHOCOLATE CHIP STREUSEL COFFEE CAKE

Streusel:
1/2 cup brown sugar
1/2 cup flour
1/4 cup margarine
1/4 cup chopped walnuts
1 cup chocolate chips

Cake:
1 (8-ounce) package cream cheese
1-1/2 cups sugar
3/4 cups margarine
3 eggs
3/4 teaspoon vanilla
2-1/2 cups flour
1-1/2 teaspoons baking powder
3/4 teaspoon baking soda
1/4 teaspoon salt
3/4 cup milk

For streusel, combine brown sugar and flour. Cut in margarine until mixture resembles coarse crumbs. Stir in walnuts and chocolate chips. Set aside. Grease and flour a 13x9x2-inch pan. Combine cream cheese, sugar, and margarine, mixing at medium speed until well-blended. Blend in eggs and vanilla. Add combined dry ingredients alternately with milk, mixing well after each addition. Spoon batter into prepared pan. Sprinkle with crumb mixture. Bake at 350 degrees for 40 minutes. Cool.

Great for large crowds! If you like cheese filling, you'll love it!
Mrs. George Franks, Millerton, Pa.

MINCEMEAT COFFEE RING

1¾ cups sifted flour
2 teaspoons baking powder
½ teaspoon salt
¼ cup sugar
⅓ cup shortening
1 egg
¼ cup milk
¾ cup prepared mincemeat

Into bowl sift flour, baking powder, salt and sugar. Cut in shortening using pastry blender. Beat egg. Add milk and mincemeat. Make a depression in flour mixture and pour liquid in. Mix quickly. Do not overmix. Pour into greased ring mold or tube pan. Bake at 400 degrees for 30–40 minutes. Ice while warm with thin confectioners' sugar icing, tinted green, letting it trickle down from the top over the sides of the ring. Decorate with candied cherries and chopped nuts.

Fantastic FRUITS

BLUEBERRY BUTTER

Makes 8 pints

8 cups blueberries, fresh or dry-
  pack frozen (rinsed and drained)
8 large green cooking apples,
  peeled, cored and sliced
8 cups sugar
4 cups water
1 teaspoon ground allspice
1 teaspoon ground mace
1 teaspoon ground nutmeg

Combine all ingredients in large
saucepan or kettle. Bring to a boil;
lower heat and simmer 1 hour, stirring occasionally. Cook until mixture
is thick. Spoon hot mixture into sterilized glasses. Seal, cool and store in
cool, dry place.

APRICOT–APPLE COMPOTE

Serves 3-4

10 dried apricot halves, soaked
4 medium apples
Lemon juice to taste
1/8 teaspoon grated lemon rind
Cinnamon to taste

Pare, quarter, and core apples. Cut
into eighths. Place apples in saucepan; add apricots and a few tablespoons of water in which apricots
have soaked. Cover and simmer until
apples are tender, about 20 minutes.
While hot, add cinnamon, lemon juice,
and grated rind. Serve hot or cold. (70
calories per serving)

Suzan L. Wiener, Spring Hill, Fla.

FRUIT WHIP

1 (8-ounce) package
  cream cheese
1 can sweetened con-
  densed milk
1 (8-ounce) container
  Cool Whip
1 (No. 2) can fruit cock-
  tail, drained
1 (No. 2) can mandarin
  oranges, drained
1 (No. 2) can chunk
  pineapple, drained
  Any fruits or nuts
  desired

Beat cream cheese and milk until
smooth. Add Cool Whip. Fold in
drained fruit. Chill and serve in attractive bowl.

Pat Habiger, Spearville, Kan.

FRESH PEACH MUFFINS

1 cup chopped peaches
1 teaspoon lemon juice
1 cup milk
1 egg
1/4 cup margarine
2/3 cup sugar
1/4 teaspoon cinnamon
3 teaspoons baking powder
2 cups unsifted flour

Sprinkle peaches with lemon juice
and set aside. Mix remaining ingredients, adding flour last. Fold in fruit.
Fill greased muffin tins 2/3 full. Bake
at 450 degrees for 20 minutes.

CHEESE–FILLED PEARS

Serves 4

4 pears, halved, peeled, and cored
1 (8-ounce) package of cream
  cheese, softened
1/4 cup honey
1/4 cup vanilla wafer crumbs
1/2 cup crushed pecans

Combine cream cheese, crushed
pecans, and honey. Beat until well-
blended. Fill pear halves with mixture. Place in shallow baking pan.
Sprinkle with vanilla wafer crumbs.
Bake 30 minutes at 350 degrees, or
until tender.

June Harding, Ferndale, Mich.

BLUEBERRY SALAD

2 packages blackberry gelatin
2 cups blueberries, fresh or frozen
1 (8-1/2-ounce) can crushed
  pineapple, drained
1/2 cup sugar
1 (8-ounce) package cream cheese
1 cup sour cream
1/2 teaspoon vanilla

In large bowl, prepare gelatin as
directed on package. Thicken. In
medium bowl mix together blueberries and pineapple. Add fruit to gelatin when thickened. In small bowl,
cream sugar, cream cheese, sour
cream, and vanilla. Spread on gelatin
mixture after it congeals. Chopped
pecans may be sprinkled on top, if
desired.

FROSTY FRESH FRUIT BOWL
Serves 10

2 cups water
1 cup sugar
1/4 cup lemon juice
1-1/2 tablespoons anise seed
1/4 teaspoon salt
1 small pineapple, cut into bite-size
  chunks
1 small honeydew melon, cut into
  bite-size chunks
1 small canteloupe, cut into bite-size
  chunks
2 oranges, cut into bite-size chunks
1 nectarine, cut into wedges
4 apricots, cut into wedges
1 purple plum, cut into wedges
2 cups seedless green grapes
1 lime, sliced

In a saucepan, combine water with sugar, lemon juice, anise seed, and salt; cook 15 minutes until mixture reaches light-syrup consistency; chill. Prepare and combine all fruit; place in a large bowl; pour chilled syrup through a strainer over fruits. Chill until frosty-cold; stir occasionally.

Gwen Campbell, Sterling, Va.

FRUITED BANANA SPLITS
Serves 2

1 1/2 cups cottage cheese
1/2 cup toasted coconut
1 1/2 cups chopped pineapple,
  drained
1 cup strawberry halves
2 bananas

Combine 1 1/2 cups cottage cheese and 1/2 cup toasted coconut; mix lightly and chill. Combine pineapple and strawberry halves; mix lightly. Slice bananas in pieces or lengthwise. For each salad, arrange bananas in individual dishes and scoop cottage cheese on top of bananas. Surround with fruit and serve with Kraft French Dressing.

To toast coconut, spread in layer pan and toast in oven at 350 degrees until lightly browned, stirring once or twice, so it will not burn.

Edna Askins, Greenville, Texas

RAISIN-NUT PIE

3 eggs
3/4 cup dark corn syrup
1/2 cup firmly packed light brown
  sugar
1/4 cup margarine, melted
1/4 teaspoon salt
1 teaspoon pure vanilla extract
1 cup raisins
1/2 cup chopped pecans
1 unbaked 9-inch pastry shell

Using a fork, beat eggs lightly in a bowl. Beat in corn syrup, brown sugar, margarine, salt and vanilla until well-blended. Stir in raisins and nuts. Pour into pastry shell and bake in preheated 350-degree oven for 40–50 minutes, or until knife inserted halfway between center and edge comes out clean. Cool and serve.

Suzan L. Wiener, Spring Hill, Fla.

PEAR BREAD
Makes 2 loaves

3/4 cup brown sugar
1/2 cup shortening
2 eggs
1/3 cup peeled, mashed, ripe pears
2 tablespoons lemon juice
1 teaspoon vanilla
2 cups flour
1 1/2 teaspoons ground ginger
1 teaspoon ground mace
1/2 teaspoon ground cinnamon
1 teaspoon baking soda
1 teaspoon salt
2 cups coarsely chopped pears
1/2 cup chopped nuts
Sugar Topping:
1/4 cup sugar
1 1/2 teaspoons soft butter

In large bowl, combine sugar, shortening, eggs, mashed pears, lemon juice and vanilla. Beat until smooth.

Combine next 6 ingredients and stir into creamed mixture. Fold in chopped pears and nuts. Pour into two greased and floured loaf pans.

Mix *Sugar Topping* ingredients to make crunchy mixture and sprinkle atop batter in pans.

Bake in preheated 350-degree oven for about 60 minutes. Cool.

Mrs. Agnes Ward, Erie, Penn.

APPLE GRUNT
Serves 5–6

2¼ cups sliced apples,
  unpeeled
2 cups flour
1 teaspoon baking
  powder
½ teaspoon soda
½ teaspoon salt
3 tablespoons soft
  margarine
½ cup sugar
1 egg
½ cup buttermilk

Butter a 10¼ x 6¼ x 2-inch baking pan. Wash apples; cut in quarters; core and thinly slice quarters. Cover with wet toweling to prevent discoloration. Sift flour; measure and resift 3 times with baking powder, soda and salt. Cream margarine and sugar; beat in egg. Add flour mixture in 2–3 portions alternately with buttermilk; begin and end with flour; beat well. Fold in apples. Turn into prepared pan and sprinkle with topping. Bake 30 minutes at 400 degrees.

Topping:
⅓ cup brown sugar
1 tablespoon flour
½ teaspoon cinnamon
2 tablespoons firm
  margarine

Combine topping ingredients; sprinkle on cake. Bake 30 minutes.

APPLE PLUMPLINGS

2 cups flour
1 teaspoon baking powder
1 cup milk
1 egg, beaten
6 large apples

Mix all ingredients, except apples. Peel apples and core; cut into 1/2-inch cubes. Add to batter. Drop mixture into deep, hot oil by tablespoonfuls. Be sure that each spoonful has some apple pieces in it. When brown, lift out of oil and drain on paper towels or brown paper. Serve while hot.

Joy Shamway, Freeport, Ill.

APPLE BUTTER
Makes 8 half-pints

6 pounds tart apples
6 cups cider *or* apple juice
1/2 teaspoon ground cloves
3 cups sugar
2 teaspoons ground cinnamon

Core and quarter unpared apples. In 4–6 quart kettle, combine apples and cider. Cook about 30 minutes, or until soft. Pass through food mill. Boil gently for 30 minutes, stirring often. Add sugar and spices. Cook and stir over low heat until sugar dissolves. Boil gently, stirring often, until desired thickness. Ladle hot apple butter into hot jars, leaving 1/2-inch headspace. Adjust lids. Process in boiling water bath for 10 minutes.

Melissa Meckley, Cata Wassa, Pa.

FRUIT TACOS WITH CREAM CHEESE
Serves 10

16 ounces cream cheese, softened
2 tablespoons grated orange rind
2–3 tablespoons sugar
3 tablespoons orange juice
2 oranges, peeled and cubed
1 cup strawberries, halved
1 kiwi, peeled, halved and sliced
1 banana, peeled, halved and sliced
1 (20-ounce) can pineapple chunks, drained
1 cup shredded coconut
1 box taco shells

In medium bowl, blend cream cheese, orange rind, sugar and orange juice; chill. Combine cut-up fruit, pineapple and coconut; chill. Heat taco shells according to package directions. Spread cream cheese mixture on shells; top with fruit mixture. Serve immediately.

Laura Hicks, Troy, Mont.

DESERT ISLAND FRUIT DESSERT
Serves 6

2 cups sliced peaches, coarsely chopped
1 apple, peeled and chopped
1/2 cup dates, chopped
1/4 cup dried apricots, chopped
1 banana, peeled and cut into 1-inch pieces
2 oranges, peeled and chopped coarsely
1 cup green seedless grapes
1 cup shredded coconut
Candied ginger
Lettuce
1 packet whipped topping mix
1/2 cup dairy sour cream

In a large bowl gently mix the first five fruits. Spread the lettuce on a large chilled platter; place the fruits on the lettuce leaves. Make the whipped topping according to package directions; fold in the sour cream. Place the orange pieces around the edge of the platter; scatter the grapes across the fruit. Dollop the whipped cream mixture here and there; sprinkle the coconut and candied ginger on the cream dollops.

Gwen Campbell, Sterling, Va.

FRESH CRANBERRY TARTLETS
6 servings

Quick Cranberry Sauce:
2 cups (1/2 pound) fresh cranberries
1 cup water
1 cup sugar
Cheesecake Filling:
1 small package (3 ounces) cream cheese, softened
1/4 cup sugar
1 egg, slightly beaten
1 tablespoon milk
1 teaspoon lemon juice
1/2 teaspoon vanilla
Coconut Pastry:
1/4 cup finely shredded coconut
6 teaspoons finely crushed cornflake crumbs
Ingredients for your favorite pastry recipe
First, make *Quick Cranberry Sauce*

by heating cranberries with water and sugar to boiling point. Stir until sugar dissolves. Boil rapidly until berries pop open (about 5 minutes). This makes 2 cups sauce. Chill.

Make *Cheesecake Filling* by beating cream cheese with sugar until smooth and creamy. Add remaining filling ingredients and again, beat until smooth.

For *Coconut Pastry*, make your favorite pastry recipe, blending in the shredded coconut. Roll out pastry and cut to fill six medium-size muffin tins, just like small pie crusts, fluting or pinching edge to stand 1/2 inch above top of muffin tin. Sprinkle 1 teaspoon cornflake crumbs in the bottom of each crust, and top each with 2 1/2 tablespoons *Cheesecake Filling* mixture.

Bake in 350-degree oven for 25 minutes; cool. Just before serving, fill each tartlet with *Cranberry Sauce*, and top with additional snips of coconut, if desired.

Mrs. Amelia Brown, Pittsburgh, Penn.

APPLE APRICOT MEDLEY
Serves 4

2 large, tart green apples
1 cup dried apricots, about 25 to 35 halves
1/2 cup water
1/3 cup orange juice
1/4 cup lemon juice
1 teaspoon almond extract
Brown sugar, optional
1/2 cup toasted, slivered almonds

Core and slice apples into wedges approximately 1/3-inch thick. In medium-size saucepan, combine apples with apricot halves. Add water, orange and lemon juices, and almond extract to saucepan. Simmer apples and apricots, covered, for 5 minutes. Remove from heat and let stand, covered, for 5 minutes. Taste for sweetness. Stir in brown sugar to taste, if necessary. Put in serving bowl and chill until serving time. Sprinkle with almonds.

Suzan L. Wiener, Spring Hill, Fla.

PEACH CLAFOUTI
Serves 6

5 tablespoons sugar, divided
3 cups sliced, peeled fresh peaches
1 cup milk
1 cup half-and-half cream
3 eggs
1/4 cup flour
Pinch of salt
1 teaspoon vanilla
Confectioners' sugar or vanilla ice cream

Sprinkle a well-buttered 1-1/2-quart shallow, oval baking dish with 2 tablespoons sugar. Distribute peaches over the sugar. In a blender, combine milk, cream, eggs, flour, and salt for 2 minutes. Add vanilla and remaining sugar. Blend mixture for a few seconds; then pour over fruit. Bake in preheated 375-degree oven for 45-50 minutes or until puffed and golden.

Sprinkle the Clafouti with confectioners' sugar or top with vanilla ice cream. Serve immediately.
Marcella Swigert, Monroe City, Mo.

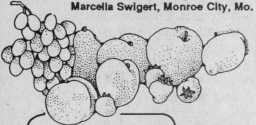

PEACH EASE
Serves 8

1 (29-ounce) can sliced peaches
3 tablespoons quick-cooking tapioca
1/2 teaspoon cinnamon
4 tablespoons butter or margarine, melted
1/2 cup flour
1/2 cup sugar
1/3 cup milk
2 teaspoons baking powder
1 teaspoon vanilla

Preheat oven to 400 degrees. Place peaches with juice in a 7x11-inch baking pan. Stir in tapioca and cinnamon. In mixing bowl, combine remaining ingredients. Spoon batter over peaches. Bake 25-30 minutes or until cake tests done.

For an extra crunch, sprinkle 1/4 cup chopped pecans over batter before baking.
Agnes Ward, Erie, Pa.

FRUIT ICE

1/2 cup orange juice or 1/3 cup pineapple juice
1 tablespoon lemon juice
1/2 cup water
1 egg white

Combine fruit juices and water; freeze. Stir mixture often while freezing. When almost hard, fold in one stiffly beaten egg white. Place in an individual mold and allow to set by returning to freezer.
Suzan L. Wiener, Spring Hill, Fla.

FRUIT PANCAKE PUFF
Serves 4

1/2 cup butter
1 cup all-purpose flour
1 cup milk
4 eggs
1/4 teaspoon salt
2 (10-ounce) packages frozen mixed fruit, thawed and drained
2 tablespoons firmly packed brown sugar
Pinch of freshly grated nutmeg

Preheat oven to 425 degrees. Melt 1/4 cup butter in heavy 10-inch skillet in oven, 3 to 5 minutes. Mix flour, milk, eggs, and salt in blender until smooth. Pour batter into hot skillet. Bake until pancake is puffed and golden brown, 20 to 25 minutes.

Meanwhile, combine remaining 1/4 cup butter, fruit, brown sugar and nutmeg in medium saucepan. Stir over low heat until butter is melted and sauce is warm, about 5 minutes. Place pancake on serving platter. Cut into 4 wedges. Top with fruit, using slotted spoon, and serve, passing sauce separately.

CHOCOLATE-COVERED STRAWBERRIES

1/2 cup semi-sweet chocolate chips
1 tablespoon corn syrup
5 tablespoons butter or margarine
36 strawberries

Place chips, syrup, and butter in saucepan. Melt over low heat. Stir until smooth. Remove from heat; place in pan of water. Dip berries into chocolate; place on waxed paper. Chill.
Lisa Varner, Baton Rouge, La.

FRITTURA DIFICHI RUSPOLI—(HOT FRIED FIGS)

8 firm black figs or extra large fresh prunes, peeled
1/2 cup dark rum
1/3 cup all-purpose flour
1/4 cup chopped walnuts
1/2 teaspoon vanilla extract
1/2 cup water (Mix vanilla and water together)
Vegetable oil for frying
Confectioners' sugar

Soak figs in the rum for 1 hour; turn often to completely even out flavor. In a bowl slowly stir the flour into the water and vanilla mixture. Beat until smooth and creamy. Add walnuts and mix well. Put about 3/4 inch of oil into skillet and set on medium high heat. When oil is hot; dip each fig or prune into the prepared batter and drop into the hot oil. Fry until golden brown on each side (about 3 minutes). Sprinkle confectioners' sugar over top and serve hot.
Marie Fusaro, Manasquan, N.J.

SPICED PINEAPPLE CHUNKS

1 (20 ounce) can juice pack pineapple chunks
1 tablespoon sugar
1 tablespoon vinegar
3 (3-inch) sticks cinnamon
6 whole cloves

Drain pineapple, reserve juice, set pineapple aside.

Combine reserved juice, sugar, vinegar, stick cinnamon and whole cloves in 1-quart container. Microwave on **HIGH** for 5 minutes. Add pineapple chunks, microwave for 4-6 minutes on **HIGH** stir once. Cool. Store in covered container. Drain. Serve on picks.

Foreign
& EXOTIC

SOPAPILLAS

1 package dry yeast
1 cup warm water
1 egg
1 cup milk
5 teaspoons baking powder (1 for each cup of flour)
½ cup sugar
1 teaspoon salt
5 cups flour

In large bowl, add yeast to water and dissolve. Add egg, milk and sugar. Mix until mixture starts to foam. Add flour, salt and baking powder, a little at a time; mix to thick dough. Let sit for 15 minutes. Put dough on floured board and roll to ¼-inch thickness. Cut in 2-inch squares or triangles. Fry in hot oil until brown, as you would doughnuts. Serve warm with melted honey.

Mrs. W.T. Gore, Aztec, N.M.

RUSSIAN MEATLOAF
Serves 4

As in most Russian recipes, potatoes and vegetables are added to stretch the meat portions of the dish. Russian foods are usually very filling and satisfying. This one is no exception.

2 pounds hamburger
3 eggs
1 medium potato, grated
2 carrots, grated
1 medium onion, diced
1/2 teaspoon salt
Pepper to taste
1/2 tablespoon parsley
1/2 teaspoon dill
2 slices dry bread, crushed
1 cup tomato sauce

Put all ingredients in large mixing bowl and mix with hands until thoroughly combined. Mold into loaf and place in an 8x12-inch casserole. Cover with foil and bake in a 350-degree oven for 1-1/2 hours. Remove cover and bake for additional 30 minutes until browned. Remove from baking dish and place on serving platter. Cover with 1 cup tomato sauce.

Roberta Rothwell, Palmdale, Calif.

FINSKA KAKOR
(Finnish cakes)
Makes 4 dozen

Mix together thoroughly:
3/4 cup soft butter
1/4 cup sugar
1 teaspoon almond extract
Stir in:
2 cups sifted flour

Mix thoroughly with hands. Chill dough. Roll out 1/4-inch thick. Cut into strips 2-1/2 inches long and 3/4 inch wide. Brush tops lightly with 1 egg white, slightly beaten. Sprinkle with mixture of 1 tablespoon sugar and 1/2 cup finely chopped, blanched almonds. Carefully transfer to ungreased baking sheet. Bake in a 350-degree oven for about 17-20 minutes, or just until cookies begin to turn a very delicate golden brown.

Leona Teodori, Warren, Mich.

TACO CASSEROLE

1 pound ground beef
1 (1 1/4-ounce) package taco seasoning mix
1/4 cup water
3 cups regular corn chips
2 cups (8 ounces) cheddar cheese
1 medium tomato, chopped
1 cup sour cream

Crumble ground beef into a 2-quart casserole; microwave on HIGH for 5–6 minutes; drain. Stir in seasoning mix and water; microwave for 2 minutes. Stir in chips and 1 1/2 cups cheese; microwave for 2 1/2 minutes, or until heated through. Stir; top with tomato and remaining cheese. Microwave for 2 minutes, or until cheese is melted. Top with sour cream.

FINNISH FLAT BREAD (RIESKA)

¼ cup oatmeal
¼ cup whole-wheat flour
3 cups all-purpose flour
¼ cup sugar
3 teaspoons soda
½ cup shortening
2 cups buttermilk

Combine dry ingredients with shortening. Mix well. Add buttermilk. Divide dough in half; shape into round loaves. Place on cookie sheet. Flatten. Bake at 450 degrees for 15–20 minutes.

Faye Hope, Detroit, Mich.

DANISH STUFFED CABBAGE
Serves 6

1 large head leafy green cabbage
1½ pounds ground beef
1 small onion, chopped
¼ cup green pepper, chopped
2 eggs
½ cup cooked rice
1 teaspoon salt
⅛ teaspoon seasoned pepper
⅛ teaspoon marjoram
Butter *or* margarine
1 (1-pound) can stewed tomatoes
½ cup water
1 tablespoon vinegar

Discard core of cabbage. Remove large leaves; reserve. Working from the bottom, use paring knife to hollow out cabbage, leaving shell and leaves in a large bowl; add boiling water to cover; let stand 10 minutes. Drain. Combine beef, onion, pepper, eggs, rice and seasonings. Fill cabbage shell, mounding mixture on top. Dot with butter. Press softened outside leaves around stuffed cabbage shell. Tie with soft cord or secure with toothpicks to hold shape. Place in Dutch oven. Combine remaining ingredients; pour around cabbage. Cover. Bake at 325 degrees for 2½ hours.

Leona Teodori, Warren, Mich.

ITALIAN FRIED BOW TIES
Makes 15-20 dozen

6 large eggs
1 tablespoon vanilla
1/2 teaspoon salt
6 cups flour
1/2 cup sugar
1/3 cup butter *or* oil
1 tablespoon baking powder

Beat eggs. Add remaining ingredients to make a soft dough. Knead well. Let stand 15 minutes. Knead 5 minutes longer. Place in bowl and keep covered. Roll out small amount of dough at a time, rolling each piece as thin as possible. Cut in narrow strips, about 4 inches long. Form in shapes of a bow tie.

Fry in deep fat, about 360 degrees until delicately browned. Drain on paper towels. Drizzle lightly with thin confectioners' sugar icing or sprinkle with confectioners' sugar. Keeps well in tightly covered container.

Diantha Susan Hibbard, Rochester, N.Y.

RANTOTT CSIRKE (HUNGARIAN OVEN-FRIED CHICKEN)
Serves 4

½ cup butter *or* margarine
½ cup all-purpose flour
1 (2–2½-pound) broiler-fryer, cut up
2 eggs
1 teaspoon salt
1 tablespoon paprika
⅛ teaspoon nutmeg
⅛ teaspoon poultry seasoning
2 tablespoons lime juice
1 cup bread crumbs

Heat oven to 350 degrees. In oven melt butter in a 13 x 9 x 2-inch baking dish. Place flour and chicken pieces in a paper bag; coat thoroughly; set aside. Combine and beat together eggs, salt, paprika, nutmeg, poultry seasoning and lime juice. Dip floured pieces, one at a time, in egg mixture. Dip in crumbs; turn to coat evenly. Place chicken in baking dish skin side down. Bake 50 minutes, or until fork-tender, turning once.

Gwen Campbell, Sterling, Va.

DEEP-FRIED CAULIFLOWER - KVETAK (CZECHOSLOVAKIA)

1 head cauliflower
2 eggs
1/4 cup milk
Salt to taste
1/2 cup flour
2 cups bread crumbs

Separate cauliflower into flowerets. Beat eggs and milk together. Season cauliflower with salt; roll in flour. Dip in egg mixture; coat with bread crumbs. Heat oil to 400 degrees; fry cauliflower until golden brown. Remove from fryer; place in 1-1/2- or 2-quart casserole. Bake at 350 degrees for about 10 minutes or until tender. Do not overcook.

Yes, this is an old family favorite brought over from Czechoslovakia, although it is a favorite among Americans and Canadians as well.

Mrs. Lewis A. Mason, Bokigo, Canada

BOBOTIE (SOUTH AFRICA HAMBURGER PIE)
Serves 10

2½ tablespoons butter *or* margarine
2 cups onion, chopped
2 cups soft bread crumbs
½ cup milk
3 pounds chuck beef (ground)
1 egg
1½ tablespoons curry powder
¼ teaspoon salt
3 tablespoons plum jam
2 tablespoons lime juice
⅓ cup blanched almonds, ground
4 bay leaves
2 lemons, sliced
4 pimiento strips

In skillet melt butter; sauté onion until golden. Soak bread crumbs in milk. Combine with next 7 ingredients. Place bay leaves on bottom of an ungreased 10-inch pie plate. Pat meat mixture on top; bake at 350 degrees for 1 hour.

To garnish:
Arrange lemon slices in a border around edge of meat pie. On center top lay a lemon slice that has been cut halfway through and twisted. Place a pimiento strip on 4 sides; cut into wedges to serve.

Gwen Campbell, Sterling, Va.

KJOTT PIE (NORWEGIAN MEAT PIE)

Serves 4–6

6 eggs
2 1/2 cups bread cubes
1 tablespoon chopped onion
5 strips bacon
1/2 cup chopped celery
1/4 teaspoon garlic salt
1 1/2 teaspoons–1 tablespoon
  Worcestershire sauce
3/4–1 pound ground beef
2 1/2 cups milk
1/2 teaspoon lemon juice
1 teaspoon salt
1/4 pound cheese, grated
1/2 teaspoon celery salt

Beat 1 egg with 1/2 cup milk. Add 2 1/2 cups bread cubes; let stand for 5 minutes. Add to ground beef. Also add Worcestershire sauce, lemon juice, salt and chopped onion; mix well. Line bottom and sides of casserole dish (7 x 11 x 2-inch) or large pie pan with mixture.

Fry bacon until crisp. Crumble and sprinkle over meat in dish; add grated cheese over this and then add chopped celery. Beat remaining 5 eggs and 2 cups milk together; add celery salt and garlic salt. Pour over mixture in dish. Bake at 400 degrees for 15 minutes. Then lower temperature to 350 degrees for 30 minutes, or until mixture is firm.

Mary M. West, Columbia, Ind.

CHICKEN SALTIMBOCCA (ITALY)

Serves 6

1½ pounds boneless
     chicken breasts (3
     whole breasts)
¼   teaspoon sage
6   thin slices boiled ham
¼   cup flour
¼   cup butter *or* margarine
½   cup white wine
1   (10¾-ounce) can
     condensed chicken
     broth

Flatten chicken breasts with the flat side of a knife; rub with sage. Top each breast with 2 slices of ham. Secure with toothpicks. Dust with flour. Brown in butter or margarine in a skillet. Add wine. Bring to a boil, stirring to loosen browned bits. Add broth and bring to a boil. Reduce heat; simmer 5 minutes, or until sauce thickens slightly.

Kenneth McAdams, El Dorado, Ark.

ORIENTAL CHICKEN BREASTS

Serves 4

1/2 cup soy sauce
1/2 cup water
Juice of 1 lime
2 cloves garlic, crushed
Dash of hot pepper sauce
1/2 teaspoon black pepper
2 tablespoons olive oil
1 tablespoon sugar
4 chicken breasts (skinned and
  boned)

Mix all ingredients, except chicken, in a glass bowl. Marinate breasts several hours in mixture (refrigerate). Cover grill with heavy aluminum foil. Pierce foil with fork. Grill chicken over hot coals, turning once, for about 15 minutes. Chicken is done when no pink shows after piercing with fork. Garnish with lime slices.

POMMES SOUFFLÉS (Puffed Potato Slices)

Serves 4

From France, this recipe is 150 years old.

2 medium-size potatoes
32 ounces cooking oil

Peel potatoes and trim into the shape of a cylinder. Cut potatoes into 1/4-to 3/8-inch slices. Rinse in cold water and dry well. Pour cooking oil into 2 frying pans (16 ounces in each). Heat 1 pan to 325 degrees and the other to 375 degrees. Drop slices in the 325-degree pan and shake back and forth for 7 minutes. Remove and drain for about 5-6 seconds. Place in 375-degree pan and brown. The potatoes will puff up as they brown. Two medium-size potatoes should yield about 30 slices. Not all slices will puff up. For best results, do not use new potatoes.

Kenneth McAdams, El Dorado, Ark.

ORIENTAL VEGETABLES

Serves 4

1 bell pepper, sliced
6 green onions, split lengthwise
12 snow peas
4 ounces fresh mushrooms, sliced
Few water chestnuts, sliced
1 can Chinese noodles

Cook on foil, alongside chicken. Baste foil generously with vegetable oil. Place pepper on foil, and gently stir-fry, using plastic spatula. When pepper appears half-done, add remaining vegetables, and continue stir-frying until done. Serve atop Chinese noodles, with soy sauce.

FINSKA KAKOR (Finnish cakes)

Makes 4 dozen

Mix together thoroughly:
  ¾ cup soft butter
  ¼ cup sugar
  1 teaspoon almond extract

Stir in:
  2 cups sifted flour

Mix thoroughly with hands. Chill dough. Roll out ¼ inch thick. Cut into strips 2½ inches long and ¾ inch wide. Brush tops lightly with 1 egg white, slightly beaten. Sprinkle with mixture of 1 tablespoon sugar and ½ cup finely chopped, blanched almonds. Carefully transfer to ungreased baking sheet. Bake in a 350-degree oven for about 17–20 minutes, or just until cookies begin to turn a very delicate golden brown.

Leona Teodori, Warren, Mich.

HUNGARIAN NOODLES OR KLUSE

Serves 5

2 cups flour
2 eggs
1 cup water
1 teaspoon salt

Beat all the above ingredients with a wooden spoon until the dough is soft, and bubbles form. Make dough somewhat stiff. Cut with a spoon into boiling salted water. Let noodles boil until they rise to the top and boil for 5 minutes. Drain and serve with chicken.

This recipe was made by my mother-in-law. She used to cool the mixture and then fry them with a pound of side pork and onion, like fried potatoes. She did this to serve a family of 15 at one time. This recipe is about 50 years old. It takes about 20 minutes to prepare.

Theresa Guillaume, Mosinee, WI

HONEY-HAM CHOW MEIN

1 medium green pepper
1 medium onion
2 ribs celery
1 small can mushrooms
2 tablespoons vegetable oil
2 cups cooked ham strips
1 cup chicken bouillon
2 tablespoons honey
1 tablespoon corn starch
1 tablespoon soy sauce
1/4 cup water

Cut green pepper in strips, onion in slices, celery in pieces (for Chinese effect, cut on the bias) and mushrooms in slices. Heat oil; add onions and ham; cook until ham is slightly browned. Add bouillon, pepper, celery and mushrooms; cover tightly; cook slowly for 6 minutes. Mix remaining ingredients; add and cook for 2 minutes, stirring constantly. Serve with crisp noodles, or over a bed of rice.

Mrs. Gwen Campbell, Sterling, VA

ITALIAN VEGETABLE SALAD

1 head cauliflower, cut into pieces
1 bunch broccoli, cut into pieces
3 zucchini, sliced
5 tomatoes, cut into chunks or 1 basket of cherry tomatoes
1 can black pitted olives, sliced
1 (16 ounce) bottle of Seven Seas Italian Dressing
1 teaspoon salt
1/2 teaspoon pepper

Mix all ingredients together and let stand overnight in refrigerator. This is a great recipe for picnics or potlucks.

Edna Mae Seelos, Niles, IL

ENCHILADA CASSEROLE

12 corn tortillas
2 pounds hamburger
2 tablespoons chili powder
1/2 teaspoon garlic powder
1 medium onion, chopped
15 ounce can tomato sauce
Salt and pepper
1 cups grated Colby or Cheddar cheese
1 can cream of chicken soup
3/4 cup milk

Brown meat, garlic and onion. Add tomato sauce, chili powder, salt and pepper. Heat 9 x 13 inch pan. Line bottom with 6 tortillas. Add meat on top. Cover with 6 more tortillas. Spread chicken soup over these and then milk. Cover with cheese. Bake 25 minutes at 350 degrees. A very easy and tasty dish!

Mrs. Carrie Orth, Burlington, IA

QUICK MEXICAN DISH

Serves 6-8

1 can cream of cheese soup
1 can cream of onion soup

16 ounce can tomatoes, chopped and drained
1 pound ground beef
1 package taco seasoning
8 ounce package Cheddar cheese, grated
11 ounce package Doritos, crushed
Onion, chopped
16 ounce can corn, drained
1 can green chilies, chopped

Brown meat and onion; drain. Add seasonings and corn. Mix together. Add soups and tomatoes. Grease an oblong baking dish. In bottom of dish crush Doritos to completely cover the bottom. Add meat mixture, then pour soup mixture over the meat. Top with cheese. Bake 350 degrees for 25 minutes.

Add sour cream on top of baked casserole, and sliced ripe olives. This is quick and easy!

Patricia Staley, Westmont, IL

ENCHILADA SQUARES

1 pound ground beef
1 cup chopped onion
4-ounce can diced green chilies, drained
4 eggs
8-ounce can tomato sauce
5-1/3-ounce can (2/3 cup) evaporated milk
1 (12-ounce) envelope enchilada sauce mix and 1 teaspoon chili powder
1 cup shredded Cheddar cheese
1/2 cup sliced black olives

Brown beef and onion, drain. Spread meat mixture in lightly buttered 10 x 6 x 2-inch baking dish. Sprinkle diced green chilies over meat mixtures. Beat eggs, tomato sauce, evaporated milk, enchilada sauce. Sprinkle sliced black olives over top.

If desired, sprinkle 2 cups corn chips over top.

Bake in a 350 degree oven for 25 minutes or until set. Sprinkle with cheese and bake 5 more minutes. Let set 10 minutes before cutting.

Barbara June Ohde, Atkinson, NE

VIENNESE POPPY SEED CAKE

Makes 1 large tube cake

1/2 pound butter, softened
4 beaten egg yolks
4 stiffly beaten egg whites (not dry)
1-1/2 cups sugar
1 teaspoon baking soda
1/2 pint sour cream
2 cups flour
2 teaspoons vanilla
2-1/4 ounces poppy seeds

Cream butter; gradually beat in sugar until fluffy. Stir in poppy seeds and vanilla with beaten egg yolks. Add sour cream that has been mixed with baking soda to creamed mixture, *alternately* with flour, ending with flour. Fold in the stiffly beaten egg whites. Pour into an ungreased 9- or 10-inch tube pan. Bake in a 350-degree oven for 1 hour or until it tests done. Cool on rack 15 minutes. Loosen and remove from pan. Completely cool on rack. This moist cake needs no frosting and freezes well.

Joan Ross, Amenia, N.Y.

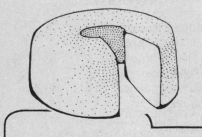

RUMANIAN APPLE TORTE

2 eggs
1/2 cup sugar
1/2 cup sifted all-purpose flour
1/2 teaspoon baking powder
1/4 teaspoon salt
1 cup chopped apples
1/2 cup chopped walnuts

Beat eggs until light, gradually add sugar and beat until fluffy. Sift dry ingredients and add to mixture. Add apples and nuts; blend well.

Bake in greased 8x8-inch pan at 325 degrees for 40 minutes. There is no shortening in this recipe. Delicious!

Mildred V. Schuler, Beaver Falls, Pa.

DUTCH TEA CAKES (KLETSKOPPEN)

This recipe is more than 400 years old and originated in the Dutch city of Leyden.

1-1/2 cups brown sugar
2 tablespoons water
1/4 cup butter
1 teaspoon cinnamon
1 cup ground almonds
1 cup flour

Mix sugar and water to make a thick paste. Add butter, cinnamon, almonds, and flour. Shape into small rounds, about 1 inch in diameter, on a baking sheet greased with unsalted fat. Place at least 2 inches apart. Bake about 15 minutes in 350-degree oven. Remove from oven; let stand 30 seconds and lift from baking sheet with spatula. If wafers become too hard to remove easily, return to oven for a minute, then remove.

Agnes Ward, Erie, Pa.

POTATO DUMPLINGS (GERMANY)

Serves 6–8

3 pounds medium potatoes
2 medium eggs
1 cup unsifted all-purpose flour
1/2 cup packaged dry bread crumbs
1/4 teaspoon nutmeg
1/4 cup chopped parsley
Salt
Dash of pepper

Cook unpeeled potatoes, covered, in boiling water just until tender—about 30 minutes. Drain; cool slightly; peel.

Put potatoes through ricer. Spread on paper towels to dry well. Turn potatoes into large bowl. Lightly toss with 2-1/2 teaspoons salt and the dash pepper. Make a well in center; break eggs into it.

Sift 3/4 cup flour over eggs. Then add bread crumbs, nutmeg, and parsley. With hands, work mixture until it is smooth and holds together. Shape into approximately 18 egg-size balls. Roll in remaining flour.

Meanwhile, in large pan, bring about 2 quarts lightly salted water to boiling point; reduce heat. Drop in at one time just enough potato balls to fit comfortably in pan. Boil gently, uncovered, 2 minutes after they rise to surface. With slotted spoon, transfer dumplings to paper towels; drain. Serve hot.

Judie Betz, Eureka, Calif.

PUACKI (POLISH DOUGHNUTS)

2 cups milk
1 scant cup butter
2 packages dry yeast
5 eggs
1-1/4 cups sugar
1-1/2 teaspoons vanilla extract
1/2 teaspoon lemon extract
1/2 teaspoon salt
8-10 cups flour
1 stick butter

Dissolve yeast in 2 tablespoons sugar and a little warm water. Scald milk; add butter to it and let cool. Beat eggs, sugar, salt, and the two extracts until very light in color, at least 7 minutes. Add flour, a little at a time; beat after each addition. This is not a sticky dough. Let rise in bowl until double, then roll out 1/2-inch thick and cut 2-inch rounds with a biscuit cutter. Let rise again, until double. Fry in hot oil (deep-fat fry) until brown on one side; turn and brown on the other; lift out of fat and drain on a brown paper sack. Melt butter; dip doughnuts in butter then shake in a paper sack with some sugar. Doughnuts are ready to eat. These can be frozen before you dip in melted butter and shake in sugar.

Kathleen Dwyer, Saginaw, Minn.

MEXICAN PIE

Crust:
2 cups beef broth
1 cup long-grain rice
1 tablespoon margarine
1 teaspoon salt
2 eggs, slightly beaten
2 tablespoons chopped pimiento

Filling:
1 pound ground beef
1 garlic clove, crushed
1 teaspoon cumin
1/2 teaspoon salt
1/2 cup mild taco sauce
1 egg, beaten

Guacamole:
1 large avocado, peeled and quartered
1 tablespoon chopped onion
1 tablespoon mild taco sauce
1/2 teaspoon salt
1/2 teaspoon lemon juice

1 cup sour cream

Crust: Grease a 10-inch pie pan. In medium saucepan, heat broth to boiling. Stir in rice, margarine and salt. Return to a boil. Cover reduce heat; simmer until rice is tender. Remove from heat; let cool slightly; stir in eggs and pimiento. Press against bottom and sides of pie plate.

Filling: Preheat oven to 350 degrees. In skillet, brown beef. Drain. Stir in garlic, cumin and salt; cook 2 more minutes. Remove from heat; stir in taco sauce and egg. Spoon filling into crust. Bake 25 minutes.

Guacamole: In small bowl, mash 3 avocado quarters (reserve 1 quarter for garnish). Stir in remaining ingredients. Cover and set aside.

Remove pie from oven. Spread guacamole over meat. Top with sour cream. Return to oven and bake 5 more minutes. Slice remaining avocado; sprinkle on pie.

Suzanne Dawson, Cypress, TX

CRAB MEAT PIES (BRIKS)
Makes 10 pies

4 tablespoons butter
2 medium sized onions, finely chopped
3 cloves garlic, crushed
1/4 cup finely chopped fresh coriander leaves
1 hot pepper, finely chopped
1 teaspoon salt
1/2 teaspoon pepper
4.5-ounce can crab meat, drained
1/2 cup Parmesan cheese
11 small eggs
10 sheets filo dough
Oil for frying

In frying pan, melt butter. Over medium heat, stir-fry onions, garlic, coriander leaves, hot pepper, salt and pepper for 10 minutes. Remove from heat. Make a filling by stirring in crab meat and cheese; set aside. Beat one of the eggs; set aside. Fold a sheet of filo dough over twice to make a square. Place 1/10 of the filling in center; form into a well. Keep dough soft by placing wet towel over sheets while making pies. Brush edges of square with beaten egg; break an egg into the well; fold over to form a triangle. Press edges together. Turn them in about 1/2"; brush again with egg to make sure they are well sealed. In frying pan, pour oil to 3/4" thickness; heat; gently slide in pies; fry over slightly higher than medium heat for about 2 minutes on each side, or until sides are golden brown. Remove and place on paper towels; drain. When all the pies are finished, serve immediately.

LUAU RIBS
Serves 6-8

1/2 cup brown sugar, firmly packed
2 teaspoons ginger
1/3 cup catsup
1/3 cup vinegar
2 cloves garlic, minced
2 (4-1/2-ounces each) cans apple and apricot baby food
2 tablespoons soy sauce or Worcestershire sauce
6 to 8 pounds meaty spareribs
1 teaspoon salt
Dash of pepper

Mix brown sugar and ginger. Combine with baby food, catsup, vinegar, soy sauce and garlic. Rub ribs with salt and pepper. Place ribs, meat side up, on rack in a shallow pan. Bake at 450 degrees for 15 minutes; pour off fat. Reduce oven temperature to 350 degrees. Baste ribs with sauce and continue baking for 1-1/2 hours (depending on your oven.) While baking, baste with sauce several times.

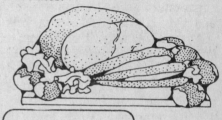

ITALIAN TURKEY LOAF

1-1/4 pounds ground turkey
1 cup egg plant, diced
1 onion, chopped
6-8 mushrooms, chopped
1 egg white, beaten
1/3 teaspoon sage
1/3 teaspoon tarragon
2 tablespoons low sodium tomato sauce
2 cups bran flakes cereal
1 medium pepper, chopped
2 medium tomatoes, peeled and chopped
1 whole egg, beaten
1/3 teaspoon oregano
1 clove garlic
1/4 teaspoon pepper

Place all ingredients, except tomato sauce, in large mixing bowl. Mix until well blended. Press mixture in loaf pan 8x5x3-inches. Spread tomato sauce evenly over top of loaf; bake at 350 degrees for 30 minutes. Remove from oven and drain off excess liquid. Return to oven for additional 45 minutes or until loaf is done. Allow to sit a few minutes before removing from pan and slicing.

Winnie Dettmer, Canfield, Ohio

SLEEK GREEK SALAD

Serves 6

1/2 pound cooked shrimp
1/2 pound feta cheese (rinsed, patted dry, and crumbled)
4 green onions, sliced
2 teaspoons fresh chopped oregano (or 3/4 teaspoon dried)
2 teaspoons fresh chopped basil (or 3/4 teaspoon dried)
1/4 cup sliced ripe olives
3 tomatoes (peeled, cored, and chopped)
1 (12-ounce) package uncooked spaghetti

In a 3-quart bowl combine the shrimp, cheese, onions, seasonings, olives, and tomatoes. Let stand at room temperature for 1 hour. Cook spaghetti in 5 quarts water until tender; drain. Toss the salad ingredients with the hot pasta and serve immediately.

This is a warm main-dish salad that is rich-tasting even though it is low in calories.

Sharon Vircks, Auburn, Wash

ORIENTAL CABBAGE SALAD

Serves 6-8

4 cups shredded cabbage
1/4 cup sliced onion
4 ounces sliced water chestnuts
1 (3-ounce) package oriental noodle soup with chicken flavor
3 tablespoons cider vinegar
2 tablespoons sugar
2 tablespoons salad oil
1/2 teaspoon pepper
1/4 teaspoon salt

Crush noodles to separate. Place in colander. Pour 2 cups boiling water over noodles to soften slightly. Combine drained noodles, cabbage, onions, and water chestnuts in large bowl.

For dressing mix together vinegar, sugar, oil, pepper, salt, and seasoning packet from soup mix. Mix well and pour over cabbage; toss. Chill a few hours before serving.

Loretta M. Brown, Birdsboro, Pa.

GATEAU AUX POIRES (PEAR CAKE)

Serves 8

2 eggs, plus 1 yolk
1 cup skim milk
2 teaspoons vanilla
1/4 teaspoon nutmeg
1 cup flour
1/3 cup sugar
1/4 teaspoon salt
1 teaspoon baking powder
3 pears
1/2 tablespoon confectioners' sugar

Preheat oven to 375 degrees. In a mixing bowl, beat together eggs, egg yolk, skim milk, vanilla, and nutmeg. Sift flour with sugar, salt, and baking powder; gradually add liquid ingredients. Pour batter into a deep 9-inch pie dish.

Peel pears; cut in half lengthwise, removing the cores and seeds. Place pears in a circle in the batter, cut sides down and with the stem ends toward center. Do not allow the bottom ends to touch the sides of the dish. The rounded sides of the pears will be above the batter level.

Place in the oven and bake for 35 minutes or until top is a deep golden brown and pears are tender when pierced with a small, sharp knife. The batter will have puffed. Pear Cake should be eaten warm or cool. Sprinkle with confectioners' sugar before serving.

Suzan L. Wiener, Spring Hill, Fla.

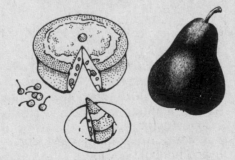

HELADO DE MANGO (MANGO SHERBET)

Serves 6

1 cup water
3/4 cup sugar
Dash salt
2 mangoes, peeled and sliced
1/2 cup light cream
1/4 cup lemon juice
2 egg whites

In saucepan combine water, 1/2 cup sugar, and salt. Cook 5 minutes; cool. In blender combine mangoes and cream, blending until smooth. Stir in cooled syrup and lemon juice. Place in freezer until partially frozen. Beat egg whites to soft peaks; gradually add 1/4 cup sugar, beating to stiff peaks. Place partially frozen mixture into chilled mixing bowl; break into chunks. Beat until mixture is smooth. Fold in beaten egg whites. Freeze until firm.

Kenneth McAdams, El Dorado, Ark.

CZECHOSLOVAKIAN COOKIES

Makes 2-1/2 dozen

1 cup butter
1 cup sugar
2 egg yolks
2 cups flour, sifted
1 cup walnuts, chopped
1/2 cup raspberry or strawberry jam

Cream butter until soft. Gradually add the sugar, creaming until light and fluffy. Add egg yolks and blend well. Gradually add flour and mix thoroughly. Then fold in nuts. Spoon half the batter into a buttered 8-inch square cake pan; spread evenly. Top with jam. Cover with remaining cookie dough. Bake in a moderately slow 325-degree oven for 1 hour or until lightly browned. Cool and cut into 1x2-inch bars.

This cookie recipe is over 100 years old and is also called Kolacky.

Ella Evanicky, Fayetteville, Texas

Holiday
DESSERTS

HOLIDAY DESSERT TORTE
Serves 8–10

1 (10¾-ounce) frozen pound cake, thawed
1 (8-ounce) package cream cheese, softened
2 cups whipped topping with real cream, thawed
⅓ cup semisweet chocolate pieces, melted
½ cup diced, mixed candied fruit

Split pound cake lengthwise into 3 layers. Combine cream cheese and whipped topping. Reserve ⅔ cup of cream cheese mixture. Stir in chocolate. Fold fruit into remaining cream cheese mixture. Spread 2 layers with fruit mixture. Stack. Top with remaining layer. Frost with chocolate mixture. Chill.

Note: This can be made ahead, wrapped securely and frozen. When ready to serve, thaw, wrapped, in refrigerator.

Joy Shamway, Freeport, Ill.

YANKEE DOODLE APPLE PIE

4 cups flour
1 tablespoon sugar
1 teaspoon salt
1 3/4 cups whipped shortening (Crisco)
1 tablespoon cider vinegar
1 egg
1/2 cup water

Mix flour, sugar and salt together. Cut in shortening with fork. In a separate bowl combine vinegar, egg and water. Combine mixtures and stir well. Divide into 5 portions and wrap in waxed paper. Chill in refrigerator for 1 hour. Shape into pie plate.

4 baking apples, cut up
1/2 cup sugar for filling
2 tablespoons flour for filling
1/2 teaspoon nutmeg
1/4 cup lemon juice
1/2 cup sugar for topping
1/4 cup butter for topping
1/2 cup flour for topping

Combine filling and mix with apples. Toss lightly. Spoon into pastry shell. Drizzle with lemon juice. Combine topping ingredients and place on pie. Bake for 1 hour at 425 degrees.

CHOCOLATE SPIDERS
Makes 3 dozen

1½ cups semisweet chocolate morsels
1 (5-ounce) can chow mein noodles
1 cup salted peanuts

Place chocolate morsels in top of double boiler; bring water to a boil. Reduce heat to low; cook until chocolate melts. Add noodles and peanuts, stirring well. Drop chocolate mixture by teaspoonfuls onto greased baking sheets. Refrigerate 8 hours or overnight. Keep chilled until ready to serve.

Mary Mitchell, Cleveland, Ohio

CUSTARD CRUNCH MINCEMEAT PIE

1 unbaked 9-inch pie shell
1 cup sugar
2 tablespoons flour
1/8 teaspoon salt
3 eggs, slightly beaten
1/4 cup butter or margarine, melted
1/2 cup chopped walnuts
1 cup prepared mincemeat

Blend dry ingredients and slowly add to eggs. Add remaining ingredients. Mix well. Pour into pastry shell and bake in a 400-degree oven 15 minutes. Reduce heat to 350 degrees and bake 30 minutes longer.

CRANBERRY CHEWS
Makes 45 bars

1-1/2 cups sifted flour
1-1/2 teaspoons baking powder
1/2 teaspoon salt
2 eggs
1 cup sugar
1 tablespoon lemon juice
3/4 cup jellied cranberry sauce
1 cup chopped pecans

Mix and sift flour, baking powder and salt. Beat eggs well. Add lemon juice, mix. Add sifted dry ingredients, mix. Beat sauce gently with fork. Add sauce and nuts to egg mixture, mix. Spread mixture in greased 9x13-inch pan. Bake in preheated 350 degree oven about 40 minutes. Cool 5 minutes; remove to cooling rack. Cool and cut into bars. Sprinkle with confectioners' sugar, if desired.

Jenni Lien, Stoughton, Wis.

CHRISTMAS APPLE BREAD PUDDING
Serves 4

- 4 slices stale bread
- 2 tablespoons butter
- 3 eggs, well-beaten
- ⅔ teaspoon cinnamon
- ½ teaspoon nutmeg
- ½ teaspoon cloves
- ½ teaspoon allspice
- 6 tablespoons brown sugar
  Pinch salt
- 2 cups apple juice
- ½ teaspoon vanilla

Butter the bread slightly and cut in ½-inch cubes. Place in buttered baking dish. Mix sugar, salt, eggs, apple juice, vanilla and spices. Pour mixture over bread cubes. Bake in a pan of water. Bake at 350 degrees for 40 minutes, or until a knife comes out clean. Sprinkle cinnamon over top, if desired.

Carmen Bickert, Dubuque, Iowa

NORTH POLE LIME-NUT PIE
Serves 6–8

- 1 (3-ounce) package lime-flavored gelatin
- 1 teaspoon lime peel, finely shredded
- ¼ cup lime juice
- 1 cup evaporated milk
- ½ cup chopped pecans
- 1 (4½-ounce) container frozen whipped topping, thawed
- 1 purchased chocolate-flavored crumb pie shell

Dissolve gelatin in ½ cup boiling water. Stir in lime peel and lime juice. Stir in evaporated milk. Chill until partially set. Fold thawed dessert topping and nuts into mixture. Chill until mixture mounds when spooned. Turn into pie shell. Refrigerate for 3 hours.

Joy Shamway, Freeport, Ill.

SNOW PUDDING
Serves 4

- 1 tablespoon (envelope) unflavored gelatin
- 2 cups low-fat milk
- 1 tablespoon instant coffee
- 1 (3¾-ounce) package vanilla instant pudding
- 2 egg whites
- 4 tablespoons low-fat whipped cream topping

Sprinkle gelatin over 1 cup milk in small pan; heat over low heat, stirring until gelatin is dissolved. Set aside.

Stir together pudding, remaining milk and coffee powder in bowl; add gelatin mixture and beat according to pudding package instructions. Beat egg whites until stiff but not dry; fold into pudding mixture. Turn into 3-cup mold; chill until set. When ready to serve, top with dollops of whipped cream topping. Very rich for the few calories involved! (200 calories per serving)

Judie Betz, Eureka, Calif.

FROZEN CHRISTMAS PUDDING

- 1-1/2 cups vanilla wafer crumbs
- 1/2 cup chopped walnuts or pecans
- 1/2 cup chopped dates
- 1/2 cup chopped candied fruit peel
- Grated rind of 1/2 lemon
- 1/4 teaspoon cinnamon
- 1/4 teaspoon nutmeg
- 8 marshmallows, quartered
- 1/4 cup hot orange juice
- 1/4 cup sugar
- 1 cup heavy cream, whipped

Combine crumbs, nuts, fruit, rind, and spices. Dissolve marshmallows in hot orange juice, add sugar and combine this mixture with first mixture. Fold in whipped cream. Place in refrigerator tray and freeze until firm. May be garnished with holly wreaths made of red cinnamon candies and bits of green gumdrops.

Mrs. Carmen J. Bickert, Dubuque, Iowa

FROSTY THE SNOWMAN'S PUMPKIN SQUARES
Serves 9

- 1½ cups graham cracker crumbs
- ¼ cup sugar
- ¼ cup butter, melted
- 1½ cups pumpkin
- ½ cup brown sugar
- ½ teaspoon salt
- 1 teaspoon cinnamon
- ¼ teaspoon ginger
- ⅛ teaspoon cloves
- 1 quart vanilla ice cream, softened
  Whipped cream
  Pecans

Mix graham cracker crumbs with sugar and melted butter. Press into the bottom of a 9-inch square pan. Combine pumpkin with sugar, salt and spices. Fold in the softened ice cream. Pour into crumb-lined pan. Cover and freeze until firm. Cut into squares and top with whipped cream and pecans.

Judy Haffner, Auke Bay, Alaska

CRANBERRIES IN THE SNOW
Serves 12

- 12 unfrosted cupcakes
- 1 cup fresh cranberries
- 1 cup sugar
- 1/2 cup water
- 6 egg whites
- 1/4 teaspoon cream of tartar
- 3/4 cup sugar

Combine fresh cranberries, sugar and water in saucepan; bring to boil. Cook 5-8 minutes; cool. Beat egg whites and cream of tartar until foamy; add sugar gradually; beat until glossy, stiff peaks form. Place cupcakes on cookie sheet; frost each with meringue. Bake 5 minutes at 400 degrees or until meringue is lightly browned; cool. Top each meringue-frosted cupcake with a dollop of the cooked cooled cranberries.

Gwen Campbell, Sterling, Va.

CHRISTMAS PIE
Serves 6–8

1 envelope unflavored gelatin
½ cup sugar
⅛ teaspoon salt
2 eggs, separated
1¼ cups milk
½ teaspoon peppermint flavoring
1 cup heavy cream, whipped
Green food coloring
1 (9-inch) chocolate cookie crust

Mix gelatin, ¼ cup sugar and salt in medium saucepan. Beat together egg yolks and milk. Stir into gelatin mixture. Place over low heat; stir until gelatin dissolves and mixture thickens slightly, about 5 minutes. Remove from heat; stir in peppermint. Chill, stirring occasionally, until mixture mounds slightly when dropped from spoon. Beat egg whites until stiff but not dry. Gradually add ¼ cup sugar; beat until very stiff. Fold into gelatin mixture; fold in whipped cream. Add enough green food coloring to make nice green shade. Pour into pie shell. Chill until firm. Garnish with cherries.

Mrs. Michael D. Carl, Fowlerville, Mich.

FILBERT CAKE
Serves 10

1/2 pound (3 cups) shelled but blanched filberts (3 pounds unshelled nuts)
10 egg yolks
1/4 teaspoon salt
1 cup sugar
1 teaspoon vanilla
6 egg whites
Whipped cream or butter icing

Finely grind shelled filberts and beat egg yolks until very light. Add salt, sugar and vanilla, mix well. Fold in filbert meat lightly. Beat egg whites until stiff and fold into the mixture. Pour into buttered and lightly-floured 10-inch angel cake

pan. Bake at 325 degrees for 1 hour. Cool slowly and remove from pan. Serve as is or with whipped cream or butter icing.

Susan Wiener, Spring Hill, Fla.

FROZEN PUMPKIN SQUARES
Serves 9–12

1¼ cups fine gingersnap cookie crumbs
¼ cup sugar
¼ cup butter *or* margarine, melted
1 (16-ounce) can pumpkin
1½ teaspoons pumpkin pie spice
¼ cup sugar
1 pint vanilla ice cream, softened
2 tablespoons lemon juice
1 (12-ounce) container frozen whipped topping, thawed

Combine crumbs and sugar. Mix in butter. Press firmly on bottom of 9-inch square pan and set aside. Combine pumpkin, spice and sugar in bowl. Spoon in ice cream and blend well. Fold in lemon juice and 4 cups of the whipped topping. Blend well. Pour over crust. Freeze about 4 hours. Garnish with remaining whipped topping.

Shari Crider, Stoughton, Wis.

CREAM PUFF HEART

1 cup water
½ cup butter
1 cup sifted flour
4 eggs
Cream Filling (recipe follows)
2 (10-ounce) packages frozen strawberries, drained
Confectioners' sugar

Fold a 9 x 8½-inch piece of paper in half lengthwise. Sketch half of a heart on it; cut out. Open paper to full heart. Grease baking sheet lightly,

and trace with greased pencil on baking sheet.

Heat water and butter in pan to boiling; reduce heat. Add flour. Stir vigorously over low heat until mixture forms a ball (about 1 minute). Remove from heat. Beat in eggs, 1 at a time; beat until smooth after each addition. Drop mixture by spoonfuls, with sides touching, along edge and entire surface of heart outline positioned on the baking sheet. Bake at 400 degrees for 45 minutes. Cool on rack. Cut off top. Fill shell with filling; top with strawberries. Replace top. Dust with confectioners' sugar. Chill until serving.

Cream Filling:
Combine 1 (3-ounce) package vanilla pudding with 1½ cups milk. Follow package directions for cooking. Cool, then fold in 1 cup heavy cream, whipped, and 1 teaspoon vanilla.

This can be refrigerated overnight. Then just dust with confectioners' sugar before serving. This is a wonderful valentine dessert.

Vickie Vogt, Kewaskum, Wis.

FRUIT CAKE PUDDING
Serves 6-8

2 cups cubed fruitcake (aged or leftovers)
Sugar to taste
3 eggs or egg substitute, well beaten
Milk
1 teaspoon vanilla
1/4 cup coconut

Place cubed fruitcake into 1-1/2 quart casserole. In 2-cup measuring cup, beat eggs with fork or wire whisk. Add enough milk to fill cup; add vanilla. Pour over fruitcake; sprinkle coconut on top. Let sit out while oven preheats to 350 degrees. Bake, uncovered, for 45 minutes or until silver knife inserted into center comes out clean. Serve with whipped cream or whipped topping, if desired.

Agnes Ward, Erie, Pa.

Kids IN THE KITCHEN

MAGIC PUDDING COOKIES

Makes 3 dozen

1 cup Bisquick baking mix
1 (4-serving) box instant pudding
¼ cup salad oil
1 egg

Combine baking mix with instant pudding. Add salad oil and egg. When the dough forms a ball, shape a teaspoonful into a ball and place onto an ungreased cookie sheet. Flatten the balls lightly and sprinkle with colored sugar. Bake at 350 degrees for 5–8 minutes.

Whenever I feel like a cookie treat, my mom lets me make this recipe. Each time you make them it's like magic—a new taste treat depending on which instant pudding flavor you use!

Dustan Neyland, Gillette, Wyo.

WHOOPIE PIES

6 tablespoons Crisco shortening
½ teaspoon salt
1 cup sugar
1 egg
1 teaspoon vanilla
1 cup milk
2 cups flour
5 tablespoons cocoa
1½ teaspoons soda

Cream together first 6 ingredients. Blend flour, cocoa and soda and add to first mixture; blend well. Drop by spoonfuls on an ungreased cookie sheet. Bake at 425 degrees for 10 minutes. Put 2 pies together with this filling:

¾ cup Crisco shortening
¾ cup confectioners' sugar
6 tablespoons marshmallow creme

Combine ingredients and beat well.
Barbara Farren, Addison, Maine

SAVORY CRACKERS

¼ teaspoon garlic powder
¼ teaspoon dill weed
1 package dry ranch-style dressing mix
1 (1-pound) package oyster crackers
½ cup salad oil

In container with tight-fitting lid, combine garlic powder, dill weed and dry dressing mix; stir to combine. Add oyster crackers; put on lid and shake until crackers are covered with seasoning. Sprinkle oil over all. Cover again and shake until oil is absorbed.

Place crackers on cookie sheet; heat in 350-degree oven for 10 minutes.
Donna K. Gore, Aztec, N.M.

NO-BAKE ORANGE SLICES

1 small can frozen orange juice concentrate
1 (17-ounce) package vanilla wafers, crushed
¼ pound soft butter (1 stick)
1 (1-pound) package confectioners' sugar
1 cup chopped nuts
2 cups coconut

Mix all ingredients; except coconut, and roll mixture into balls. Roll balls in coconut.

Barbara Hurlocker, Rock Hill, S.C.

COCONUT BALLS

¼ cup shortening
1 egg
1 teaspoon vanilla
¼ pound graham crackers, crushed
¼ cup sugar
¼ cup coconut

Mix shortening and egg and cook until thickened. Add remainder of ingredients; mix and roll into balls.
Marguerite Myers, Germantown, N.Y.

SEVEN-LAYER BARS

½ cup butter
1½ cups crushed graham crackers
1 cup flaked coconut
1 (6-ounce) package chocolate chips
1 (6-ounce) package butter-scotch chips
1 cup nuts
1 can sweetened condensed milk

Melt butter in bottom of 9 x 13-inch pan. Put all other ingredients in pan in layers in order given, pouring milk over the top of last layer. Bake 15–20 minutes in 350-degree oven.
Mrs. Roger Krueger, Neshkoro, Wis.

OATMEAL CRACKERS

3 cups rolled oats
1 cup wheat germ
2 cups flour
3 tablespoons sugar
1 teaspoon salt
¾ cup oil
1 cup water

Combine all ingredients and place onto cookie sheets. Cut into squares and sprinkle with salt. Bake for 30 minutes at 300 degrees, or until crisp.

Heather Grauer, Seneca, Kan.

CARAMEL APPLES

1 package caramels (10 ounces)
4 teaspoons water
4–5 medium-size apples

Put caramels and water on top of double boiler. Place over low heat until melted, about 15 minutes, stirring occasionally. Insert sticks into clean apples. Dip into melted caramels; twirl until apples are coated; set on butter-coated waxed paper. Refrigerate until cool.

Mrs. Harold Kramer, Parkersburg, Iowa

YOGURT FRUIT CRUNCH
Serves 4

It's smooth, crunchy and sweet.

2 cups plain low-fat yogurt
1 cup dry cereal (granola type *or* dry crunchy cereal)
1 cup fruit, fresh *or* canned in light syrup or natural juices

Spoon layers of cereal, yogurt and fruit into 4 individual bowls.

Betty Poorman, Springfield, Ill.

NO-BAKE CHOCOLATE COOKIES

2 cups sugar
½ cup butter or margarine
½ cup milk
5 tablespoons cocoa
3 cups quick-cooking oatmeal
1 cup walnuts
½ teaspoon vanilla

Mix and cook together for 1 minute, the sugar, butter and milk. Remove from heat and add cocoa, oats and nuts. Add vanilla and stir until it can be dropped from a spoon onto waxed paper.

Genevieve Burns, McMinnville, Ore.

QUICK GRAHAM TREATS

2 cups confectioners' sugar
½ stick margarine *or* butter, softened
1 teaspoon vanilla
Milk (1 *or* 2 tablespoons)
Graham crackers

Combine sugar, margarine or butter, vanilla and 1 tablespoon milk; blend until smooth. If too thick, add more milk. Spread about 1 tablespoon frosting on a graham cracker and top with a second cracker. The number of sandwich cookies this makes depends upon whether you spread the frosting or the children spread it. Kids love this!

Georgia Bender, Kittanning, Pa.

GOOFY BARS

1 package white cake mix
2 eggs
Water
1 cup brown sugar
1 cup chocolate chips
1 cup miniature marshmallows

Place dry cake mix in a bowl. Put eggs in a glass measuring cup and add enough water to make ⅔ cup; add to cake mix with brown sugar. Beat until blended and spread in a greased 9 x 13-inch pan. Sprinkle chocolate chips and marshmallows on top. Bake at 350 degrees for 30–40 minutes.

Cheryl Santefort, Thornton, Iowa

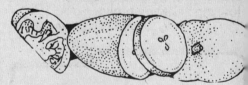

FUDGE BARS

1 cup shortening
2 cups sugar
4 eggs
½ teaspoon salt
1½ cups flour
½ teaspoon baking powder
4 tablespoons cocoa
2 teaspoons vanilla
½ cup nuts

Combine all ingredients and spread in greased and floured 9 x 13-inch pan. Bake at 350 degrees until toothpick comes out clean.

Mrs. Roger Krueger, Neshkoro, Wis.

AMISH HAT

4 Ritz crackers
1 large marshmallow *or* 4 small marshmallows
Peanut butter

Spread peanut butter on crackers and add marshmallows. Place in microwave or under broiler and broil until marshmallow is soft.

Betty Klopfenstein, Waterman, Ill.

FINGER JELL-O

1½ cups boiling water
1 (3-ounce) package orange Jell-O
2 packages Knox unflavored gelatin
1½ cups cold orange juice

Dissolve Jell-O and gelatin in boiling water and add the cold orange juice. Pour into a square dish and chill until set. Cut into squares.

Mary Hale, Tulsa, Okla.

EASY PEANUT BUTTER COOKIES

This is a favorite with children!

1 cup peanut butter
1 cup sugar
1 egg
1 teaspoon vanilla

Mix peanut butter and sugar; stir in remaining ingredients. Shape in 1-inch balls and put on ungreased cookie sheets. Press with fork to flatten slightly and bake in a 350-degree oven for 12–15 minutes.
Note: There is no flour in this recipe.
Elizabeth McJunkin, Toronto, Kan.

PEANUT BUTTER S'MORES

Split hamburger buns
Peanut butter
Marshmallow creme *or* marshmallows

Split hamburger buns and spread each half with peanut butter. Top with a big teaspoon of marshmallow creme or marshmallows. Place bun halves on broiler pan and broil until marshmallow top is lightly brown.
Betty Klopfenstein, Waterman, Ill.

WHIZZ BARS

1 (6-ounce) package chocolate chips
1 (6-ounce) package butterscotch chips
½ cup peanut butter
1 (10½-ounce) package miniature marshmallows
1 cup salted peanuts
½ cup Rice Krispies

Combine chips and peanut butter; melt. Pour over remaining ingredients and press into a 9 x 13-inch pan. Refrigerate until set. This makes a quick snack when you don't have time to bake.
Cheryl Santefort, Thornton, Ill.

NO-BAKE MARSHMALLOW COOKIES

1 (12-ounce) package chocolate morsels
2 tablespoons butter
3 eggs
2 cups confectioners' sugar
1 cup chopped walnuts
1 (10½-ounce) bag miniature marshmallows
Coconut

Melt chocolate morsels with butter in heavy pan over low heat, or in double boiler. Cool. Beat eggs; add sugar, walnuts and marshmallows. Mix all together in large bowl. Shape into balls; roll in coconut and refrigerate. Will keep about 1 month. Butterscotch morsels may be substituted for chocolate.

Marg Ondus, Southwest, Pa.

OATMEAL COOKIES

¾ cup flour
1 teaspoon baking powder
½ teaspoon salt
¾ cup oatmeal
½ teaspoon cinnamon
½ cup sugar
¼ cup shortening
½ cup raisins *or* nuts
1 egg
3 tablespoons milk

Sift flour, baking powder, salt and cinnamon. Cream shortening and sugar together until smooth. Add egg and beat until blended. Stir in oatmeal, raisins or nuts, and milk. Mix well. Add flour mixture. Mix. Drop by teaspoonfuls onto a greased cookie sheet. Bake about 12 minutes in a 375-degree oven.
David Andrews, Butler, Pa.

COCONUT MACAROONS
Makes 2½ dozen

2 cups shredded coconut
⅓ cup sweetened condensed milk
½ teaspoon vanilla extract
1 egg white, stiffly beaten

Blend coconut, milk and vanilla thoroughly; stir in egg white. Drop from teaspoon onto greased cookie sheets; bake in 350-degree oven for 15 minutes. Remove from pan while warm.
Elsie Swanson, Bar Harbor, Maine.

LUSCIOUS LIME WHIP

1 (3-ounce) package lime gelatin
1 (13¼-ounce) can crushed pineapple, drained
8 ounces creamed cottage cheese
1 (4¼-ounce) container Cool Whip

Gently combine all ingredients and refrigerate until well-chilled.
Note: Gelatin is used directly from package. It is not dissolved.
Molly Cairnes, Germantown, Wis.

SEASONED CEREAL SNACKS
Makes 4 cups

⅓ cup margarine, melted
½ teaspoon garlic salt
2 teaspoons Worcestershire sauce
2½ cups Kellogg's Most® cereal
1 cup thin pretzel sticks
½ cup salted peanuts

Combine melted margarine, garlic salt and Worcestershire sauce in a 13 x 9-inch pan. Stir in cereal, peanuts and pretzels. Bake in 250-degree oven for 40–45 minutes. Cool and store in airtight container.

Mary Bell, Cincinnati, Ohio

NO-BAKE PEANUT SQUARES

1 cup light corn syrup
1 cup white sugar
1 cup peanut butter
4 cups cornflakes
4 cups Cheerios
1 cup peanuts

In a 2-quart pan melt together just until smooth the first 3 ingredients, stirring constantly. Do not boil. Remove from heat. Measure the last 3 ingredients into a large bowl. Pour over peanut butter mixture. Stir, coating cereal and nuts. Spread in buttered large pan. Cut into squares. Press down.

Travis Williams, Stockton, Kan.

FINGER GELATIN

4 (1-ounce) packages unflavored gelatin
Fruit-flavored diet pop (16 ounces)

Dissolve gelatin in half the pop. Heat the remaining pop slightly. Add to softened gelatin. Pour into square pan. Chill in refrigerator for about 10 minutes. Cut into squares. Eat with your fingers!

Diane Cole, Cleveland, Ohio

CRAB-CHEESE FONDUE

1½ sticks butter *or* margarine
1 (8-ounce) package Velveeta cheese
1 small can crabmeat
French bread

Melt butter or margarine and cheese over low heat. Stir well until cheese and butter are combined. Stir in crabmeat. Spear French bread with fondue forks and dip in mixture.

Mrs. John Clifford, Grafton, Wis.

NO-BAKE CHOCOLATE BARS

1 cup chopped walnuts
4 cups graham cracker crumbs
½ cup sifted confectioners' sugar
1 (12-ounce) package semisweet chocolate chips
1 cup evaporated milk
1 teaspoon vanilla

Combine nuts, crumbs and sugar in a large bowl. Melt chocolate and evaporated milk over low heat stirring constantly. Blend well. Add vanilla and then set aside ½ cup chocolate mixture. Stir in crumbs mixture and spread in a well-buttered, 9-inch square pan. Spread rest of chocolate mixture over top. Chill and cut into bars.

Lucille Wardlow, Oxnard, Colo.

CANDY COOKIES

1 cup white sugar
1 cup white Karo
1 cup peanut butter
2 cups cornflakes
1½ cups Cheerios
1½ cups Rice Krispies

Combine sugar and syrup; boil until clear. Mix in peanut butter. Combine cereals and mix well. Pour peanut butter-syrup mixture over cereals; drop by spoonfuls onto waxed paper. Store in cool place.

Elva Henderson, Presque Isle, Maine

BUTTERSCOTCH COOKIES
Makes 5 dozen

2 cups granulated sugar
¾ cup margarine
⅔ cup evaporated milk
1 (3¾-ounce) box butterscotch instant pudding mix
3½ cups quick oatmeal

Mix sugar, margarine and evaporated milk in saucepan and bring to a rolling boil on low heat, stirring constantly. Remove from heat and add pudding mix and oatmeal. Mix thoroughly. Cool 3 minutes; drop by teaspoonfuls onto waxed paper. Let sit until cool. Chocolate, chocolate fudge, lemon, or coconut instant puddings may be substituted.

Mrs. Herman A. Strasser, Evans, Colo.

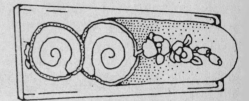

COCOA PEANUT LOGS

1 cup semisweet chocolate pieces
⅓ cup peanut butter
4 cups cocoa-flavored corn puffs cereal

Butter a 9-inch square pan. Melt chocolate with peanut butter in heavy, medium pan over low heat, stirring constantly. When well-blended remove from heat. Stir in cocoa corn puffs to coat well. Press mixture into prepared pan. Cool or refrigerate until mixture is hardened. Cut into log-shaped bars.

Mrs. M. Piccinni, Ozone Park, N.Y.

HOPSCOTCH CRUNCHIES
Makes 1½ dozen

1 (6-ounce) package butterscotch morsels
½ cup peanut butter
1 (3-ounce) can chow mein noodles
1 cup miniature marshmallows

Melt over hot water in double boiler 1 package butterscotch morsels and ½ cup peanut butter. Remove from heat; stir in 1 can chow mein noodles and marshmallows. Drop by teaspoonfuls onto waxed paper. Chill until set.

Lisa Bauman, Fort Wayne, Ind.

RICE KRISPY TREATS
Makes 24

No more standing over a double boiler waiting for the marshmallows to melt. This treat can be ready to chill in 10 minutes, and that includes getting out the ingredients. They have been a favorite of kids for years.

½ cup butter *or* margarine
45 large marshmallows (*or* 4 cups miniature)
5 cups rice cereal

Place butter and marshmallows in a 3-quart casserole. Do not cover. Microwave on HIGH for 3 minutes, stirring often. Add cereal. Mix until completely coated with marshmallow mixture. With buttered hands, press into 8 x 12-inch or 9 x 13-inch pan. Cool. Cut into bars.

Mary Fran Williams, Dayton, Ohio

CUTOUT COOKIES
Makes 10 dozen

3 cups flour
¼ teaspoon salt
½ teaspoon nutmeg *or* 1 teaspoon vanilla
1 cup butter *or* margarine
½ cup milk
1 cup sugar
1 teaspoon soda

Mix first 4 ingredients as you would pie crust. Heat milk, sugar and soda until it foams. Cool mixture; add to flour mixture. Chill dough thoroughly. Roll out on floured board. Cut in various shapes. Bake on greased cookie sheet at 375 degrees for 3–5 minutes, or until lightly browned.

The dough is very easy to roll out so the recipe is ideal for the young cook.

I make the cookies all year long using the shape cutters according to what special day is coming up.

Phyllis Last, Green Bay, Wis.

SOFT PRETZELS
Makes 8–10

Fun to twist any way you like!

1 loaf frozen bread dough
Poppy *or* sesame seeds

Thaw covered dough overnight in refrigerator, or for several hours at room temperature, until soft enough to shape. On a floured surface, cut dough the long way into 8 strips. Cover and let rise 10 minutes. Roll each strip on floured surface or between floured hands until ½ inch thick and 18 inches long. Shape strips into pretzel shape and place on greased cookie sheets. Brush with lukewarm water. Sprinkle lightly with sesame or poppy seeds.

Let rise, uncovered, for 15–20 minutes in warm, draft-free place. Place a shallow pan of water on bottom shelf of oven. Preheat to 425 degrees. Bake pretzels on center shelf of oven for 18–20 minutes, or until golden brown.

Mabel Phillips, Dallas, Texas

SAVORY SUNFLOWER SNACK
Makes 2 cups

3¾ cups sunflower seeds
3 tablespoons oil
¼ teaspoon cayenne
3 tablespoons soy sauce
½ teaspoon ground celery seed
¼ teaspoon paprika

Combine sunflower seeds with other seasonings in a shallow baking pan. Stir well. Bake in preheated 350-degree oven for 20 minutes, stirring after 10 minutes.

Remove pan from oven. Drain on paper towels to blot excess oil. Cool and store in tightly covered container.

To double recipe, bake about 30 minutes.

Mary Bell, Cincinnati, Ohio

MIXED DRY CEREAL AND NUTS
Serves 9–10

2 tablespoons margarine
1¼ cups unsalted roasted peanuts
2½ cups assorted unsweetened, ready-to-eat cereals
1 teaspoon paprika
¼ teaspoon onion powder
⅛ teaspoon garlic powder
1¼ teaspoons chili powder

Preheat oven to 250 degrees. Melt margarine in large baking pan in oven. Remove pan from oven; stir in nuts and cereals; mix well. Sprinkle with seasonings; stir well. Bake, uncovered, in oven 20–30 minutes, or until light-colored cereals begin to brown. Stir every 10 minutes. Serve warm or cooled. Store cooled cereal snack in tightly closed containers. If snack needs re-crisping, reheat in 250-degree oven for a few minutes.

A crunchy, low-salt treat that is a sure crowd pleaser.

Heather Williams, Dayton, Ohio

STRAWBERRY SPREAD

1 jar strawberry jam
1 pint marshmallow creme

Combine ingredients and mix well. Use on hot rolls, toast or as an ice-cream topping.

Rebbie Baker, Killbuck, Ohio

SNOW-CONE SYRUP

2 cups sugar
¾ cup water
1 package unsweetened Kool-Aid

Bring sugar and water to a full boil. Remove from heat and stir in Kool-Aid. Chill. It's now ready for the crushed ice.

Sue Hibbard, Rochester, N.Y.

CHOCOLATE PEANUT BUTTER APPLES

Makes 6–8

6–8 medium-size apples
6–8 wooden skewers
1 cup semisweet chocolate mini chips
1 cup peanut butter-flavored chips
1 tablespoon vegetable oil

Wash apples and dry thoroughly. Insert wooden skewer into each apple. Set aside. Melt mini chips and peanut butter chips with oil in top of double boiler or in a heavy 1½-quart saucepan over low heat; stir constantly until smooth. Remove from heat; dip apples in mixture (tilting pan as needed). Twirl to remove excess coating; place apples on waxed-paper–covered cookie sheet. Refrigerate until firm.

Peggy Fowler Revels, Woodruff, S.C.

LEMONADE COOKIES

1 cup margarine
1 cup sugar
2 eggs
1 (6-ounce) can lemonade concentrate, thawed
1 (3¼-ounce) size (French's or McCormicks) yellow decorator's sugar
3 cups flour
1 teaspoon soda

Cream margarine and sugar; add eggs and mix well. Add flour and soda alternately with ½ cup lemonade concentrate. Drop by teaspoonfuls on ungreased cookie sheet. Bake at 400 degrees for 8–10 minutes. Paint with remaining lemonade and sprinkle with sugar. Remove to rack and cool. Sugar sticks better if you brush 1 or 2 at a time with pastry brush and then sprinkle sugar on them immediately.

Diane Cole, Cleveland, Ohio

WHIPPER-SNAPPERS

1 (18½-ounce) package lemon cake mix
2 cups frozen whipped topping, thawed
1 egg, beaten
1 teaspoon lemon flavoring
Confectioners' sugar

Combine dry cake mix, whipped topping, egg and flavoring. Stir together until well-mixed. With hands dusted with confectioners' sugar, shape dough into small balls and roll in confectioners' sugar.

Bake in preheated 350-degree oven on greased cookie sheets for 10 minutes. These will puff up, and when they begin to settle down they are done. They should be slightly soft when you take them from the oven. Do not overbake.

These freeze well. Vary the recipe with a chocolate cake mix and vanilla flavoring.

Florence Satterfield, Greenfield, Ohio

JIFFY RAISIN SQUARES

1 (8-ounce) package cake mix, spice *or* vanilla
1 (3½-ounce) package butterscotch pudding
2 eggs
½ cup milk
1 cup seedless raisins

Beat in bowl, the cake mix, pudding mix, eggs and milk until smooth. Add raisins and pour into jelly roll pan. Bake at 350 degrees for 20 minutes. Cut into squares. Makes squares ½–¾-inch thick. Two may be spread with jelly or jam and put together as a "sandwich" for easy packing in a lunch box.

STRAWBERRY GEMS

1 cup margarine
1 (3-ounce) package strawberry gelatin
¼ cup sugar
2 cups flour

Cream margarine with gelatin and sugar. Beat until well-mixed. Blend in flour with wooden spoon or pastry blender until dough forms. Press into an 8-inch square on ungreased cookie sheet. Cut into 1-inch squares. Do not separate.

Bake in preheated 325-degree oven for 25 minutes. Cool 5 minutes. Recut. Roll in confectioners' sugar.

Sharon Crider, Evansville, Wis.

ROCKY ROAD BROWNIES

Makes 48 bars

You may begin with your favorite brownie recipe, but it is easier to start with a mix.

1 (22-ounce) package brownie mix
2 cups miniature marshmallows
1 (1-ounce) square unsweetened chocolate
2 tablespoons margarine
1 teaspoon vanilla
Dash salt
2 cups confectioners' sugar
¼ cup water

Prepare brownie mix according to package directions. Spoon into an 8 x 12-inch pan and smooth the top. Microwave on HIGH for 6 minutes. Remove from the oven. Sprinkle marshmallows over the top. Cool. Put chocolate and margarine into a glass bowl. Microwave on HIGH for 1 minute to melt. Add remaining ingredients and beat. Carefully spread frosting over the marshmallows. Cut into bars when cool.

Mabel Phillips, Dallas, Texas

Micro-
MAGIC

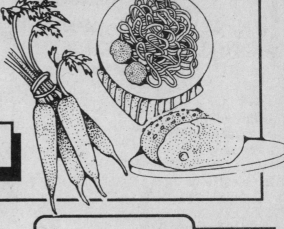

ORANGE YOGURT CAKE
Serves 8–10

1 egg, slightly beaten
1 (8-ounce) carton orange yogurt
1 (9-ounce) package yellow *or* white cake mix (Jiffy cake mix)
1/2 teaspoon grated orange peel (optional)

Grease an 8-inch round baking dish lightly; line with waxed paper. Combine egg, yogurt and orange peel; add cake mix and blend. Beat 2 minutes. Pour into baking dish. Place in microwave on inverted pie plate. Microwave on SLOW-COOK (30 percent power) for 6 minutes; make 1/2 turn. Microwave on HIGH (100 percent power) for 6 minutes. Let stand flat on counter to cool for 5–10 minutes. Turn onto serving place and frost when completely cooled.
Note: Try chocolate cake mix with vanilla or cherry yogurt, or spice cake mix with apple or peach yogurt.
Karen Blunt, Mason City, Iowa

CHILLED FRUIT AMBROSIA
Serves 6–8

1 (10-ounce) package frozen strawberries, thawed
1 (8-1/4-ounce) can pineapple chunks
5 tablespoons brown sugar
1 tablespoon cornstarch
1 (11-ounce) can sliced mandarin oranges, drained

1/2 cup thinly sliced apples
1/4 cup green seedless grapes
1/4 cup shredded coconut
1/4 cup quick-cooking oats
2 tablespoons flour
1/4 teaspoon cinnamon
2 tablespoons butter *or* margarine

Drain strawberries and pineapple; reserve syrup; combine to make 1 cup liquid. In a 10 x 6-inch microwave-safe dish mix 2 tablespoons of the sugar with cornstarch; blend in juices. Microwave, uncovered, 3–4 minutes on HIGH; stir after each minute; add fruits and coconut. Mix remaining sugar, oats, flour and cinnamon. Cut in butter; sprinkle over fruits. Microwave, uncovered, 3 minutes on HIGH; turn dish 1/2 turn after 1-1/2 minutes. Chill well before serving.
Gwen Campbell, Sterling, Va.

PASTA AND TUNA SALAD
Serves 6

1 (7-ounce) package pasta shells or elbow macaroni, cooked
1 (10-ounce) package frozen peas, prepared as directed
1 (6-ounce) can tuna, drained
1 cup creamy ranch dressing
3 green onions, sliced
10 cherry tomatoes, halved (optional)

Combine pasta and peas with tuna, dressing, onions, and tomatoes in serving bowl; mix gently to coat evenly. Cover and refrigerate.

CIDER SNAP
Serves 2

2 cups apple cider *or* apple juice
4 teaspoons red cinnamon candies
Thin apple slices, optional

In a 4-cup measure combine apple cider and cinnamon candies. Microwave, uncovered, on 100 percent power or HIGH for 4–5 minutes or until candies dissolve and the cider is steaming hot, stirring once. Serve in mugs. Garnish with apple slices, if desired.
Laura Hicks, Troy, Mont.

SALMON CASSEROLE
Serves 2-3

1 small can salmon
1/2 cup fresh bread crumbs
1/4 cup minced celery
1 tablespoon minced onion
1 tablespoon parsley
1 tablespoon margarine
2 cheese slices

Rinse salmon in cold water to remove as much salt as possible. Drain; flake in a 3-quart bowl. Blend in bread crumbs, celery, onion, parsley, and margarine; mix together. Press into a small tube pan or shape into a ring in a small dish. Decorate top with cheese slices, cut into strips. Microwave on HIGH for 10 minutes. For the last 3 minutes of cooking time, fill center of ring with peas.

HONEY AND LEMON MICROWAVE ENGLISH MUFFIN BREAD

Makes 2 loaves

5 cups flour
2 packages dry yeast
1 teaspoon salt
1/4 teaspoon soda
2 tablespoons grated lemon rind
1-3/4 cups milk
1/2 cup water
1/3 cup honey
Cornmeal

In a large bowl combine 3 cups flour, dry yeast, salt and soda. Stir in lemon rind. Combine milk, water and honey in a saucepan. Heat until very warm (120–130 degrees). Add to dry ingredients and beat well. Stir in remaining flour to make a stiff batter. Spoon into 2 (8-1/2 x 4-1/2 x 2-1/2-inch) loaf dishes which have been greased and sprinkled with cornmeal. Sprinkle tops with cornmeal. Allow to rise to top of dish. Microwave on HIGH for 6-1/2 minutes. Allow to rest 5 minutes. Surface will be pale. Toast and serve.

Ruth Meinert, Davis, Ill.

PARMESAN-BUTTERED ROLLS

Makes 6–8 rolls

1/4 cup butter *or* margarine, softened
2 tablespoons grated Parmesan cheese
1 teaspoon dried parsley flakes
1/4 teaspoon garlic salt
6–8 dinner rolls

Combine margarine, cheese, parsley flakes and garlic salt. Cut each roll crosswise, two-thirds of the way to the bottom. Spoon or spread about 1 rounded teaspoon margarine mixture on cut surface of each roll. Microwave, uncovered, on HIGH (100 percent) until warm, 30 seconds to 1 minute.

Sharon M. Crider, Stoughton, Wis.

CHOCOLATE CRACKLES

Makes 4 dozen

1/2 cup plus 2 tablespoons Butter Flavor Crisco
6 tablespoons cocoa
1 cup sugar
2 teaspoons baking powder
1/2 teaspoon salt
2 eggs
1 teaspoon vanilla
2 cups flour
1/2 cup chopped nuts
1/2 cup confectioners' sugar in sifter

In medium bowl microwave Butter Flavor Crisco on HIGH power for 45–60 seconds or until melted. Add cocoa; blend. Beat in sugar, baking powder, salt, eggs and vanilla. Stir in flour and nuts. Mix well. Cover and refrigerate until firm. Shape dough into 1-inch balls; roll in confectioners' sugar. Arrange 8 balls, 2 inches apart, in a circle on waxed-paper-lined plate.

Microwave at MEDIUM power for 1-1/2–2 minutes or until cookies are puffed and surface is dry, but cookies should be soft to touch. Cool on waxed paper on countertop. Before serving, sprinkle with confectioners' sugar, if desired.

Sue Thomas, Casa Grande, Ariz.

ANYTIME CRUNCH BARS

Makes 16 bars

6 ounces (1 cup) semisweet chocolate chips
1/2 cup peanut butter chips
1/3 cup margarine
1 teaspoon vanilla
2 cups crisp rice cereal
1 cup quick-cooking rolled oats

Glaze:
1/4 cup peanut butter chips
1 teaspoon oil

Grease 9-inch square or round pan. In medium, microwave-safe bowl, combine chocolate chips, 1/2 cup peanut butter chips and margarine. Micro-

wave on MEDIUM for 2–3 minutes, stirring once halfway through cooking. Stir until smooth. Remove from heat; stir in vanilla. Add cereal and oats; stir until well-coated. Press in greased pan.

To prepare glaze, in small, microwave-safe bowl, combine glaze ingredients. Microwave on MEDIUM for 1–2 minutes; stir until smooth. Drizzle over bars. If desired, refrigerate until set. Cut into bars.

Barbara Nowakowski, North Tonawanda, N.Y.

CARAMEL CHEERIOS BARS

14–16 ounces caramel candies
1/4 cup water
1/2 cup peanut butter
4 cups Cheerios
1 cup salted peanuts

Topping:
1 cup chocolate chips
1/4 cup peanut butter
2 tablespoons margarine

Combine caramels, water and peanut butter in large mixing bowl. Microwave on HIGH for 3–5 minutes until melted; stir every minute. Stir in cereal and peanuts; press into buttered 13 x 9-inch pan. Melt topping ingredients in a 2-cup glass measure by microwaving them for 2 minutes on 50 percent power or MEDIUM. Stir, then microwave 2 more minutes on MEDIUM; blend well. Spread over bars. Cool before cutting.

Mrs. Merle Mishler, Hollsopple, Pa.

ORANGE TEA

1 cup orange juice
2 cups water
1 tablespoon sugar
2 tea bags
4 orange slices

In a 2-quart measure, microwave the orange juice, water and sugar for 7–9 minutes. Stir; add tea bags and let stand, covered, for about 5 minutes. Serve with an orange slice.

CRUNCHY-TOPPED PUMPKIN CAKE

Serves 12

2 eggs
1 (16-ounce) can or 2 cups cooked and mashed pumpkin
3/4 cup evaporated milk
1/2 cup firmly packed brown sugar
1 teaspoon cinnamon
1/4 teaspoon nutmeg
1 (9-ounce) package yellow cake mix
1/2 cup margarine

In 2-quart microwave-proof bowl or casserole, whisk 2 eggs. Blend in pumpkin, milk, sugar, cinnamon and nutmeg. Microwave on HIGH, uncovered, 4 minutes, or until hot and slightly thickened, stirring once halfway through. Pour into microwave-proof 8-inch square baking dish. Sprinkle with dry cake mix.

Microwave margarine in a microwave-proof small bowl on HIGH for 1 minute, or until melted. Drizzle evenly over cake mix. Microwave, uncovered, on HIGH for 8 minutes, or until top is set, rotating dish twice. Place dish under conventional broiler for 2 minutes, or until lightly browned. Cool and refrigerate. Cut in squares.

June Harding, Ferndale, Mich.

APPLE CAKE

Serves 8

1-1/2 cups flour
1 teaspoon baking powder
1 teaspoon cinnamon
1/4 teaspoon salt
1/2 cup butter or margarine
3/4 cup sugar
2 eggs
1/4 cup vegetable oil
1 large tart apple (1-1/2 cups), peeled, cored and chopped
1/2 cup chopped walnuts
1/2 teaspoon vanilla

Glaze:
1/2 cup confectioners' sugar
2 teaspoons milk

Mix flour, baking powder, cinnamon and salt. Melt butter in an 8-inch square glass baking dish. Add sugar, eggs and oil. Mix with fork until blended. Stir in flour mixture, then apple, walnuts and vanilla; smooth top. Place on inverted plate. Microwave on HIGH for 8–10 minutes turning twice, until pick inserted comes out clean. Cool 30 minutes. Mix glaze ingredients and drizzle over cake.

Ruth Meinert, Davis, Ill.

PINEAPPLE DREAM CAKE

Serves 10–12

1-1/2 cups shredded coconut
1 package yellow cake mix (without pudding)
1 (3-ounce) package instant vanilla pudding
1 (8-ounce) can crushed pineapple, undrained
1 cup sour cream
2 eggs

In a pie plate, spread coconut; microwave 5–7 minutes on HIGH; stir 3–4 times until golden. Cool. Grease bundt pan, coat with the toasted coconut. In a large mixing bowl, place cake mix, pudding, undrained pineapple, sour cream and eggs. Blend well; pour into greased bundt pan, on top of coconut. Microwave on 70 percent power for 14–17 minutes. Let stand 10 minutes. Cakes in the microwave will not brown, but the toasted coconut adds some color.

Mrs. Merle Mishler, Hollsopple, Pa.

CARAMEL COFFEE RING

Serves 8

1/2 cup packed brown sugar
1/4 cup butter
1 tablespoon water
1/2 cup chopped nuts
1 (10- or 12-ounce) can refrigerated buttermilk biscuits

In a ring-shaped microwave baking dish put the sugar, butter and water. Microwave on HIGH for 1–1-1/2 minutes until melted; stir to blend. Sprinkle nuts around ring; arrange biscuits on top, slightly overlapping. Microwave on MEDIUM for 4–6 minutes, turning dish after half the time, until dough springs back when lightly touched and top looks dry. Invert on a serving plate. Let stand 2 minutes before removing pan. Serve warm.

Ruth Meinert, Davis, Ill.

POPEYE'S FRENCH BREAD

Serves 6

4 cups fresh spinach leaves
1 small onion, chopped
1 clove garlic, minced
3 tablespoons butter or margarine
1 teaspoon Worcestershire sauce
1 (8-ounce) loaf French bread
1 tomato, thinly sliced
1 cup shredded mozzarella or Monterey Jack cheese

Wash spinach well and remove thick stems. Place in a 1-quart microwave-safe casserole and cover with lid. Cook on HIGH 2–2-1/2 minutes, or until wilted. Drain well and squeeze to remove excess liquid. Chop coarsely and return to casserole. Place onion, garlic and butter in 1-cup glass measure. Cook on HIGH for 1-1/2–2 minutes or until tender. Add to spinach along with Worcestershire sauce; mix well. Cut bread almost in half lengthwise. Open up and spread spinach mixture over bottom half. Top with tomato slices; sprinkle with cheese. Close bread and wrap in paper towels. Microwave on HIGH for 1-1/2 minutes or until cheese starts to melt, rotating loaf once. Cut into 6 slices and serve at once.

Mrs. A.S. Warren, Charlotte, N.C.

SOUTH-OF-THE-BORDER CHOCOLATE CAKE
Serves 8

1 package microwave chocolate cake mix with round pan
2/3 cup water
1/3 cup vegetable oil
1 egg
1 teaspoon cinnamon

Topping:
1 cup semisweet chocolate chips
2 teaspoons almond extract mixed with 2 tablespoons water
1/2 cup whipping cream
2-1/2 teaspoons confectioners' sugar
1/2 teaspoon vanilla extract
1/4 cup almonds

Using solid shortening grease round pan provided with mix. In medium bowl, combine all cake ingredients. Beat with spoon about 1 minute or until well-blended. Pour into pan. Microwave on HIGH for 6-1/2 minutes; if microwave oven is under 600 watts microwave on HIGH for 8 minutes. Cake is done when top no longer has any wet spots and it pulls away from sides of pan. If cake is not done, add additional time in 30-second intervals. Immediately invert cake onto serving plate. Cool completely.

In microwave-safe bowl, combine chocolate chips, almond extract and the 2 tablespoons water; microwave on MEDIUM for 1-1/2–2-1/2 minutes or until chocolate chips are melted, stirring once halfway through cooking. Beat until smooth. Cool 20 minutes, or until slightly thickened. Spread onto top of cake.

In small bowl, beat whipping cream until soft peaks form. Blend in confectioners' sugar and vanilla; beat until stiff peaks form. Spread over chocolate icing on cake. Stick almonds into whipped cream. Store in refrigerator.

Frances Allen, Mount Juliet, Tenn.

TOFFEE COFFEE CAKE
Serves 8–10

1/2 cup butter or margarine
1 cup sugar
2 eggs
1 teaspoon vanilla
1 cup sour cream
1-1/2 cups sifted all-purpose flour
1/2 teaspoon baking powder
1/2 teaspoon baking soda
1/4 teaspoon salt
3 tablespoons sugar
3/4 teaspoon cinnamon
1/2 cup almond brickle chips or crushed Heath bars
Almond Glaze (recipe follows)
1 tablespoon sliced almonds

Place butter in 2-quart glass measure and cook on HIGH for 20–30 seconds, or until softened. Cream in 1 cup sugar. Add eggs, 1 at a time, beating well after each. Blend in vanilla and sour cream. Add flour, baking powder, soda and salt; beat until smooth. Grease a 10–12 cup microwave-safe tube pan. Combine 3 tablespoons sugar with cinnamon; sprinkle pan with 1 tablespoon of mixture. Spoon half of batter into pan; sprinkle with brickle chips and remaining cinnamon-sugar. Spoon remaining batter on top, spreading evenly. Cook on MEDIUM (50 percent), uncovered, for 13–14 minutes, or until edges are set, rotating pan once. Then cook on HIGH 1-1/2–2-1/2 minutes, or until no longer doughy, rotating pan once. Let stand 10 minutes; invert onto serving plate and let cool. Spoon Almond Glaze over cake; sprinkle with almonds.

Almond Glaze:
2 tablespoons butter or margarine
1 cup unsifted confectioners' sugar
1–2 tablespoons hot water
1/4 teaspoon almond extract

Place butter in a 2-cup glass measure; cook on HIGH for 10–20 seconds, or until softened. Mix in sugar; add hot water until of drizzling consistency. Stir in almond extract.

Mrs. A.S. Warren, Charlotte, N.C.

BARK COOKIES
Makes 4 dozen

2 pounds almond bark
1 cup peanut butter
2 cups dry roasted peanuts
3 cups Rice Krispies
2 cups miniature marshmallows

In an 8-cup microwave-safe dish melt almond bark on MEDIUM heat. Add rest of ingredients, 1 at a time, stirring well after each addition.

Drop by spoonfuls onto waxed paper.

Sue Thomas, Casa Grande, Ariz.

BROWNIE NUT CUPCAKES
Makes 1-1/2 dozen

1 cup milk
1/2 cup cocoa
1/2 cup shortening
1-1/2 cups flour
1 cup sugar
1 teaspoon baking powder
1/2 teaspoon baking soda
1 egg
1/2 cup semisweet chocolate chips
1/2 cup chopped walnuts

Line 6 medium muffin cups, 2 x 2 x 1-1/4 inches, or 6 (6-ounce) custard cups with paper baking cups. Arrange cups in circle on 12-inch plate.

Put milk and cocoa in 2-1/2-quart bowl; add shortening. Microwave, uncovered, on HIGH for 2 minutes; stir until shortening is melted. Stir in flour, sugar, baking powder, baking soda and egg. Add chocolate chips and walnuts; mix until smooth. (Mixture will be thick.) Fill muffin cups half full. Sprinkle with additional chocolate chips and walnuts, if desired.

Microwave, uncovered, on HIGH for 2–3 minutes, rotating plate 1/4 turn after 1 minute, until wooden pick inserted in center comes out clean. (Parts of cupcakes will appear moist, but will continue to cook while standing.) Let stand, uncovered, for 1 minute; remove to rack. Repeat with remaining batter.

Barbara Nowakowski, North Tonawanda, N.Y.

STEAK-VEGETABLE POCKETS
Serves 2

1/2 pound beef top round steak
2 tablespoons cold water
1 tablespoon soy sauce
1 teaspoon cornstarch
1 small carrot, thinly sliced
1 tablespoon water
1/2 cup broccoli buds
6 fresh mushrooms, sliced
2 tablespoons green onion, sliced
1 tablespoon cooking oil
1 small tomato, chopped
2 pita bread rounds

Partially freeze meat. With a sharp knife thinly slice meat across the grain, into bite-size strips. In a small bowl stir together 2 tablespoons water, soy sauce and cornstarch; set aside. Place carrots in shallow baking dish; sprinkle with 1 tablespoon water. Cover with vented plastic wrap. Microwave on 100 percent power on HIGH for 2 minutes. Stir in broccoli, mushrooms and green onion. Microwave, covered, on 100 percent power or HIGH for 1–2 minutes more, or until crisp-tender. Drain; cover and set aside.

Preheat a 10-inch microwave browning dish on 100 percent power or HIGH for 3 minutes. Add oil; swirl to coat dish. Add beef. Microwave, uncovered, on 100 percent power or HIGH for 2–3 minutes or until meat is done, stirring twice. Stir the soy sauce mixture. Stir into beef. Microwave, uncovered, on 100 percent power or HIGH for 1–2 minutes or until mixture is thick and bubbly, stirring every 30 seconds. Gently toss the beef mixture with broccoli mixture and chopped tomato. Halve the pita bread. Carefully spoon some of the mixture into each of the 4 pita bread halves.

Laura Hicks, Troy, Mont.

FISH CREOLE

1   pound sole or orange roughy fillets

1   (8-ounce) can tomato sauce
1   (2.5-ounce) jar sliced mushrooms
1/2 green pepper, diced
1/4 teaspoon garlic powder
1/4 teaspoon oregano
3   green onions, sliced
1   stalk celery, diagonally sliced
3   tablespoons water
1   teaspoon instant chicken bouillon

Rinse fish and pat dry. Arrange in 3-quart oblong baking dish with thicker portions toward outside of dish. Combine remaining ingredients in a 4-cup glass measure; pour evenly over fish. Cover with plastic wrap; microwave on HIGH for 8–10 minutes, or until fish flakes easily. Let stand 5 minutes.

FLORENTINE NOODLES

1/2 cup chopped onion
1 (10-ounce) package frozen chopped spinach
1 (10-ounce) can cream of celery soup
1/2 cup sour cream

1/2 cup grated Parmesan cheese
1/8 teaspoon pepper
1/8 teaspoon ground nutmeg
Dash of cayenne pepper
2 cups cooked wide egg noodles (6 ounces uncooked)

Place onion in 2-quart casserole; cover with lid; microwave on HIGH for 3 minutes; stir once. Add spinach; cover and microwave on HIGH about 5 minutes; stir once. Stir in soup, sour cream, cheese, pepper, nutmeg, and cayenne. Cover and microwave on 50% power for about 8 minutes; stir once. Add hot noodles. Toss to coat.
Suggestion: Add 2 cups cooked ham or sausage to make a complete meal.

SAUCY GINGER CHICKEN
Serves 4

4 chicken breasts, skinned and deboned
1/4 teaspoon onion powder
1/2 teaspoon garlic powder
1/8 teaspoon ground ginger
2 eggs, beaten lightly
2 tablespoons apple juice
1/4 cup Parmesan cheese
2 cups seasoned bread crumbs
1/2 stick butter *or* margarine

Season chicken breasts with spices. Mix eggs and apple juice; dip breasts in egg mixture. Combine cheese and bread crumbs; roll breasts in crumb mixture. Place chicken in 8 x 8 x 2-inch square, microwave-safe baking dish; pour butter over all. Cover; cook on HIGH for 25 minutes, rotating dish twice during cooking. Remove chicken to warmed platter; pour sauce over chicken breasts.
Gwen Campbell, Sterling, Va.

SHORTCUT SEAFOOD AND CHICKEN CASSEROLE
Serves 6

1 (16-ounce) can whole tomatoes, undrained
1 (10-ounce) package frozen green peas
1 (6-1/2-ounce) can minced clams, undrained
1 (5-ounce) can chunk chicken, drained
1 (4-1/4-ounce) can broken shrimp, rinsed and drained
2 cups uncooked instant rice
2 tablespoons instant minced onion
1 teaspoon chicken bouillon granules
1 teaspoon paprika
1/4 teaspoon turmeric
1/4 teaspoon ground red pepper

Mix all ingredients in 3-quart casserole, breaking up tomatoes with fork. Cover tightly and microwave on HIGH for 11–14 minutes, stirring after 5 minutes, until liquid is absorbed.
Barbara Nowakowski, North Tonawanda, N.Y.

HOT CHICKEN SALAD IN CHEESE TARTS
Serves 6

2 cups coarsely cut up cooked
  chicken *or* turkey
1 cup celery, thinly sliced
2 tablespoons lemon juice
1 tablespoon onion, finely chopped
1/2 teaspoon salt
1/4 teaspoon pepper
3/4 cup mayonnaise
1 cup seedless green grapes, halved
1/2 cup slivered almonds, toasted

Cheese Tarts:
1/4 cup plus 2 tablespoons margarine
1 cup flour
1/2 teaspoon salt
1/2 cup (2 ounces) finely shredded
  cheddar cheese
2–3 tablespoons cold water

Prepare Cheese Tarts. Toss chicken, celery, lemon juice, onion, salt and pepper in 1-1/2-quart bowl. Stir in mayonnaise. Fold in grapes and 1/4 cup of the almonds carefully. Cover loosely and microwave on MEDIUM (50 percent) for 6–7 minutes, stirring after 3 minutes, until hot. Spoon chicken mixture into tarts. Sprinkle with remaining almonds.

Cheese Tarts: Cut margarine into flour and salt until particles are size of small peas. Stir in cheese. Sprinkle in water, 1 tablespoon at a time, tossing with fork until all flour is moistened and pastry cleans side of bowl (1–2 teaspoons water may be added, if necessary).

Gather pastry into a ball; shape into flattened round on lightly floured surface. Roll into 13-inch circle about 1/8-inch thick. Cut into 6 (4-1/2-inch) circles. Shape pastry circles over backs of 6 (6-ounce) custard cups, making pleats so pastry will fit closely. Prick with fork to prevent puffing.

Arrange custard cups in circle on 12-inch plate. Microwave, uncovered, on HIGH about 5 minutes, rotating plate 1/2 turn after 3 minutes, until tart shells are dry and flaky. Let stand, uncovered, 5 minutes. Loosen edge of each tart with tip of knife; remove each tart from cup carefully. Let cool on rack.

Barbara Nowakowski, North Tonawanda, N.Y.

MAKE-AHEAD MASHED POTATOES
Serves 6

6 medium potatoes (about 2 pounds)
1-1/2 cups creamed cottage cheese
1/2 cup sour cream *or* Lite sour
  cream
1/8 teaspoon garlic powder
1/2 teaspoon salt
2 teaspoons dried chopped chives
Pepper to taste
Butter
Parmesan cheese
Paprika

Peel and quarter potatoes. In a 1-1/2-quart casserole combine potatoes and 1/2 cup water. Cover casserole and microwave on HIGH (100 percent power) for 15–20 minutes, or until very tender, stirring once. Drain. Transfer potatoes to a large bowl. Beat with electric mixer on low speed. Add cottage cheese, sour cream, garlic powder, salt, pepper and chives and beat until smooth and fluffy. Turn into a greased 1-1/2-quart casserole. Brush with butter and sprinkle with Parmesan cheese and paprika. Chill up to 24 hours. Cover and microwave on HIGH (100 percent power) for 8–10 minutes, or until heated through.

Karen Blunt, Mason City, Iowa

PORK CHOW MEIN
Serves 6–8

1 pound pork, cut in 1/2-inch cubes
2 cups celery, thinly sliced
1 cup onion, chopped
2 tablespoons cornstarch
1/4 cup water
1 (16-ounce) can Chinese vegetables, drained and rinsed
1 tablespoon brown sauce *or* molasses
2 tablespoons soy sauce
1/4 teaspoon ginger, ground
1 tablespoon cornstarch
1 cup beef broth

Place pork cubes in covered 3-quart casserole dish. Microwave on HIGH for 4 minutes, stirring once. Add celery and onion; cover; cook on HIGH for 3 minutes. Blend 2 tablespoons cornstarch and 1/4 cup water; stir into meat mixture. Add Chinese vegetables, brown sauce or molasses, 2 tablespoons of soy sauce and 1/4 teaspoon ginger.

Blend 1 tablespoon cornstarch with 1/4 cup beef broth. Add the rest of the beef broth to the casserole. Heat on LOW for 20–25 minutes, stirring twice. Mix in cornstarch and beef broth mixture, stirring well. Cook for 2–3 minutes more.

Kathleen Dwyer, Saginaw, Minn.

HOT GERMAN POTATO SALAD
Serves 8–10

8 medium potatoes
8 strips lean bacon
1 medium onion, finely chopped
3 tablespoons flour
1/4 cup sugar
1 teaspoon salt
1/2 teaspoon celery seed
1 cup water
1/3 cup vinegar

Pierce potatoes and microwave in a circle for 12–15 minutes on HIGH. Turn over and rearrange after 5 minutes. Be sure they are cooked through. Peel and slice. Cut bacon in pieces and put in casserole with onion. Cover with paper towel and microwave on HIGH for 8 minutes, or until crisp. Stir after 4 minutes. Remove bacon and drain. Stir flour, sugar, salt and celery seed into bacon fat until smooth. Microwave on HIGH for 1–2 minutes until bubbly. Stir in water and vinegar. Microwave on HIGH 5 minutes. Stir after 1 minute. Cook until it boils and thickens. Stir until smooth. Add potatoes and bacon; stir. May be made ahead and reheated.

Mrs. Merle Mishler, Hollsopple, Pa.

CHEESEBURGER-VEGETABLE CASSEROLE

Serves 4–6

1 pound ground beef
1/2 cup chopped onion
1/4 cup butter *or* margarine
1/4 cup flour
1 teaspoon salt
Dash pepper
    1-1/2   cups   milk
1-1/2 cups shredded sharp American cheese
1 teaspoon Worcestershire sauce
1 (10-ounce) package frozen mixed vegetables
1/4 cup chopped canned pimiento
Packaged instant mashed potatoes, enough for 4 servings

In a large bowl crumble the beef. Add onion. Microwave, covered, until meat is brown, about 5 minutes, stirring several times to break up meat. Drain off fat. In a 4-cup measure, melt butter about 45 seconds. Stir in flour, salt and pepper. Gradually stir in milk. Microwave, uncovered, 1 minute; stir. Microwave until thick and bubbly, about 3 minutes, stirring every 30 seconds. Stir in 1 cup of the cheese and Worcestershire sauce. Add to meat mixture. Break up frozen vegetables. Stir vegetables and pimiento into meat mixture. Turn into an 8 x 8 x 2-inch baking dish. Microwave, covered, 10 minutes, turning after 5 minutes.

Prepare the instant potatoes according to package directions, except decrease water by 1/4 cup. Spoon the prepared potatoes around the edge of the casserole. Sprinkle remaining cheese over potatoes. Microwave, uncovered, until cheese is melted, about 1 minute.

Laura Hicks, Troy, Mont.

CHICKEN AND BEAN CASSEROLE

1 pound chicken cutlets (no thicker than 1/4 inch)
2 eggs, beaten
1 cup bread crumbs
1 (8-ounce) can tomato sauce
1 small onion, chopped
1 clove garlic, minced
1 teaspoon mustard
1 teaspoon Worcestershire sauce
Dash pepper
1 (8-ounce) box frozen Italian beans, thawed

If cutlets are thicker than 1/4 inch, just flatten with a rolling pin. Dip each cutlet into beaten eggs and then in bread crumbs. Place chicken cutlets in 2-quart microwave dish and cook, covered, on HIGH for 5 minutes. While chicken is cooking combine tomato sauce, onion, garlic, mustard, Worcestershire sauce and pepper. Remove chicken from baking dish. Place thawed beans in bottom of baking dish. Top beans with chicken. Then top all with tomato sauce mixture. Cover and cook for 10 minutes on HIGH.

Maria Balaklaw, Cortland, N.Y.

CHICKEN CORDON BLEU

Serves 6

3 large chicken breasts, deboned, skinned and halved lengthwise (about 1-1/2 pounds)
6 thin slices boiled ham
6 thin slices Swiss cheese
2 tablespoons butter
1 (10-3/4-ounce) can cream of mushroom soup
2 tablespoons milk *or* white wine
1 (2-1/2–3-ounce) can sliced mushrooms, drained
1 tablespoon minced parsley

Pound chicken breasts with mallet until 1/4-inch thickness. Place 1 slice ham and 1 slice cheese on each. Tuck in

sides and roll up, jelly-roll fashion. Skewer with 2 toothpicks; set aside. Melt butter in 8 x 12-inch glass baking dish, in microwave. Microwave breasts in melted butter on HIGH for 3 minutes, uncovered. Turn chicken over so seam side is down; microwave on HIGH for 3 minutes. Combine soup with milk and mushrooms. Pour over chicken. Cover with waxed paper. Microwave on HIGH for 7 minutes, rotating dish after 3-1/2 minutes. . Garnish with minced parsley.

Mrs. Merle Mishler, Hollsopple, Pa.

CHEESY ENCHILADA CASSEROLE

Serves 6–8

1 pound ground chuck
1 teaspoon garlic salt
1 teaspoon onion salt
1 tablespoon chili powder
2 cups shredded Velveeta cheese
1 (10-3/4-ounce) can mushroom soup
1 (10-ounce) can enchilada sauce (mild)
2/3 cup evaporated milk
8 large corn tortillas

Preheat an 8-1/4-inch browning skillet for 5 minutes on HIGH. Turn after 2-1/2 minutes. Place ground chuck in skillet and microwave on HIGH for 3 minutes. Add garlic salt, onion salt and chili powder, and cook for 1-1/2 minutes; turn skillet. Add enchilada sauce, mushroom soup and evaporated milk. Stir well. Cook for 1-1/2 minutes; stir; turn skillet and cook for 1-1/2 minutes.

Remove from oven. Tear 8 corn tortillas into fourths. Place in 9 x 13-inch glass microwave dish. Spoon mixture over tortillas until all are covered. Return to oven and cook for 4 minutes on MEDIUM. After 2 minutes, turn skillet; do not stir. Add 2 cups shredded Velveeta cheese and cook for 1-1/2 minutes, or until cheese is melted. Remove from oven and serve with tossed salad and your favorite beverage.

Joan D. Sisk, Warner Robins, Ga.

DOUBLE CHOCOLATE BARS

Makes 2 dozen

First Layer:
1/2 cup butter *or* margarine
3/4 cup sugar
2 eggs
1 teaspoon vanilla
3/4 cup flour
2 tablespoons cocoa
1/4 teaspoon baking powder
1/4 teaspoon salt
1/2 cup pecans

Second Layer:
2 cups miniature marshmallows

Topping:
6 ounces chocolate chips
1 cup peanut butter
1-1/2 cups Rice Krispies

Mix all first-layer ingredients together. Pour into an 11 x 9-inch dish. Microwave on SIMMER (50 percent) power for 6 minutes, then on HIGH power for 3 minutes.

Spread 2 cups miniature marshmallows on top and put in microwave on HIGH for 1-1/4 minutes. Spread the melted marshmallows, let cool.

Melt 6 ounces chocolate chips and 1 cup peanut butter; stir in Rice Krispies. Microwave on HIGH for 1–1-1/4 minutes. Spread on bars, let cool.

Mary Ann Donlan, Waterloo, Iowa

APPLE NUT TORTE

4 eggs
1 cup sugar
¾ cup flour
1 teaspoon baking powder
½ teaspoon salt
4 cups sliced apples
½ teaspoon cinnamon
1 cup chopped nuts
½ teaspoon vanilla

Beat eggs at high speed until frothy,

about 1 minute. Gradually add sugar; beat until mixture forms soft mounds, about 5 minutes. Fold in flour, baking powder, cinnamon and salt. Fold in apples, nuts and vanilla. Grease only bottom of 12 x 8-inch pan; spoon batter into dish; spread evenly. Cover with waxed paper. Microwave 8–9 minutes. Preheat broiler. Broil about 3 inches from heat for 2–3 minutes.

CHOCOLATE CHIP BARS

1/2 cup butter or margarine
3/4 cup brown sugar
1 egg
1 tablespoon milk
1 teaspoon vanilla
1-1/4 cups flour
1/2 teaspoon baking powder
1/8 teaspoon salt
6 ounces chocolate chips (1 cup)
1/2 cup nuts (optional)

Mix all ingredients together, except the chips, but use only 1/2 cup in the mixture; the other half, place on top of batter. Microwave in an 8- or 9-inch glass pan, for 6-1/2 minutes.

POPCORN BALLS

1/4 cup (1/2 stick) butter or margarine
1 (10-1/2-ounce) bag miniature marshmallows
1 package (4-serving-size) Jell-O Brand gelatin, any flavor
3 quarts (12 cups) popped popcorn

Heat butter and marshmallows in large microwave bowl at HIGH 1-1/2 to 2 minutes or until marshmallows are puffed. Add gelatin; stir to blend. Pour marshmallow mixture over popcorn and stir to coat. Shape into balls or other shapes with buttered hands.

APPLE MUFFINS

1/3 cup melted shortening
1/2 cup sugar
1 egg, beaten
1/2 cup milk
1 1/2 cups flour
1 tablespoon baking powder
1 teaspoon cinnamon
1 cup finely chopped apples
1/4 cup sugar
1/2 teaspoon cinnamon

In a large bowl, beat shortening and sugar; stir in egg and milk. Add flour, baking powder, cinnamon and apples; stir until just blended. Fill 6 paper-lined muffin cups, 1/2 full. Sprinkle tops with sugar-cinnamon mixture and microwave for 2 1/2 minutes; turn once, if necessary.

LOUISIANA POPCORN

Makes 2 quarts

3 tablespoons butter
1/2 teaspoon salt
1/4 teaspoon garlic powder
1/4 teaspoon chili powder
1/4 teaspoon crushed thyme
1/8 teaspoon ground red pepper
2 tablespoons grated cheddar cheese
2 quarts popped popcorn

In a 1-cup glass measure, combine butter, salt, garlic and chili powders, thyme, pepper and cheese. Cook on MEDIUM, 1-1/2–2 minutes, or until melted. Stir well and pour over popped corn. Toss to coat evenly.

Cecilia Rooney, Point Pleasant, N.J.

SWISS FILLET ROLLS
Serves 4

1 small onion, chopped
2 cups (8 ounces) sliced fresh mushrooms
2 tablespoons butter *or* margarine
1 cup herb-seasoned stuffing mix
1 pound white fish fillets (flounder, sole, etc.)
Salt and pepper

Sauce:
1 tablespoon butter *or* margarine
1 tablespoon flour
1/8 teaspoon salt
1/2 cup milk
1/4 cup shredded Swiss cheese
1 tablespoon dry white wine
Snipped fresh parsley, if desired

Combine onion, mushrooms and butter in 1-quart glass measure. Cook on HIGH for 2-1/2–3 minutes, or until tender. Mix in stuffing mix; set aside. Place fillets on flat surface; sprinkle with salt and pepper. Divide stuffing evenly among fillets. Roll up with stuffing inside; place seam side down in shallow glass baking dish (1-1/2-quart) and cover with vented plastic wrap. Cook on HIGH for 4–4-1/2 minutes, or until fish flakes easily with fork. Set aside. Place butter in 2-cup glass measure; microwave on HIGH for 30-40 seconds, or until melted. Blend in flour and salt; stir in milk. Cook on HIGH for 1–1-1/2 minutes, or until mixture boils and thickens, stirring once. Stir in cheese and wine. Spoon sauce over fillets; garnish with parsley.

Mrs. A.S. Warren, Charlotte, N.C.

MEXICAN BEEF AND RICE

1 pound ground beef
Salt and pepper to taste
8 whole green onions, sliced
1 (15-ounce) can tomato sauce
1 cup water
1/4 cup sliced, pitted ripe olives
1 tablespoon chili powder
1-1/2 cups Minute Rice
Hot peppers, if desired
Tortilla chips

Combine all ingredients except tortilla chips in a microwave dish. Cover and cook on HIGH for 5 minutes. Stir and cook for 5 minutes longer. Let stand 5 minutes; fluff with a fork.

Serve with tortilla chips. Salt and pepper to taste.

Mrs. W.O. Tucker, Jonesboro, Ark

CRUSTLESS QUICHE LORRAINE
Serves 6

10 slices bacon
1/4 cup finely chopped onion *or* 1 tablespoon instant minced onion
1 cup shredded cheddar cheese
4 eggs
1 (13-ounce) can evaporated milk
3/4 teaspoon salt
1/4 teaspoon sugar
1/8 teaspoon cayenne pepper

Cook bacon between layers of paper towels for about 8–10 minutes on HIGH. Crumble bacon. Sprinkle cheese, bacon and onion in 9-inch glass pie plate. Beat remaining ingredients with rotary beater until well-blended. Pour over bacon mixture. Microwave on HIGH for 9 minutes. Turn dish, 1/4 turn, every 3 minutes of cooking time. Let stand 10 minutes for center to finish cooking.

Mary Ann Donlan, Waterloo, Iowa

BARBECUED PORK CHOPS
Serves 4

6 pork chops, 1/2-inch thick
1 cup barbecue sauce
1/2 cup chopped onion
1/8 teaspoon minced garlic
1/2 teaspoon salt
1/8 teaspoon pepper

Arrange chops in a 12 x 8-inch dish. Combine remaining ingredients. Pour over chops. Cover with plastic wrap and microwave on HIGH for 5 minutes. Let stand, covered, for 5 minutes. Repeat 2 more times, basting with sauce during rest times. If need be, chops can be cooked 5 minutes more after the last standing time. Turn the dish 1/4 turn after each rest period.

Shari Crider, Stoughton, Wis.

TACO MAIN DISH
Serves 2–4

1 pound ground beef
1 medium onion, diced
1 (1-pound) can kidney beans, drained
1/2 package dry taco seasoning mix
1 can olives (black *or* green)
1 package frozen corn *or* 1 can whole-kernel corn
1 cup Doritos, crushed
1 (8-ounce) can tomato sauce

Brown first 2 ingredients in 1-1/2-quart baking dish in microwave on HIGH for 5 minutes. Add remaining ingredients. Heat through. Cover with grated cheese. Microwave on HIGH, or until cheese melts and bubbles.

Sue Thomas, Casa Grande, Ariz.

SALAMI
Serves 6–8

2 pounds lean ground beef
1/4 teaspoon salt
1/4 teaspoon pepper
1/8 teaspoon garlic powder
1 tablespoon mustard seed
2 tablespoons Morton Tender Quick salt
1 tablespoon Liquid Smoke
3/4 cup water

Mix all ingredients well. Divide into 2 rolls; wrap in plastic wrap and twist ends securely. Cook on MEDIUM HIGH for 34 minutes. Let stand 5 minutes. Refrigerate. If microwave is not equipped with turntable, turn 2 or 3 times during cooking time.

Ann Elsie Schmetzer, Madisonville, Ky.

MILLION-DOLLAR CHEESECAKE
Serves 8–10

Crust:
10 chocolate sandwich cookies with filling, crushed
2 tablespoons margarine, melted

Combine crushed cookies and margarine. Press on the bottom of a 9-inch round glass dish. Rotating pan midway through cooking, microwave on HIGH for 2 minutes.

Cheesecake Filling:
2 (8-ounce) packages cream cheese
1/2 pound white chocolate, cut into small pieces
3 large eggs
3/4 cup plus 1 tablespoon sugar
1-1/2 tablespoons white creme de cacao
3/4 cup sour cream
1 (8-ounce) container non-dairy whipped topping
Dark chocolate shavings for garnish

Put cream cheese and white chocolate into a large glass mixing bowl. Stirring midway through cooking time, microwave on MEDIUM for 4 minutes, or until cheese is softened and chocolate is melted. Add eggs and beat with mixer or whisk. Add 3/4 cup sugar and 1 tablespoon creme de cacao; mix well. Pour over prepared crust. Rotating pan 1/4 turn after 3 minutes, microwave on MEDIUM HIGH for 10–12 minutes, or until center jiggles only slightly. Combine sour cream with remaining sugar and liqueur; spread over top of cheesecake. Microwave on MEDIUM HIGH for 1 minute. Let cool and refrigerate. Spread whipped topping over top and garnish with dark chocolate shavings before serving.

LEMON BARS
Makes 15

Crust:
1/2 cup butter *or* margarine, at room temperature
1/4 cup confectioners' sugar

1 cup all-purpose flour
1/8 teaspoon salt

Topping:
2 large eggs
1 cup granulated sugar
1 teaspoon freshly grated lemon peel
1/4 cup fresh lemon juice
2 tablespoons all-purpose flour
1/4 teaspoon baking powder

Spray bottom of an 8-inch square glass baking dish with vegetable cooking spray. To make crust, beat butter and sugar in a medium-size bowl with electric mixer or wooden spoon until blended. Stir in flour and salt until well-blended. With lightly floured fingertips press mixture evenly in bottom of prepared dish. Place dish on plastic trivet or inverted saucer in microwave oven. Microwave, uncovered, on HIGH 3–5 minutes, rotating dish 1/2 turn once. Crust will look dry on top with some wet spots on bottom (lift dish to check) and will not be browned. Let stand 15 minutes or until slightly cooled.

To make topping, slightly beat eggs in small bowl. Stir in remaining ingredients until blended. Pour over crust. Microwave, uncovered, on HIGH 3–5 minutes, rotating dish 1/2 turn once, until edges are set. Top will have some foamy spots and center will be slightly loose. It will set on standing. Cool completely in baking dish on flat heatproof surface. Cut into 2-1/2 x 1-1/2-inch bars. Remove carefully with narrow metal spatula.

Karen Waldo, Mendota, Ill.

RAISIN-NUT DROPS
Makes 2 dozen

1 (6-ounce) package semisweet chocolate chips
1 cup jumbo peanuts
1 cup seedless raisins

Place chocolate, peanuts and raisins in a 2-1/2-quart casserole dish. Place in microwave and cook 1–3 minutes on HIGH until chocolate chips melt. Stir to cover peanuts and raisins completely. Drop by teaspoonfuls onto waxed paper. Place in refrigerator to set.

Barbara Penland, Goshen, Ind.

PECAN SPREAD
Serves 12

1 (8-ounce) package cream cheese
2 tablespoons milk
1/4 cup chopped green pepper
1/2 teaspoon garlic salt
1/4 teaspoon pepper
2 tablespoons dry onion flakes
1/2 cup sour cream
1 tablespoon melted butter *or* margarine
1/3 cup chopped pecans
1/2 teaspoon salt

Place cream cheese in a medium, micro-safe bowl; microwave on HIGH power for 30–45 seconds. Add milk, green pepper, garlic salt, pepper, onion flakes and sour cream; mix well.

Microwave butter *or* margarine in small micro-safe dish for 15 seconds on HIGH power to melt; stir in pecans and salt. Microwave 1 minute on HIGH power to toast pecans. Sprinkle buttered pecans over cheese mixture in serving dish. Serve with crackers or crisp vegetables.

Yvonne Schilling, Wauwatosa, Wis.

CHUNKY GRANOLA

6 cups rolled oats
1/2 cup sunflower seeds *or* nuts
1/2 cup coconut
1/2 cup wheat germ
1/2 cup powdered milk
2/3 cup honey
2/3 cup oil
1 teaspoon vanilla

In microwave heat rolled oats 3 minutes on HIGH. Stir together vanilla, oil and honey; add to dry ingredients. Heat on HIGH for 6 minutes, stirring 3 times.

Raisins, dates or dried fruit may be added with nuts, etc. Spread to cool.

Sue Thomas, Casa Grande, Ariz.

STRAWBERRY MOUSSE
Serves 4–6

1 (10-ounce) package frozen strawberries, defrosted
1 envelope unflavored gelatin
1/4 cup granulated sugar
1/2 teaspoon lemon juice
1/4 teaspoon lemon peel
2 egg whites
1/4 teaspoon cream of tartar
1 cup frozen whipped topping, thawed

Mash strawberries; press through sieve *or* blend in an electric blender until smooth (puréed). Sprinkle gelatin over puréed fruit. Microwave on HIGH (100 percent) for 2–3 minutes, or until the gelatin dissolves. Stir in 2 table-spoons sugar, lemon juice and lemon peel. Chill for 20 minutes, or until thick-ened, but not set.

Beat egg whites and cream of tartar until foamy. Gradually add remaining sugar. Beat until stiff, but not dry. Fold beaten egg whites into strawberry mixture. Then fold in whipped topping. Pour into a 1-quart serving dish or 4 individual serving dishes. Refrigerate for 4 hours, or until set. Garnish with whipped topping and a dab of orange marmalade, if desired.

Marie Fusaro, Manasquan, N.J.

FROSTED MEAT LOAF DINNER
Serves 4

This makes a very attractive and complete meal on one plate.

2 cups bread crumbs
1/2 cup chopped onion
Salt and pepper to taste
1/2 cup milk
2 pounds ground beef
2 eggs, beaten
4 cups mashed potatoes
1-1/2 cups cheese, shredded
Paprika
1 or 2 packages frozen mixed vegetables, cooked

Mix all ingredients together, except the last 4. Shape and form into a ring loaf. Bake in microwave according to directions of your oven. Remove loaf from microwave and invert onto a plat-ter. Frost loaf ring with mashed pota-toes. Sprinkle cheese over top. Return to oven to melt cheese. Sprinkle with paprika and fill center of ring with mixed vegetables.

Ann Elsie Schmetzer, Madisonville, Ky.

CHEESY ASPARAGUS
Serves 3–4

2 (14-1/2-ounce) cans cut, well-
  drained asparagus
1/4 teaspoon salt
1/8 teaspoon pepper
2 hard-cooked eggs, sliced
1 (4-ounce) can mushrooms, drained
1 (10-1/2-ounce) can cheddar cheese
  soup
5 crushed soda crackers
2 ounces slivered almonds
1/2 cup cheddar cheese
Pinch of paprika

Place half of asparagus in 1-1/2-quart casserole. Sprinkle with half of salt and pepper. Top with half of egg slices. Add half of mushrooms. Beat cheese soup with fork. Spoon half of soup over mushrooms. Top with half of crackers. Sprinkle almonds over all. Repeat layers. Microwave 8–10 min-utes at 70 percent power, MEDIUM; should be hot and bubbly. Top with cheese and paprika. Microwave at 50 percent power, 4–6 minutes until cheese melts. Let sit, covered, 10 minutes before serving.

Sue Thomas, Casa Grande, Ariz.

SOUR CREAM BURGERS
Serves 2

1/4 cup sour cream
2 tablespoons sliced green onion
4 teaspoons fine dry bread crumbs

1/4 teaspoon salt
Dash of pepper
1/2 pound ground beef
2 hamburger buns, toasted
Lettuce leaves
Sliced tomatoes

Stir together sour cream, green on-ion, bread crumbs, salt and pepper. Add ground beef, mixing well. Shape mix-ture into 2 (3/4-inch-thick) patties. Place patties in a small baking dish. Loosely cover with plastic wrap or waxed pa-per. Microwave on 100 percent power or HIGH for 3 minutes. Turn patties over; rotate baking dish 1/2 turn. Micro-wave on 100 percent power or HIGH for 2–3 minutes more, or until done. Drain off fat. Serve patties on toasted buns with lettuce and tomato. Dollop with additional sour cream, if desired.

Laura Hicks, Troy, Mont.

SCALLOPED CHEESE POTATOES
Serves 5–6

1/4 cup margarine
3 tablespoons flour
2 teaspoons dried chives *or* green
  onion
1/2 teaspoon salt
1/2 teaspoon dry mustard
1/8 teaspoon pepper
1-3/4 cups milk
4 medium potatoes, peeled and sliced
1 cup grated cheese

Microwave margarine in 2-quart cas-serole for 45 seconds, or until melted. Stir in flour, chives, salt, dry mustard and pepper. Blend in milk. Microwave on HIGH 6–7 minutes, or until thick-ened, stirring often. Mix in potatoes and cheese; cover. Microwave on HIGH for 15–20 minutes until potatoes are tender, stirring 2–3 times.

Mrs. Warren G. Anderson, Fremont, Neb.

Party
FARE

SMOKY CHEESE BALL

1/2 teaspoon Worcestershire sauce
Several drops Liquid Smoke®
1 roll cheese spread (bacon, garlic or sharp cheese flavor)
2 small packages (3 ounces each) cream cheese, softened
1 cup shredded sharp cheddar cheese
1/2 cup chopped fresh parsley
1/2 cup chopped pecans.

Unwrap cheese spread and microwave on "High" for 1 minute in a large casserole. Add cream cheese and microwave again for 1 minute, or until cheeses mix well. Add Liquid Smoke® and Worcestershire sauce and blend well. Stir in shredded cheddar. Chill for about 15 minutes in freezer, or for about 1 hour in refrigerator. Roll mixture into a ball. Roll in parsley, then in chopped pecans to cover ball. Chill for several hours. Serve with crackers.

Monica W. Cox, Cleveland, Miss.

DRIED FRUIT CHEESE BALL

Makes 2 9-ounce cheese balls

1 large package (8 ounces) cream cheese, softened
1 cup (4 ounces) grated sharp cheddar cheese
1 tablespoon honey
6-ounce package dried fruits and raisins, cut up

Beat cheeses and honey together until light and smooth. Stir in 1 cup dried fruit. Wrap tightly. Chill until firm. Divide in half and shape each into a ball. Garnish with remaining dried fruit. Wrap tightly. Keeps for up to 2 weeks in refrigerator.

CHEESE BALL

1 large package (8 ounces) cream cheese, softened
4-ounce package blue cheese, softened.
1/2 cup shredded cheddar cheese
1 teaspoon Worcestershire sauce
2 teaspoons dry onion-soup mix
Pinch of paprika
Pinch of dried parsley
Crushed salted peanuts

Cream softened cheeses together. Add seasonings and mix well. Roll into a ball, then roll in crushed salted peanuts. Serve with crackers.

Mrs. Ronda Oborne, Packwood, Wash.

HOT BEEF DIP
Makes 2 cups

1 cup (2 1/2-ounce jar) dried beef
1/4 cup chopped onion
1 tablespoon margarine
1 cup milk
1 large package (8 ounces) cream cheese, cubed
1/2 cup sliced mushrooms, drained
1/4 cup grated Parmesan cheese
2 tablespoons chopped parsley

Rinse dried beef in hot water; drain and chop. Cook onion in margarine until tender. Stir in milk and cream cheese; mix until well-blended. Add dried beef and remaining ingredients. Mix well. Serve hot.

Mrs. Agnes Ward, Erie, Penn.

MARSHMALLOW FRUIT DIP

1 large package (8 ounces) cream cheese
13-ounce jar marshmallow creme
1/2 teaspoon ginger
2 tablespoons grated orange rind
Dash of nutmeg
Pineapple juice
Red and green apples

Cream together cream cheese, marshmallow creme, orange rind and spices. Wash, core and slice apples into wedges. Dip wedges in pineapple juice to prevent discoloration. Serve apple wedges with dip.

Mary Kauphusman, Rochester, Minn.

SALMON BALL

1-pound can salmon, drained (2 cups)
1 large package (8 ounces) cream cheese
1 tablespoon lemon juice
2 teaspoons grated onion
1 tablespoon prepared horseradish
1/4 teaspoon salt
1/4 teaspoon paprika
1/2 cup chopped pecans
3 tablespoons chopped parsley

Combine all ingredients except pecans and parsley; blend mixture well. Roll into a ball; roll tightly in plastic wrap; chill for several hours. Roll in combined parsley and pecans. Chill until ready to serve. May be frozen.

CHILI DIP

2 pounds process American cheese, cubed
2 4-ounce cans green chilies, seeded and chopped
1 large tomato, peeled, seeded and chopped
3 tablespoons minced onion
1/2 teaspoon Worcestershire sauce
1/8 teaspoon garlic powder
1/8 teaspoon salt
1/8 teaspoon oregano
1/8 teaspoon pepper

Melt cheese in top of a double boiler over hot (*not* boiling) water, stirring constantly. Combine remaining ingredients in blender container. Process at medium speed until smooth. Add to cheese and cook over low heat, stirring occasionally, for about 15 minutes, or until hot. Serve with corn chips.

Margaret Russo, Winsted, Conn.

CUCUMBER DIP

1 cucumber
1 small package (3 ounces) cream cheese, softened
1/2 cup chopped nuts
Mayonnaise

Grate cucumber; drain well. Add cream cheese; mix well. Add nuts and enough mayonnaise to moisten mixture. Mix until blended.

JALAPENO CRACKER SPREAD

Makes about 2 1/2 cups spread

2 small packages (3 ounces each) cream cheese, softened
1/2 pound grated sharp cheddar cheese
7 1/2-ounce can chopped tomatoes with jalapeno peppers
1 tablespoon ground cumin
1 teaspoon garlic powder
1/8 teaspoon hot pepper sauce

Beat cheeses together to blend well. Gradually beat in remaining ingredients to blend well. Chill. Stores in refrigerator up to one week.

SPICY BEEF DIP

Makes 12 party servings

1 pound ground beef
1/2 cup chopped onion
1 clove garlic, minced
8-ounce can tomato sauce
1/4 cup catsup
1 teaspoon sugar
3/4 teaspoon dried oregano
1 large package (8 ounces) cream cheese, softened
1/3 cup grated Parmesan cheese

Cook beef, onion and garlic in a skillet until meat is browned and onion is tender. Drain off fat. Stir in next 4 ingredients. Cover and simmer gently for 10 minutes. Spoon off excess fat. Add cheeses. Heat until cream cheese melts and is well-combined.

It's easy to double this recipe; keep warm in a slow cooker on low heat for easy serving during your party.

Mrs. Marion Frost, Princeton, Wis.

VEGETABLE-COFFEE DIP

Makes 1 1/2 cups dip

1 large package (8 ounces) softened cream cheese
3 tablespoons cold brewed coffee
1 tablespoon finely grated carrot
1 tablespoon finely chopped parsley
2 teaspoons finely chopped onion
1/4 teaspoon salt
1/2 teaspoon Worcestershire sauce

Combine cream cheese and coffee until smooth. Stir in remaining ingredients and blend well. Chill. Serve with raw vegetables.

CURRY DIP

Makes 1 cup

1 cup mayonnaise
1 tablespoon minced onion
1/2 teaspoon curry powder
Dash of salt

Combine all ingredients. Chill. Sprinkle with extra curry, if desired. Serve with raw vegetables.

HOT CRAB MEAT DIP

1 large package (8 ounces) cream cheese, softened
7-ounce can crabmeat (drained, flaked, cartilage removed)
Dash of white horseradish
1 tablespoon milk
2 tablespoons chopped onion
1/2 teaspoon salt
1/3 cup sliced almonds

Blend all ingredients together until well-mixed, except almonds. Spoon mixture into greased baking dish; sprinkle almonds on top. Bake in a preheated 375-degree oven for 15-20 minutes. Serve hot with chips, crackers, or raw vegetables.

Margaret Russo, Winsted, Conn.

NACHO DABS

Makes 6 1/2 dozen

8-ounce bag tortilla chips
16-ounce can refried beans
1-2 cups (4-8 ounces) shredded cheddar cheese
5-6 jalapeno peppers, sliced into rings
Preheat oven to 400 degrees.

Set aside 6 1/2 dozen whole tortilla chips, reserving any broken ones for another use. Place chips on cookie sheet and top each with about 1 teaspoon beans, some cheese, and a jalapeno pepper ring.

Bake at 400 degrees for 2-3 minutes, or until cheese melts. Serve at once.

CHILI PEPPER DIP

1 can cream of chicken soup
1 can green chilies, chopped
1 cup grated cheddar cheese
2 teaspoons instant minced onion

Combine all ingredients in saucepan; stir over low heat to melt the cheese. Serve with chips.

QUICK CHEESE BALLS

2 cups flour
2 cups shredded cheddar cheese
1 cup margarine, softened
Salt and pepper to taste
2 cups crispy rice cereal

Preheat oven to 350 degrees. Combine all ingredients; mix well. Roll into balls and place on an ungreased baking sheet; flatten slightly. Bake at 350 degrees for 10-12 minutes. These may be frozen after baking; place in the oven for several minutes to crisp before serving.

CHEESE CRISPS

1/2 cup butter
1 roll (3 ounces) sharp cheese
1 cup sifted flour
1/8 teaspoon dry mustard
1 teaspoon Worcestershire sauce
1/2 teaspoon garlic salt
2 drops hot pepper sauce (optional)

Combine and mix all ingredients, working together with fingers to form dough. Shape into 3/4-inch balls; place on ungreased cookie sheets. Bake in preheated 450-degree oven for 10 minutes. Serve hot.

These may be prepared the day before and refrigerated until baking time.

CHOCOLATE POPCORN
Makes about 4 quarts

2 cups sugar
1 cup water
1/2 cup light corn syrup
2 ounces unsweetened chocolate
4 quarts freshly popped corn

Combine sugar, water, corn syrup and chocolate in saucepan. Cook, stirring constantly, until syrup hardens when dropped in cold water. Pour over fresh popcorn and stir to coat well. Shape into balls and store in tightly covered container.

Louise Hicks, Chicago, Ill.

CARAMEL POPCORN I
Makes about 8 quarts

1 cup sugar
1 cup packed brown sugar
4 tablespoons corn syrup
8 tablespoons water
2 cups butter
8 quarts popped popcorn

Combine all ingredients except popcorn in a large saucepan. Cook over medium heat, stirring occasionally, to soft-ball stage on a candy thermometer. Cool until the bubbles subside. Pour over popcorn. Cool and break up. Store in covered containers.

Eileen DeBeukelar, DePere, Wis.

PRETTY PARTY TARTS
Yield: 24

1/3 cup butter
1 cup confectioners' sugar, sifted
1 egg, well beaten
Dash salt
1/3 cup red raspberry jam
1-1/2 tablespoons lemon juice
1/3 cup blanched, chopped almonds
24 small baked party tarts

Cream butter; add confectioners' sugar, egg, salt, jam and lemon juice. Beat together until light and blended. Stir in almonds. Spoon into tart shells. Chill for 1-2 hours; serve.

Agnes Ward, Erie, Pa.

HARVEST MOON POPCORN
Makes about 2 1/2 quarts

1/3 cup melted butter
1 teaspoon dill weed
1 teaspoon Worcestershire sauce
1 teaspoon lemon pepper
1/2 teaspoon onion powder or onion salt
1/2 teaspoon garlic powder or garlic salt
1/4 teaspoon salt
2 quarts popped popcorn
2 cups canned shoestring potatoes

Combine all ingredients except popcorn and potatoes. Put popcorn and potatoes in a large bowl. Pour seasoned butter over all and toss well.

Spread mixture in a 15x10x1-inch pan. Bake in a preheated 350-degree oven for 8-10 minutes, stirring once.

Mary Kauphusman, Rochester, Minn.

SPICED NUTS

4 cups pecans or walnuts or mixture of both
1 cup sugar
1 tablespoon ground cinnamon
1/2 teaspoon salt
1 egg white
1 tablespoon water

Put nuts in large bowl; set aside. Mix sugar, cinnamon and salt in small bowl. In another bowl, beat egg white and water until almost stiff; add to nuts and stir until nuts are well coated. Add sugar mixture and stir. Grease cookie sheet. Pour nuts in pan; bake in 300 degree oven for 30 minutes, stirring after 15 minutes. When cool, separate nuts; store in tightly-covered container.

Patricia Habiger, Spearville, Kan.

PEANUT BUTTER PARTY MIX
Makes 4 cups

2 tablespoons butter
1/3 cup creamy peanut butter
2 cups Wheat Chex cereal
2 cups Rice Chex cereal
1/4 cup dry roasted peanuts

Melt butter and then add peanut butter; stir until well mixed. Toss cereal and nuts in mixture until coated. Remove from heat.

Spread on ungreased cookie sheet. Bake at 375 degrees for 8 minutes or until golden brown. Drain on paper towels. A very healthful snack!

Vickie Vogt, Kewaskum, Wis.

SUNSHINE SWEET POTATO BALLS

Makes 18-20 balls

1/4 cup butter, melted
1/4 cup milk
2 tablespoons sugar
1/2 teaspoon salt
1/4 teaspoon pepper
4 cups cooked, mashed sweet potatoes
18-20 miniature marshmallows
3 cups coarsely crushed cornflakes

Beat butter, milk, sugar, salt, and pepper into mashed sweet potatoes. Form 2-inch balls with a center of a marshmallow. Roll in cornflakes. Place in greased 9-1/2x12-3/4-inch baking pan. Bake in moderate oven of 375 degrees for 25-35 minutes. May be frozen first, then baked without defrosting for 45 minutes at 375 degrees.

Audrey L. Reynolds, Lumberport, W.V.

POTATO 'N BROCCOLI SUPREME

Serves 8

3 cups hot mashed potatoes (5-6 medium)
1 (3-ounce) package cream cheese, softened
1/4 cup milk
1 egg
2 tablespoons margarine
1 (2.8-ounce) can Durkee French fried onions
2 (10-ounce) packages frozen broccoli spears, cooked and drained
1 cup (4 ounces) shredded American cheese

Whip together first 5 ingredients until smooth. Season to taste with salt and pepper. Fold in 1/2 can onions. Spread potato mixture over bottom and sides of a buttered 8x12-inch baking dish; form a shell. Bake, uncovered, at 350 degrees for 20-25 minutes. Arrange hot broccoli in potato shell. Sprinkle with cheese and remaining onions. Bake, uncovered, 5-10 additional minutes.

Lonetta Natale, Madison, N.J.

BUBBLE AND SQUEAK (CABBAGE AND POTATOES)

3 cups unpeeled potatoes, boiled (approximately 3 large)
4 cups cabbage, chopped, par-boiled, and drained well
1 small onion, chopped
4 slices bacon, cut up and fried

With paring knife chop cooked, unpeeled potatoes. In large skillet, fry cut-up bacon; drain on paper towel. Add onion and sauté until golden brown; add chopped, cooked cabbage and chopped, cooked potatoes. Sprinkle bacon bits over top surface. Allow potatoes to become golden brown on bottom over medium heat, about 20 minutes or less. Invert skillet over large serving plate and serve. Garnish with parsley, if desired.

Donna Holter, West Middlesex, Pa.

SPINACH MASHED POTATOES

6-8 large potatoes
3/4 cup sour cream
1 teaspoon sugar
1 stick butter
2 teaspoons salt
1/4 teaspoon pepper
2 tablespoons chopped dried chives
1/4 teaspoon dill leaves
1 (10-ounce) package spinach (cooked)
1 cup shredded Cheddar cheese

Cook and mash potatoes; add sour cream, sugar, butter, salt, and pepper. Beat with mixer until light and fluffy. Add chives, dill, and drained spinach. Place in casserole and sprinkle with cheese. Bake at 400 degrees for 20 minutes. Delicious!!

Kristy Schemrich, Shreve, Ohio

CRUNCHY-TOP POTATOES

6 tablespoons butter or margarine
3 or 4 large potatoes
3/4 cup crushed cereal flakes (non-sweet)
1 cup shredded Cheddar cheese
1 teaspoon salt
1 teaspoon paprika

Place butter/margarine in casserole and put in oven that is pre-heated to 375 degrees. Peel potatoes and slice into 1/4 inch crosswise slices. Place slices in melted butter, coating well. Mix remaining ingredients; sprinkle over top of sliced potatoes. Bake 30 minutes, or until potatoes are done and tops are crisp

CREAMY CHIVE-STUFFED POTATOES

Serves 8

8 medium baking potatoes
Vegetable oil
1/2 cup butter or margarine, softened
1 (2-ounce) carton frozen chopped chives, thawed
2 tablespoons chopped onion
1 (16-ounce) carton commercial sour cream
1/2 teaspoon salt
1/4 teaspoon pepper
Paprika

Scrub potatoes thoroughly, and rub skins with oil; bake at 400 degrees for 1 hour or until done.

Allow potatoes to cool to touch. Slice skin away from top of each potato. Carefully scoop out pulp, leaving shells intact; mash pulp.

Combine potato pulp, butter, chives, onion, sour cream, salt, and pepper; mix well. Stuff shells with potato mixture; sprinkle with paprika. Wrap in heavy-duty aluminum foil; bake potatoes at 400 degrees for 10 minutes or until heated thoroughly.

Gloria Pedersen, Brandon, Miss.

PIZZA TURNOVERS
Makes 3 dozen

1/3 cup chopped mushrooms
1/4 cup chopped green pepper
1/4 cup chopped onion
2 tablespoons margarine
1 (6-ounce) can tomato paste
1/4 cup water
1 teaspoon oregano leaves
1/2 teaspoon salt
1/4 teaspoon garlic powder
1 cup shredded mozzarella cheese
Pastry for double-crust 9-inch pie

Saute mushrooms, green pepper, and onion in margarine. Stir in tomato paste, water, and seasonings; simmer 15 minutes. Stir in cheese. On lightly floured board, roll pastry to 1/8-inch thickness; cut into 3-1/2-inch rounds. Spoon 1 teaspoon mixture onto center of each round. Fold in half; press edges together with fork. Bake at 450 degrees, 10-15 minutes or until lightly browned.

Diantha Susan Hibbard, Rochester, N.Y.

PUMPKIN MUNCH

8 cups unsalted popped corn
1/2 cup butter
1 (3-ounce) package orange gelatin
1/4 cup light corn syrup
1/4 teaspoon soda

In 4-quart bowl place popped corn. Set aside. In a 1-quart bowl place butter and microwave on HIGH power, 30-60 seconds or until melted. Stir in gelatin and corn syrup. Microwave on HIGH, 2-3 minutes, or until mixture comes to a boil, stirring once. Mix in soda until well blended. Pour over popped corn. Toss to coat evenly. Microwave on HIGH, 4-5 minutes or until mixture is evenly coated, stirring 3-4 times. Turn onto waxed paper. Spread out and allow to cool. Break into small pieces. Store in covered container.

Donna Holter, West Middlesex, Pa.

GHOSTLY CRUNCH

8 cups unsalted popped corn
3 cups pretzel sticks
1 (6-ounce) package cheese-flavored goldfish crackers
4 cups toasted-oat cereal
1/3 cup butter
1/2 teaspoon onion salt
1/4 cup Parmesan cheese

In a 4-quart bowl combine popped corn, pretzels, crackers, and cereal. Set aside. In a 1-cup glass measure, place butter and microwave on HIGH power 45-60 seconds or until melted. Drizzle over popped corn mixture. Sprinkle with onion salt and cheese. Toss to coat. Microwave on HIGH power 3-4 minutes or until mixture is lightly toasted, stirring 2 or 3 times. Cool. Store in tightly covered container, or make *individual ghost* by placing 1/2 cup of mixture on a white paper napkin. Tie with yarn or string forming a head and allow the remainder of the paper to hang free for the body.

This could be used for Halloween, and is a great treat for the kids instead of candy.

Donna Holter, West Middlesex, Pa.

CHEWY DIPS

2/3 cup peanut butter
1/4 cup margarine
2 cups powdered sugar
1/2 teaspoon salt
1 cup chopped nuts
1 cup flaked coconut
12 maraschino cherries, chopped
3-1/2 tablespoons shaved paraffin wax
1 (12-ounce) package chocolate chips

Combine peanut butter, margarine, powdered sugar, salt, nuts, coconut, and cherries; shape mixture into 1-inch balls. Combine paraffin and chocolate chips in double boiler; stir over hot water until melted. Dip balls in chocolate mixture; place on wax paper to cool.

Sharon Crider, Evansville, Wis.

GORP
Makes 6 cups

3 cups fruit-and-nut granola cereal
3/4 cup unsalted peanuts, pecans, or walnuts
1/2 cup semisweet chocolate morsels
1/2 cup raisins
1 cup peanut butter pieces
1 cup toasted coconut

Combine all ingredients; store in airtight container.

TV HASH

2 cups Rice Chex
2 cups Wheat Chex
2 cups Cheerios
4 ounces thin stick pretzels
1 cup salted peanuts
1 cup butter, melted
1 tablespoon Worcestershire sauce

Mix cereal, pretzels, and peanuts in large roasting pan. Combine butter and Worcestershire; pour over. Cover; bake in 225-degree oven for 1-1/2 hours.

Dorothy E. Snyder, Pine Grove, Pa.

CRACKLY CORN

4 quarts popped corn
1 cup brown sugar
1/2 cup butter
1/2 cup dark corn syrup
1/2 teaspoon salt
1/2 teaspoon vanilla

Put popped corn in large greased pan. Combine sugar, butter, corn syrup, salt, and vanilla. Cook over medium heat, stirring constantly, until mixture boils. Boil 5 minutes. Pour over corn. Stir to coat well. Bake at 250 degrees for 1 hour. Stir every 15 minutes while cooling. Store in tightly covered container.

Mrs. Jay Spyker, Dallastown, Pa.

Potato
DISHES

OVEN-FRIED SWEET POTATOES
Serves 8

- 6 medium potatoes (3 pounds)
- ½ cup vegetable oil
  Sugar (optional)

Preheat oven to 450 degrees. Scrub potatoes under cold running water. Peel and cut up into ½-inch pieces. In a bowl coat all pieces evenly with oil and arrange on baking sheet not touching each other as much as possible. Bake about 20 minutes, or until tender, turning once. Sprinkle with sugar (optional).

May be cut into long slices like french fries, if desired.

Edna Askins, Greenville, Texas

APRICOT YAMS
Serves 6–8

- 6 cooked, pared yams *or* sweet potatoes
- 1½ cups brown sugar
- 1½ tablespoons cornstarch
- 1 teaspoon grated orange peel
- ¼ teaspoon ground cinnamon
- 1 cup apricot juice
- 1 cup canned apricots, drained
- 3 tablespoons butter *or* margarine
- ½ cup chopped pecans

Cut yams in half. Arrange in a buttered baking dish. Combine brown sugar, cornstarch, orange peel, cinnamon and apricot juice in a saucepan. Cook and stir until sauce thickens. Stir in apricots, butter and pecans. Pour apricot mixture over yams. Bake at 375 degrees for 25 minutes, or until heated.

Shari Crider, Stoughton, Wis.

PARTY POTATO SALAD
Serves 12-14

- 1 (2-pound) bag frozen hash-brown potatoes
- 1 can cream of potato soup
- 1 can cream of celery soup
- 1/2 cup sour cream
- 1 cup shredded cheddar cheese
- 1 (8-ounce) package cream cheese
- 1/2 green pepper, finely chopped
- 1/2 cup chopped onion
- 2 teaspoons salt
- 1/4 teaspoon pepper
- 1 teaspoon paprika

Combine soups with softened cream cheese. Add sour cream, green pepper, onion, and seasonings. Put potatoes in a 3-quart shallow baking dish. Pour soup mixture over potatoes and stir. Spread out evenly; sprinkle with cheddar cheese. Bake at 325 degrees for 1-1/2 hours.

Laura Braun, Fond du Lac, Wis.

POTATO SALAD

- 6 large potatoes, baked
- 5 hard-cooked eggs, chopped
- 3 sticks celery, chopped
- 1 small onion, minced
- 1/4 cup French dressing
- 2 tablespoons mayonnaise
- 1/2 cup pickle relish

Place potatoes, eggs, celery, and onion in a large bowl and toss lightly. In a separate bowl, combine French dressing, mayonnaise, and pickle relish. Mix together and chill.

QUICK POTATOES

- 5 large potatoes
- 1/4 cup melted butter
- 3/4 cup shredded cheddar cheese
- 3 tablespoons grated Parmesan cheese

Slice potatoes and place in casserole dish. Pour butter over potatoes. Sprinkle with cheeses. Bake covered for 25 minutes at 475 degrees. Serve hot.

HASH BROWN POTATOES

- 5 cups cooked potatoes, cubed
- 1/3 cup butter
- 1 teaspoon salt
- 1 teaspoon minced onion

Heat the butter in a skillet and brown potatoes, stirring constantly. Add the remaining ingredients and cook well. Sprinkle parsley on top and serve immediately.

WINTER POTATOES ANNA
Serves 6

6 tablespoons margarine, melted
2 medium white potatoes, peeled and sliced
1 medium sweet potato, peeled and sliced
1 cup winter squash (your choice), peeled and sliced
1 apple, peeled and sliced
1 tablespoon thyme, crushed
Salt and pepper

Slice all vegetables and apple very thin, about ⅙ inch thick. A food processor works well. Cut waxed paper to cover bottom of an 8-inch cast iron skillet or baking dish. Brush the bottom and sides of skillet with margarine. Arrange a layer of one white potato in the bottom of the skillet. Put 1 slice in center and arrange overlapping circles of potatoes around it, from center to sides. Spoon 1 tablespoon of margarine over them; sprinkle with thyme, salt and pepper. Continue layering sweet potatoes, squash, apples and other white potato, seasoning each layer and spooning margarine over it, along with thyme, salt and pepper. Pour any leftover margarine on top.

Bake at 375 degrees for 45 minutes, or until vegetables are crisp and brown around the edges and tender when pierced with a fork. Remove from oven and run a knife around edge to loosen. Put a plate on top of the pan and quickly invert it so the cake unmolds onto platter. Remove waxed paper. To serve, cut into wedges.

Alternate: Use only white potatoes or half white and half sweet potatoes. I never knew how good sweet potatoes and winter squash tasted until I tried this dish.

Leone Keune, Maryland Heights, Mo.

QUICK-FIX POTATO SALAD FOR 20
Serves 20

1 (24-ounce) package frozen hash-brown potatoes with onions and peppers
1-1/2 cups chopped celery
1 (8-ounce) container sour cream dip with chives
2/3 cup mayonnaise or salad dressing
1 tablespoon sugar
1 tablespoon white wine vinegar
1 tablespoon prepared mustard
1/2 teaspoon salt
3 hard-cooked eggs, coarsely chopped

In covered 3- to 4-quart saucepan, cook potatoes with onions and peppers in large amount of boiling water 6-8 minutes, or until potatoes are tender. Drain well. In large bowl, combine cooked potatoes and celery. Set aside.

To make dressing: In small bowl, stir together sour cream dip, mayonnaise or salad dressing, sugar, vinegar, mustard, and salt. Add dressing to potato mixture. Toss gently to coat. Gently fold in chopped eggs. Turn into a 2-1/2-quart moisture-proof container. Cover and chill several hours, or overnight.

SPIRITED POTATO SALAD

3/4 cup mayonnaise
3/4 cup sour cream
1/4 cup beer
6 cups peeled, cubed, cooked potatoes
1/2 cup onions, chopped
3/4 cup celery, chopped
1/2 pound bacon, crisped and crumbled
Salt and pepper to taste

Blend mayonnaise, sour cream, and beer. Toss lightly with potatoes, onion, celery, and bacon. Add salt and pepper to taste. Chill 3 hours and serve cold or heat at 275 degrees for 20 minutes and serve hot.

Joy Shamway, Freeport, Ill.

MASHED POTATO CASSEROLE

8 to 10 medium potatoes, peeled
1 (8-ounce) carton sour cream
1 (8-ounce) package cream cheese
1 stick margarine
2 tablespoons chives
2 teaspoons salt
Paprika

Cook, drain, and mash potatoes. Beat cream cheese until smooth with electric mixer. Add remaining ingredients, except paprika; stir just to combine. Put in buttered 2-quart casserole and refrigerate overnight. Next day, sprinkle with paprika and bake, uncovered, at 350 degrees, just long enough to heat through.

Brenda Peery, Tannersville, Va.

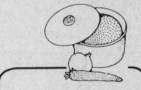

OVEN–FRIED POTATOES
Serves 4

4 large baking potatoes, unpeeled
1/4 cup vegetable oil
1-2 tablespoons Parmesan cheese
1/2 teaspoon salt
1/4 teaspoon garlic powder
1/4 teaspoon paprika
1/8 teaspoon pepper

Wash unpeeled potatoes and cut lengthwise into 4 wedges. Place skin side down in 13x9x2-inch baking dish or pan. Combine remaining ingredients; brush over potatoes. Bake at 375 degrees for 1 hour, brushing with oil/cheese mixture at 15-minute intervals. Turn potatoes over for last 15 minutes. (These are wonderful with any type of roasted meat.)

This change-of-pace way to make potatoes tastes good with just about every meal—from sloppy joes to barbecue-grilled meat, poultry, or fish. They are also a tasty snack. These days, it's nice to have something quick to make for supper!

Marcella Swigert, Monroe City, Mo.

SWEET 'TATER CASSEROLE

Medium sweet potatoes, canned *or* fresh (8–10)
1 (29-ounce) can Bartlett pear halves
½ cup butter
1 cup maple syrup
½ teaspoon cinnamon
¼ teaspoon nutmeg (optional)

If potatoes are canned, drain. If fresh, cook in boiling, salted water until tender. Peel; slice as desired. Combine butter, syrup, cinnamon and nutmeg. Arrange potatoes and drained pears in a shallow buttered casserole. Pour syrup mixture over all. Bake at 350 degrees for 35–40 minutes, or until glazed, basting several times with syrup in casserole.

Kit Rollins, Cedarburg, Wis.

POTATO KISSES
Serves 2

3 cups water
⅛ teaspoon plus ¼ teaspoon salt
½ pound potatoes, pared and cut into 1-inch cubes
¼ cup shredded Swiss cheese
1 tablespoon butter *or* margarine
⅛ teaspoon pepper
1 egg, beaten
2 tablespoons half-and-half
1½ teaspoons chopped parsley

Grease a baking sheet and set aside. Bring water and the ⅛ teaspoon salt to a boil over high heat. Add potatoes. Simmer 10–12 minutes, or until potatoes are tender; drain.

Preheat oven to 350 degrees. In medium bowl, mash potatoes. Stir in cheese, butter, the ¼ teaspoon salt and pepper until cheese is melted. Stir in egg, half-and-half and parsley; cool 10 minutes. Fit a pastry bag with a star-shaped tube. Spoon potatoes into bag. Pipe into 6 mounds on baking sheet. Bake 20–25 minutes or until lightly browned.

Gall Jordon, Sturgis, Mich.

SWEET 'N' SOUR POTATO MEDLEY
Serves 6

2 slices bacon
2 cups water
1 tablespoon sugar
3 tablespoons vinegar
1 medium clove garlic, crushed
4–5 drops red pepper sauce
1 can condensed cream of mushroom soup
1 package au gratin potatoes
1 cup thinly sliced carrots
1-1/2 cups frozen green peas
1 cup chopped tomato

Fry bacon until crisp; crumble. Stir water, sugar, vinegar, garlic, pepper sauce and soup into bacon fat in skillet. Stir in potatoes, sauce mix and carrots. Heat to boiling, stirring frequently; reduce heat. Cover and simmer about 25 minutes, or until potatoes are tender, stirring occasionally. Add peas and cook 5 minutes longer. Stir in chopped tomato. Garnish with crumbled bacon.

Laura Hicks, Troy, Mont.

POTATO SOUP

4 cups water
3 baking potatoes
1 small onion, chopped
3 tablespoons margarine
1/2 cup chopped celery
2 cups milk

In a large Dutch oven, boil water; add peeled potatoes that have been sliced and cook until potatoes are tender. Add the remaining ingredients, except milk, and cook about 20 minutes. Add milk to warm and serve.

BRAISED POTATOES

4 medium potatoes, peeled and quartered lengthwise
3 tablespoons corn oil
1 chicken bouillon cube
1 cup boiling water
Paprika

Fry potatoes in oil until lightly browned on all sides. Dissolve the bouillon cube in boiling water. Pour over potatoes. Cook, covered, over medium heat for 10-15 minutes, or until potatoes are done. (Since only a small amount of liquid is used, take care that the potatoes do not boil dry.) Sprinkle with a little paprika and serve hot. I am sure these will be a family favorite!

Lillian Smith, Montreal, Quebec, Canada

POTATO BOATS
Serves 2

2 large potatoes, boiled and cooled
2 pieces fried bacon, crisp and crushed
2 tablespoons sour cream
½ cup shredded cheddar cheese
1 tablespoon chives

After the potatoes have been boiled and cooled, take a sharp knife and cut a circle in the potato. Then take a spoon and hollow the potato out leaving very little of the meat or potato around the sides of the skin. Place in hot oil and deep-fry until golden brown and slightly crispy. While still very hot, add half of the sour cream and 1 piece of bacon (crushed). Then sprinkle half of the cheddar cheese and half of the chives over the top. Serve warm.

This makes a wonderful appetizer and is also good as a snack.

Shannon Justice, Johnson City, Texas

TWICE-BAKED POTATOES

6 baking potatoes
1/2 teaspoon salt
1/2 teaspoon pepper
3 tablespoons margarine
3 ounces cream cheese
1 egg, beaten
1/3 cup cream

Bake potatoes for 1 hour at 450 degrees. Scoop out potato from skin and mash. In a separate bowl, combine all other ingredients and beat well. Combine the two mixtures and blend until creamy smooth. Fill the potato skins and bake for 25 minutes at 400 degrees. Serve hot.

COMPANY MASHED POTATOES
Serves 6

4 cups hot, seasoned, mashed potatoes
1 cup sour cream
1/3 cup chopped onions
4 ounces sharp cheddar cheese, grated
1/2 teaspoon seasoned salt

Combine all ingredients, except seasoned salt, in greased 1-1/2-quart casserole. Sprinkle with seasoned salt. Bake at 350 degrees for 25 minutes.

Can be made ahead of time and refrigerated.

Helen Weissinger, Levittown, Pa.

RED FLANNEL HASH
Serves 4

1 large or 2 medium-size baking potatoes
1 onion, diced
1 (12-ounce) can corned beef
1 (15-ounce) can diced beets

Thinly peel potatoes, and dice them. Peel and dice onion. Cook them for 10 minutes in enough boiling water to barely cover and in a pan with lid ajar to let onion vapors escape.

Cut the hash into bits. Drain the potato-onion mixture and the can of beets, saving the juices for soup.

Combine all ingredients in a baking dish. Bake at 350 degrees for 25 minutes. Garnish with parsley sprigs, if desired.

SOUR CREAM SCALLOPED POTATOES
Serves 6

1/2 cup chopped onion
2 tablespoons butter, melted
1 cup dairy sour cream
2 eggs, well-beaten
1 teaspoon salt
Dash of pepper
4 cups cooked, sliced new potatoes
1 cup shredded sharp cheddar cheese

Saute onion in butter; combine with sour cream, eggs, salt, and pepper. Place potatoes in buttered 1-quart casserole and pour sour cream sauce over top. Top with shredded cheddar. Bake 20 to 25 minutes at 350 degrees.

Kit Rollins, Cedarburg, Wis.

CREAMED POTATOES

6 large potatoes
1/2 pound butter, melted
1/2 teaspoon salt
1/2 teaspoon pepper
1/2 cup heavy cream
3/4 cup shredded Swiss cheese

Cook potatoes for about 20 minutes in boiling water. Let cool and peel. Break up coarsely, but do not mash. Add butter, salt, and pepper; combine and mix ingredients. Put into baking dish or 9-inch pie plate. Pour heavy cream over potatoes and butter mixture; let stand about 20 minutes. Sprinkle with cheese. Bake 20 minutes in a 175-degree oven or until cheese is melted.

Sheila Symonowicz, Loganville, Pa.

CRAB-STUFFED POTATOES
Serves 4–6

4 baking potatoes
½ cup butter (no substitute)
½ cup light cream
1 teaspoon salt
4 tablespoons grated onion
1 cup sharp cheese, grated
1 (5-ounce) can crabmeat
Tabasco sauce
Pepper to taste

Bake potatoes at 350 degrees for 1½ hours, until tender. Cut in half lengthwise; scoop out potato and whip with remaining ingredients. Refill shells and reheat at 425 degrees for 15 minutes. These freeze nicely.

Pat Habiger, Spearville, Kan.

FESTIVE POTATO WEDGES
Serves 6

2 tablespoons margarine
3 medium potatoes, unpeeled
1 tablespoon Parmesan cheese
1 teaspoon dry salad dressing mix
1 teaspoon parsley flakes
¼ teaspoon salt, optional

Microwave margarine on HIGH in an 8-inch round microwave dish for 30–45 seconds, or until melted.

Scrub potatoes. Cut each in half lengthwise; cut each half into 4 wedges. Coat each potato in margarine, arrange in dish.

Combine Parmesan cheese, dry salad dressing mix, parsley flakes and salt in small dish. Sprinkle evenly over potatoes. Cover with plastic wrap.

Microwave on HIGH for 8–10 minutes, or until potatoes are tender, rotating dish once. (85 calories per serving)

Mrs. John S. Novak, Melrose Park, Ill.

Relishes
& PRESERVES

CORN RELISH

3 dozen ears sweet corn
1/2 pound cabbage
4 onions
1 quart vinegar
2 cups sugar
3 green peppers
1/2 cup salt
3 tablespoons mustard
3 pimientos
1/2 teaspoon pepper

Cut corn from ear and chop cabbage, onions, peppers and pimientos. Mix all ingredients together and boil 1 hour. Pour into sterilized jars and seal.

Suzan L. Wiener, Spring Hill, Fla.

APRICOT RHUBARB JAM

8 cups finely chopped rhubarb
4 cups sugar
1 can apricot pie filling
1 (3-ounce) package orange-
   flavored gelatin

Combine rhubarb and sugar in a bowl (not metal). Allow to stand overnight. In the morning transfer to a pan; bring to a boil and simmer 10 minutes. Add the apricot pie filling and bring to a boil. Add the gelatin and stir until dissolved. Put in jars; cover and refrigerate or freeze.

TOMATO PEACH CHUTNEY

2 1/2 cups fresh tomatoes (canned may be used)
2 cups chopped peaches
1/2 cup white seedless raisins
1 cup chopped bell pepper
1/2 cup chopped onions
1 cup brown sugar
3/4 cup white sugar (more may be used)
3/4 cup white vinegar
1/2 teaspoon ground ginger
1 teaspoon curry powder

Remove skins from fresh tomatoes and peaches. If using canned, include juice. Combine all ingredients. Cook slowly, about 1 hour, until thickened. Pack boiling hot in sterilized jars and seal tightly. Process in boiling water bath, 5 minutes for half-pints and 10 minutes for pints.

TOMATO PRESERVES

11 cups chopped tomatoes
4 pounds granulated sugar
2 lemons, thinly sliced

Put tomatoes and juice, accumulated while chopping, into pan. Cover with water; add sugar and stir. Let this sit overnight. Drain off moisture and boil rapidly until it spins a thread when dropped from spoon. Add tomatoes and lemons; continue to boil until thick and clear.

FREEZER PICKLES

7 cups sliced, unpeeled cucumbers
   (1/4 inch thick)
1 cup chopped green bell pepper
1 cup thinly sliced onions
2 tablespoons pickling salt
2 cups sugar
1 cup cider vinegar
1 tablespoon celery seed

Put cucumbers, green pepper and onions in large bowl. Sprinkle 2 tablespoons pickling salt over mixture in bowl and distribute. Set in refrigerator for 2 hours. Drain well. Then mix sugar, vinegar and celery seed. Stir to dissolve sugar. Place cucumbers in freezer containers, tightly packed. Cover with syrup, just enough to cover. Leave 1-inch head space.

Peggy Fowler Revels, Woodruff, S.C.

SPRING COMBINA-TION MARMALADE

2 pounds strawberries
3 oranges
1 pound fresh pineapple
Grated rind of 1/2 orange
3 1/2 pounds granulated sugar

Wash and stem strawberries. Peel, core and grate fresh pineapple. Dice pulp of orange. Combine pineapple, oranges and grated rind with sugar. Boil 15 minutes. Add strawberries and continue cooking 12 minutes, or until mixture is transparent and thick, approximately 225 degrees. Cool and pour into sterilized jars.

SPICED PRESERVED CANTALOUPE

Makes 4 (1/2-pint) jars

1 tablespoon whole allspice
1 tablespoon chopped crystallized ginger
3-1/2 cups sugar
1 cup Karo light corn syrup
1 lemon, thinly sliced and seeded
1/2 cup water
1/2 cup dry white wine
1/4 teaspoon uniodized salt
6 cups cantaloupe, cut in 1-inch cubes

Tie allspice and ginger in cheese-cloth bag. In 5-quart saucepan place spice bag, 2 cups sugar and next 5 ingredients. Stirring occasionally, bring to boil over medium-high heat. Add fruit. Stirring occasionally, boil gently for 20 minutes. Remove from heat; place plate on fruit to hold below syrup level. Let stand overnight. Stir in remaining sugar. Stirring occasionally, bring to boil and boil gently for 20 minutes, or until fruit is transparent and syrup is thick. Skim surface; remove spice bag. Immediately pack fruit in clean, hot half-pint jars. Add boiling syrup, covering fruit and leaving 1/4-inch headspace. Wipe top edges with damp towel. Seal according to jar manufacturer's directions. Process in boiling-water bath for 5 minutes.

PEAR RELISH

4 pounds pears, peeled and cored
6 green sweet peppers
6 red sweet peppers
6 onions
1 tablespoon celery seed
1 tablespoon salt
3 cups sugar
3 cups vinegar
1 tablespoon allspice

Grind pears, peppers and onions in food chopper or processor. Add all the ingredients to the vinegar and sugar. Boil 30 minutes. Put in jars and seal.

Diantha Susan Hibbard, Rochester, N.Y.

MIXED VEGETABLE RELISH

Makes 5–6 (1/2-pint) jars

3 cups finely chopped carrots
1-1/2 cups finely chopped onion
3/4 cup finely chopped green pepper
3/4 cup finely chopped red pepper
3/4 cup finely chopped cabbage
2 cups cider vinegar
2 cups Karo light corn syrup
1 tablespoon uniodized salt
1-1/2 teaspoons mustard seed
1-1/2 teaspoons celery seed

Place first 5 ingredients in 5-quart saucepan. Cover with boiling water; let stand 5 minutes. Drain well. Return to saucepan; stir in remaining ingredients. Stirring frequently, bring to boil over medium heat. Reduce heat. Stirring occasionally, boil gently 20 minutes, or until mixture thickens. Immediately ladle into clean, hot half-pint jars, leaving 1/4-inch headspace. Wipe top edges with damp towel. Seal according to jar manufacturer's directions. Process in boiling-water bath for 10 minutes.

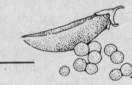

HOMEMADE PICNIC RELISH

Makes 3 cups

1 1/2 cups onion, chopped
1 cup green pepper, chopped
2 tablespoons salad oil
4 firm tomatoes, peeled and chopped
2 tablespoons white vinegar
1/4 teaspoon salt
1/2 teaspoon sugar
1/4 teaspoon dry mustard
1/4 teaspoon pickling spice
1/4 teaspoon pepper

In large skillet, cook and stir onion and green pepper in oil over medium heat until tender. Stir in remaining ingredients; heat to boiling; cool; cover and refrigerate several days.

Gwen Campbell, Sterling, Va.

PEAR LIME PRESERVES

Makes 4 (12-ounce) jars

8 cups pears, peeled, cored and chopped
1/2 cup water
1 tablespoon lime juice
1 package powdered pectin
1 tablespoon grated lime peel
1 thinly sliced lime
5-1/2 cups sugar

Prepare home-canning jars and lids according to manufacturer's instructions. Combine pears, water and lime juice in a large saucepan. Simmer, covered, for 10 minutes. Stir in pectin and bring to a full rolling boil, stirring frequently. Add lime peel, lime slices and sugar. Return to a full rolling boil. Boil hard 1 minute, stirring frequently. Carefully ladle into hot jars, leaving 1/4-inch headspace. Adjust caps. Process 15 minutes in a boiling-water bath canner.

COLD-PACKED PICKLES

Prepare sterile quart jars. Wash, and pack into the jars small cucumbers. Add to each quart jar:

1 tablespoon sugar
1 tablespoon salt
1 teaspoon mustard seed
1/2 teaspoon celery seed
2 saccharin tablets (1-grain)
Mixture of: 1 part vinegar and 2 parts cold water

Seal; place in cold water bath. Heat to very hot, just to a boil. Turn off heat and let stand until cucumbers turn color. Remove from water and let cool, out of a draft. Allow to age 3 weeks before using.

For variety, use sliced cucumbers, onions, and green or red peppers. This combination makes a very pretty mixed pickle.

Alice Dick, Montpelier, Ohio

Salad
DRESSINGS

LOW-CALORIE SALAD DRESSING
Makes 1 cup

1 egg yolk
½ teaspoon garlic powder
½ teaspoon dry mustard
½ teaspoon seasoned salt
1 teaspoon Worcestershire sauce
1 teaspoon Bakon yeast
1 teaspoon dehydrated horseradish
¾ cup soybean oil
¼ cup lemon juice
2 teaspoons arrowroot *or* cornstarch
  Chopped parsley
  Chopped chives

Blend ingredients in blender; add soybean oil. Mix 2 teaspoons arrowroot or cornstarch in water; boil until clear. Let cool; add to dressing. Add chopped parsley and chives; blend. (50 calories per tablespoon)

Ruby Pate Bodkin, Jacksonville, Fla.

VINAIGRETTE DRESSING
Makes 1 cup

½ cup olive oil
⅓ cup balsamic vinegar
1 tablespoon Dijon mustard
⅛ teaspoon nutmeg

In a small bowl, whisk together ingredients. Add to salad and toss well.

Kenneth McAdams, El Dorado, Ark.

SPINACH SALAD DRESSING AND DIP
Makes 2 cups

1 (10-ounce) bag fresh spinach
1 cup oil
1/4 cup fresh lemon juice
4 teaspoons Worcestershire sauce
1 teaspoon salt
1 teaspoon sugar

Thoroughly rinse, drain, and remove stems from spinach. Place spinach in the jar of an electric blender (it will need to be packed down). Add remaining ingredients. Cover and blend until smooth, 30 to 60 seconds, turning blender on and off. Use as a salad dressing or as a dip for fresh vegetables.

CREAMY ITALIAN DRESSING

1 cup light mayonnaise
½ small onion
3 packs Equal *or* Sweet and Low
½ teaspoon garlic salt
2 tablespoons red wine vinegar
1 teaspoon Italian seasoning
¼ teaspoon pepper *or* paprika

Put all ingredients in blender and run until smooth. Refrigerate. Shake well before serving.

Marjorie Baxla, Greenfield, Ohio

AVOCADO DRESSING
Makes 2½ cups

2 avocados, peeled
1 (8-ounce) carton plain yogurt
½ cup mayonnaise
¼ cup chopped onion
2 tablespoons lemon juice
1 tablespoon honey *or* sugar
1 tablespoon Worcestershire sauce
½ teaspoon garlic salt
½ teaspoon salt
  Dash Tabasco sauce

In blender combine ingredients; purée until smooth. Store, covered, in refrigerator.

Laura Hicks, Troy, Mont.

BUTTERMILK HERB DRESSING
Makes 1 cup

1 cup buttermilk
1 teaspoon chives, finely chopped
1 teaspoon fresh chervil, finely chopped *or* 1/2 teaspoon powdered chervil
1 teaspoon watercress
1/2 teaspoon tarragon
1/4 teaspoon dry mustard
Salt, to taste

Mix all ingredients and keep in refrigerator. Chill for at least 30 minutes before using. (6 calories per tablespoon)

Shari Crider, Stoughton, Wis.

MY OWN SLAW DRESSING
Makes 1 quart

1 cup ready-made salad dressing
1 cup cider vinegar
2 cups white sugar
1 teaspoon salt
½ teaspoon pepper
1 tablespoon yellow mustard
1 tablespoon lemon juice
½ cup Carnation evaporated milk

Put all together in mixer or blender and run until well-blended. Keep in refrigerator. Combine with shredded cabbage, carrots and slaw ingredients just before serving.

Marjorie Baxla, Greenfield, Ohio

ITALIAN DRESSING MIX POWDER

(One envelope of commercial dressing mix equals this entire recipe)

2 teaspoons onion powder
1 tablespoon white sugar or sugar substitute
1/8 teaspoon black pepper
1/8 teaspoon powdered allspice
1 teaspoon dry minced onions
1 teaspoon dry celery flakes
1/8 teaspoon crushed marjoram leaves
1/4 teaspoon dry oregano, crushed
1 clove garlic peeled, sliced fine or 2 teaspoons bottled minced garlic
1/8 teaspoon paprika
2 squares of soda crackers (1-1/2" x 1-1/2")

Mix all ingredients in blender. Keep covered. Will keep up to 3 months.

To Use: Combine all the above with 1/2 cup vinegar, 2/3 cup cold water and 1/3 cup corn oil. Mix well. Keeps in refrigerator up to 1 month. Shake well before using. Makes 1-1/2 cup prepared dressing.

K. Dwyer, Saginaw, MN

CREAMY SALAD DRESSING
Makes 2½ cups

1 teaspoon dry mustard
1 teaspoon salt
1 cup vinegar
1 egg
1 can sweetened condensed milk

Combine mustard, salt and vinegar. Add egg, beating it in well with rotary beater. Stir in sweetened condensed milk; beat to mix thoroughly. Cook over hot water, stirring constantly, until thickened. Cool before serving. Excellent on potato salad, coleslaw, etc.

Agnes Ward, Erie, Pa.

DILLED YOGURT DRESSING

1 cup non-fat plain yogurt
2 tablespoons vinegar
1/2 small onion
1/2 teaspoon dill seeds
1/4 teaspoon dry mustard
1/4 to 1/2 teaspoon fresh garlic

Combine all the ingredients in blender until smooth. Great topping for salads, vegetables, or dip for crackers or chips.

Susan L. Wiener, Spring Hill, Fla.

TARRAGON DIP OR DRESSING

¼ cup sour cream
¼ cup Hellmann's mayonnaise
¾ teaspoon crushed tarragon
⅛ teaspoon onion powder
⅛ teaspoon salt
Dash of pepper
1 teaspoon lemon juice

Combine ingredients and mix well. Chill before serving. This is so good I triple the recipe.

Wanda Harrison, Fremont, Wis.

vegetables are finely chopped. Refrigerate dressing for proper storage.

Agnes Ward, Erie, PA

CREAMY LOW-CAL DRESSING
2 cups of dressing

1/2 cup skim milk
2 tablespoons lemon juice
1 tablespoon vegetable oil
1-1/2 cup low-fat cottage cheese (12 ounce)
1 small onion, chopped
1 cloves garlic, crushed
1/2 teaspoon salt
1/4 teaspoon pepper
1/4 teaspoon paprika

Place all ingredients in blender container in order listed above. Cover and blend on medium speed until smooth, about 1 minute. Cover and refrigerate.

Judy Owen, Fairmount, GA

CHILI FLAVORED DRESSING

1/2 teaspoon chili powder
1 tablespoon wine vinegar
2 tablespoons orange juice
3 tablespoons mashed green chilies
1-1/4 cups mayonnaise

Blend chili powder with wine vinegar and orange juice. Then add green chilies and stir into mayonnaise.

Susan L. Wiener, Spring Hill, Fla.

VINAIGRETTE DRESSING
Makes 1-1/2 cups

1 cup oil and vinegar dressing
2 tablespoons chopped parsley
1/4 cup finely chopped pickle
2 teaspoons chopped onion
2 teaspoons capers (optional)

Blend above ingredients thoroughly.

PINEAPPLE-CHEESE SPREAD FOR SANDWICHES

Makes 3/4 cup

3-ounce package. cream cheese, softened
1/2 cup crushed pineapple, drained
1/4 cup finely chopped pecans

Beat cheese until light and fluffy. Stir in pineapple and pecans; mix well.

Edna Askins, Greenville, TX

TEENAGE SUBMARINE

Serves 4-6

1/2 pound boiled ham, cubed
1/2 pound sharp Cheddar cheese, cubed
1/3 cup sliced scallions
2 hard-cooked eggs, peeled and sliced
1/2 cup thinly sliced pimiento stuffed olives
3 tablespoons mayonnaise or salad dressing
1/2 cup chili sauce
12 frankfurter rolls

Preheat oven to 400 degrees. Combine first 7 ingredients in a bowl. Mix well. Spread mixture on frankfurter rolls. Wrap each roll in aluminum foil, twisting ends securely. Bake for 10 minutes.

Marcella Swigert, Monroe City, MO

GRILLED MEXICAN-STYLE BURGERS

Makes 4 servings

1 pound ground beef
2 teaspoons instant minced onion
3/4 teaspoon dried oregano leaves
3/4 teaspoon ground cumin
3/4 teaspoon salt
1/4 teaspoon pepper
4 taco shells or flour tortillas
1 cup shredded lettuce

1 small tomato, cut into 8 thin slices
1/4 cup salsa

In large bowl, combine ground beef, onion, oregano, cumin, salt, and pepper, mixing lightly but thoroughly. Divide beef mixture into 4 equal portions; form each into an oval-shaped patty. Broil patties on grill over medium coals, turning once. Broil 10 minutes for rare; 12 minutes for medium. To assemble, arrange two tomato slices with a grilled burger in each taco shell. Top each with 1/4 cup lettuce and 1 tablespoon salsa.

Susan L. Wiener, Spring Hill, FL

BIG MIX BURGERS

Serves 8

2 pounds ground beef
1/2 can consomme (10-1/2 ounce)
1/2 cup cracked wheat
1/4 cup hot water
2 tablespoons dry minced onion
2 tablespoons finely chopped green pepper
Salt and Pepper to taste

Combine the above ingredients. Form patties from the mixture. Fry until done the way you like. For special treat serve on home made mustard buns.

Mrs. James Williams, Brainerd, MN

CHEESE PUFFWICHES

1/4 cup margarine
1 egg
1 tablespoon pimiento
1 jar (5 ounce) Old English cheese
10 slices bread

In a bowl mix together margarine, egg, pimiento, and cheese well. Trim crusts off bread and cut each slice into 4 squares. Spread filling on each. Bake on ungreased cookie sheet until lightly puffed and slightly brown.

Alice McNamara, Eucha, OK

CONEY ISLAND HOT DOGS

Serves 8

1 - No. 2 can chili con carne
1 - 6 ounce can tomato paste
1 teaspoon mustard
1/2 teaspoon salt
8 frankfurters
8 frankfurter rolls
Butter or margarine

Mix chili con carne, tomato paste, mustard, and salt in a pan. Heat thoroughly. Slit frankfurters, diagonally in four or five places. Brown in broiler. Split rolls; spread with butter; then toast. Place a frankfurter in each roll and cover generously with chili con carne.

Lou Roehr, Hammond, IN

FRANKWICHES

Makes 12

8 - 10 frankfurters, chopped
1 can tomato soup
1 cup shredded American cheese
1/4 cup chopped onion
1/4 cup pickle relish
1 tablespoon prepared mustard
12 hamburger buns, split and toasted

Combine frankfurters, tomato soup, shredded cheese, onion, pickle and prepared mustard; mix thoroughly. Spoon about 1/3 cup filling onto each hamburger bun. Wrap each sandwich in foil; place sandwich on baking sheet. Heat sandwiches at 400 degrees for 15 minutes.

Sharon M. Crider, Evansville, WI

Sandwich
TASTIES

BARBECUED BEEF

6 pounds boneless chuck (*or* pork),
  cut in pieces
2 stalks celery, chopped
2 medium onions, chopped
1 green pepper, chopped
1 medium bottle ketchup
3 tablespoons barbecue sauce
3 tablespoons vinegar
1 tablespoon Tabasco sauce
1 tablespoon chili powder
1 tablespoon salt
1 teaspoon pepper

Cut meat into pieces and place in large oven roaster. Place remainder of ingredients in large mixing bowl and stir well. Pour over meat and cook in a slow oven (250 degrees) for 6 or more hours. When meat is tender, shred with 2 forks. Serve on hamburger buns.

This is a great dish to prepare on busy weekends!

Phyliss D. Dixon, Fairbanks, Alaska

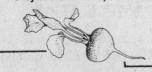

ENGLISH MUFFIN SNACKWICHES

1 can chopped ripe olives
1/2 cup chopped green onions
1-1/2 cups grated cheddar cheese
1/2 cup mayonnaise
1/2 teaspoon curry powder
1/2 teaspoon chili powder
6 split English muffins

Mix all ingredients and spread on muffins. Broil until bubbly. Quarter

and serve. Variations: May add shrimp, crab, or tuna to the spread.

Sue Thomas, Case Grande, Ariz.

BEEF MUSHROOM PASTIES
Serves 8

1 loaf frozen bread dough
1 pound lean ground beef
1 can condensed cream of mushroom soup
1 (4-ounce) can sliced mushrooms,
  drained
2 tablespoons dried, chopped onion
2 tablespoons Worcestershire
  sauce

Thaw dough until pliable. Cook beef until well-browned; drain grease. Add soup, mushrooms, onion and Worcestershire sauce to beef.

Cut loaf of bread dough crosswise, into 8 slices. Using a little flour on board and rolling pin, pat and roll dough pieces out to 5-inch circles. Place filling in centers of dough circles. Pull all dough edges up to the center and pinch tightly to seal filling inside. Place buns, smooth sides up, on greased baking sheet. Using a sharp knife, make a large cut on top of each bun for steam to escape. Bake at 375 degrees for 35 minutes, or until well-browned.

Good hot or cold. A picnic treat.

Mrs. W.T. Gore, Aztec, N.M.

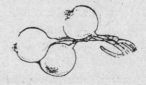

OPEN-FACED EGG AND CHEESE SANDWICHES
Makes 6 sandwiches

1 tablespoon butter
2 tablespoons onions
2 tablespoons green pepper, finely
  chopped
6 eggs, beaten
1/3 cup milk
1/4 teaspoon salt
1/8 teaspoon pepper
6 English muffin halves, toasted
1 tablespoon butter
6 1-ounce slices American cheese

Melt 1 tablespoon butter in frying pan; saute onion and green pepper, stirring often, until tender. Combine eggs, milk, salt and pepper. Pour over onion and green pepper in frying pan and cook over low heat, stirring often to let uncooked portion of eggs flow beneath cooked portion. Continue cooking until eggs are set but still moist.

Divide eggs into six portions. Spread toasted muffin halves with remaining tablespoon of butter, and top muffin halves with egg mixture and a slice of cheese. Broil until cheese melts and is lightly browned (about 5 minutes).

Charlotte Adams, Detroit, Mich.

Supreme
SALADS

EASY FRUIT SALAD

1 cup seedless grapes
1 (11-ounce) can mandarin oranges
    (chill and drain)
1 (8-ounce) can pineapple chunks
    (chill and drain)
1 red apple, sliced
Yogurt Dressing (recipe follows)

Combine grapes, oranges, apple and pineapple. Spoon onto salad greens. Serve with Yogurt Dressing.

Yogurt Dressing:
2/3 cup plain yogurt
1 tablespoon honey
1 tablespoon lemon juice

Mix all ingredients together.
Cheryl Santefort, South Holland, Ill.

GREEN AND GOLD SALAD
Serves 4-5

1 (10 ounce) package frozen green
    peas
1/2 cup shredded natural cheddar
    cheese
2 tablespoons chopped onion
2 tablespoons mayonnaise or salad
    dressing
1-1/2 teaspoons prepared mustard
1/4 teaspoon salt
Crisp salad greens

Rinse peas with small amount of running cold water to separate and remove ice crystals; drain. Mix all ingredients, except salad greens. Serve salad on greens.
Substitution: For frozen green peas use 1 (8-ounce) can green peas, drained.
Marcella Swigert, Monroe City, Mo.

PINEAPPLE CHANTILLY

1-1/2 cups pineapple juice
1 cup water
1/4 cup tapioca
1/2 cup sugar
1 teaspoon salt
2 tablespoons lemon juice
1 (13-1/2-ounce) can crushed pine-
    apple, undrained
1 cup heavy cream, whipped
Maraschino cherries for garnish

In saucepan combine pineapple juice, water, tapioca, sugar, and salt. Bring to boil. Stir constantly over medium heat until tapioca is cooked. Stir in lemon juice and pineapple. Refrigerate 2 hours before serving; fold whipped cream into pineapple mixture. Chill. Garnish with maraschino cherries.
Sharon M. Crider, Evansville, Wis.

SPAGHETTI SALAD

1 pound spaghetti, cooked in
    unsalted water
1 medium onion
1/2 bottle Italian salad dressing
1 package pepperoni, diced
1 medium green pepper, diced
1 medium tomato, chopped
3–4 stalks celery, thinly sliced

Mix spaghetti, green pepper, onion, tomato, dressing, pepperoni and celery; let sit overnight or at least several hours before serving. Mix well again before serving.
Sandra Russell, Gainesville, Fla.

CHERRY CREAM SALAD
Serves 6

1   (1-pound) can pitted,
    dark sweet cherries,
    drained
¾   cup chopped pecans
2   (11-ounce) cans
    mandarin oranges,
    drained
1   cup dairy sour cream

Combine ingredients; chill thoroughly. If desired, garnish with additional cherries, oranges and pecan halves.
Sharon Crider, Stoughton, Wis.

LIME SALAD
Serves 6

1 (3-ounce) package lime gelatin
1 cup boiling water
1 cup pineapple juice
2 tablespoons vinegar
1/2 teaspoon salt
3 slices pineapple, diced
1 pimiento, finely cut
1 orange, in sections
1/2 cup finely cut celery

Dissolve gelatin in 1 cup boiling water. Add pineapple juice, vinegar, and salt to gelatin mixture. Mix well and add remaining ingredients. Pour into molds. Serve on curly endive.
Lucy Dowd, Sequim, Wash.

MARINATED ZUCCHINI SALAD
Serves 12

- 2 medium-size zucchini, halved lengthwise and sliced
- 1 pint cherry tomatoes
- ½ bunch broccoli, cut in florets
- ½ medium-size head cauliflower, cut in florets
- 4 large ribs celery, sliced diagonally
- 4 large carrots, cut in strips
- 1 (8-ounce) jar pickled baby corn, drained
- 1 cup olive oil
- ½ cup white wine vinegar
- ½ cup water
- 1 teaspoon sugar
- 1 teaspoon dried thyme
- 1 teaspoon marjoram
- 1 teaspoon basil
- 2 teaspoons salt
- 1 teaspoon pepper
- 1 small clove garlic, peeled
- 1 bay leaf

Place vegetables in large bowl. Mix remaining ingredients; pour over vegetables; refrigerate several hours, tossing occasionally. Before serving, drain vegetables; discard garlic and bay leaf.

Leona Teodori, Warren, Mich.

PERFECTION SALAD

- 2 (3-ounce) packages lemon gelatin
- 2 cups finely chopped celery
- 12 chopped sweet pickles
- 4 tablespoons vinegar
- 4 finely chopped pimientos
- 1 teaspoon salt
- 2 cups finely chopped cabbage

Prepare gelatin according to directions. Add vinegar; refrigerate until partially set. Add remaining ingredients and refrigerate several hours.

Julie Habiger, Manhattan, Kan.

TANGY FRUIT SALAD
Serves 6-8

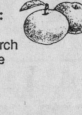

Fruit Salad Dressing:
- 1/2 cup sugar
- 2 tablespoons cornstarch
- 3/4 cup pineapple juice
- Juice of 1 lemon
- Juice of 1 orange
- Grated rind of orange

In small saucepan, mix together sugar and cornstarch. Add the remaining ingredients and cook until thickened. Boil about 1 minute. Cool.

Salad:
- 2 red apples, cut into wedges
- 2 green apples, cut into wedges
- 1/2 cup green seedless grapes
- 1/2 cup red seedless grapes
- 1 (11-ounce) can mandarin oranges, drained
- 1 (16-ounce) can peach slices, drained
- 1 (16-ounce) can pineapple chunks, drained

In a glass bowl, mix together the apples, grapes, oranges, peaches, and pineapple chunks. When the dressing has cooled, pour over the fruit and mix well. Refrigerate several hours before serving.

Sharon Jones, Indianapolis, Ind.

BROCCOLI AND MUSHROOMS ELEGANT SALAD

- 2 bunches (stalks) fresh broccoli
- 1 pound fresh mushrooms
- 1 bottle Zesty Italian dressing

Cut broccoli into flowerets. Add thickly sliced mushrooms. Pour Italian dressing over broccoli and mushrooms. Add tight-fitting cover. Refrigerate several hours or overnight, turning occasionally. This is very good and is really elegant-looking when served in a pretty dish. Perfect for potluck dinners and church suppers. Only you will know how easy it is!

Brenda Peery, Tannersville, Va.

CREAM CHEESE AND CUCUMBER MOUSSE

- 2 envelopes unflavored gelatin
- 2 1/2 tablespoons white wine vinegar
- 1/3 of a long English cucumber, unpeeled
- 12 ounces cream cheese
- Salt and pepper to taste
- 6 egg whites

Sprinkle gelatin over the vinegar in a small saucepan. Dice cucumber and liquify in a blender or grate by hand. Soften cream cheese with a fork; add cucumber, and mix together well. Place softened gelatin over low heat and stir constantly until gelatin dissolves, about 3–5 minutes. Remove from heat and add to the cream cheese. Whip egg whites until fluffy and fold into mixture. Add salt and pepper. To garnish, place very thin cucumber slices in the bottom of a large mold or 6 individual ones; then pour in a small amount of additional dissolved gelatin and allow to set before pouring in the mixture. Chill 3–4 hours before unmolding. This is a very pretty and refreshing salad.

Lillian Smith, Montreal, Canada

RHUBARB RASPBERRY SALAD

- 3 cups cut-up rhubarb pieces
- 1 cup water
- 1 (3-ounce) package raspberry-flavored gelatin
- 1 cup sugar
- 1 cup diced celery
- 1 cup chopped nuts

Cook rhubarb in the water about 10 minutes, until rhubarb is tender. Add gelatin and sugar; stir until dissolved. Cool until syrupy. Add celery and nuts. Chill until firm. (Do not try to mold this salad, because it does not get that firm).

24-HOUR SALAD
Serves 8–10

1 (17-ounce) can pitted sweet cherries, drained
2 (13-ounce) cans pineapple tidbits, drained (reserve 2 tablespoons syrup)
2 (11-ounce) cans mandarin oranges, drained
1 cup miniature marshmallows
Old-Fashioned Fruit Dressing (recipe follows)

Prepare dressing. Combine fruits and marshmallows. Pour dressing over ingredients and toss. Cover and chill 12–24 hours.

Old-Fashioned Fruit Dressing:
2 eggs, beaten
2 tablespoons lemon juice
1 tablespoon butter
2 tablespoons sugar
2 tablespoons reserved pineapple juice
Dash of salt
2 cups Cool Whip, thawed

Combine all ingredients, except Cool Whip, in small saucepan. Heat just to boiling, stirring constantly. Remove from heat and cool. In a chilled bowl with Cool Whip in it, fold in the cooled egg mixture.

Sharon Lucas, Johnstown, Pa.

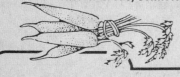

PINEAPPLE CARROT SALAD
Serves 6

1 large package lemon or orange gelatin
1 cup pineapple juice
1 cup boiling water
1 cup crushed pineapple
1-1/2 cups grated raw carrots
1/2 cup nuts (optional)

Dissolve gelatin in boiling water and add pineapple juice. Chill. When this begins to thicken, add other ingredients. Pour mixture into mold and chill until set. Unmold on a plate of lettuce and serve with mayonnaise.

Jean Hugh, Pittsburgh, Pa.

MANDARIN LETTUCE SALAD
Serves 6

1/4 cup sliced almonds
1/2 head lettuce
1 (11-ounce) can mandarin oranges
2 green onions, thinly sliced
2 tablespoons **plus** 1 teaspoon sugar
1 cup chopped celery

Cook almonds and sugar over low heat until sugar is dissolved, stirring constantly. When almonds are coated remove from heat. Cool and break apart. Keep at room temperature. Place lettuce, which is broken into bite-size pieces, celery and onions in a bowl. Pour the following dressing over this just before serving and toss. When serving individually or in a large bowl, sprinkle the caramelized almonds over top.

Dressing:
1/4 cup vegetable oil
2 tablespoons sugar
2 teaspoons vinegar
1 tablespoon snipped parsley

This recipe has been used for a number of benefit dinners as the salad. It has received many compliments from those who enjoyed it.

Sister Mary Kenneth Hemann, Dubuque, Iowa

BANANA YOGURT SALAD

2 large bananas
2 cups yogurt
¼ cup nuts, chopped
Orange sections
Lettuce

Peel and split bananas; place in serving dishes. Spoon 1 cup yogurt onto each banana. Sprinkle with nuts and surround with orange sections and shredded lettuce.

Suzan L. Wiener, Spring Hill, Fla.

CALICO COLE-SLAW FOR 10

1 cup mayonnaise
1 cup sour cream
1/3 cup sugar
3 tablespoons oil (preferably olive)
2 tablespoons lemon juice
1 tablespoon Old Bay Seasoning
1 teaspoon Dijon mustard
1/2 teaspoon dried basil, crumbled
Dash of hot pepper sauce
Salt and pepper
1 head cabbage, thinly sliced
1 onion, diced
1/2 apple, peeled and chopped
1 carrot, chopped

Combine first 9 ingredients in bowl. Season with salt and pepper. Let dressing stand 15 minutes. Meanwhile, mix remaining ingredients together in bowl. Mix in enough dressing to season to taste. Cover and refrigerate 1 to 8 hours. Stir. Serve chilled.

MY FAVORITE CUCUMBER SALAD

3 medium cucumbers
1/4 teaspoon salt
1 teaspoon sugar
4 tablespoons sour cream *or* mayonnaise
3 tablespoons chopped green onions
1 teaspoon lemon juice
2 tablespoons vinegar
1/2 teaspoon dry mustard
1 tablespoon minced parsley

Peel cucumbers and thinly slice. Spread cucumbers over bottom of a colander and sprinkle salt and sugar on top. Let them drain for 30 minutes; press gently to remove excess liquid, then chill. Blend sour cream or mayonnaise, onions, lemon juice, vinegar and dry mustard together. Add salt to taste. Toss dressing with cucumbers. Sprinkle parsley on top and serve chilled.

Lucille Roehr, Hammond, Ind.

PINEAPPLE CARROT SALAD

1 (#2 can) crushed pineapple, drained
1/4 teaspoon salt
1 cup finely-grated carrots
1 (3 ounce) package lemon gelatin
1/2 cup sugar
2 tablespoons lemon juice
1 cup whipping cream

Add enough water to pineapple syrup to make 1-1/2 cups liquid. Heat to boiling. Remove and stir in gelatin; stir until dissolved. Add sugar, salt, and lemon juice. Chill until slightly thickened. Add pineapple and carrots. Whip cream; fold into gelatin mixture. Pour into mold or bowl; chill until firm. Unmold onto lettuce leaves. This is an attractive holiday salad.

Viola C. Prinsen, Cedarburg, Wis.

WISCONSIN CRANBERRY SALAD
Serves 8

1 cup ground fresh cranberries
1 cup ground MacIntosh apples or other tart apples
1 cup sugar

Combine in a bowl. Cover and chill 24 hours. Next day add:
1 cup mini-marshmallows
1/2 cup finely-chopped, toasted pecans
1 cup whipped cream or Cool Whip

Mix and chill. Serve cold. This is a very refreshing salad, tangy, light in texture, and full of crunch—a super side dish!

Mrs. Larry Morris, Bradenton, Fla.

STRAWBERRY NUT SALAD

2 (3 ounce) packages strawberry jello
1 cup boiling water
2 (10 ounce) packages frozen strawberries, thawed and undrained
2 mashed bananas
1 can (1 pound-4 ounce) crushed pineapple, drained
1 cup pecan pieces
2 cartons (8 ounce) sour cream

Dissolve jello in boiling water. Add strawberries with juice, drained pineapple, bananas, and nuts. Put 1/2 of mixture in rectangular glass dish; refrigerate until firm. When congealed, spread sour cream over top of this layer. Pour balance of jello mixture over sour cream. Refrigerate until firm. To serve: cut into squares; arrange on lettuce.

Agnes Ward, Erie, PA

TAFFY APPLE SALAD
Serves 8-10

1 large can pineapple chunks, in natural juice (reserve juice)
2 cups miniature marshmallows
1 (8 ounce) container Cool Whip
2 red apples, pared
2 green apples, pared
1-1/2 cups chopped pecans or walnuts
1 tablespoon flour
1 egg, beaten
1-1/2 tablespoons vinegar
1/2 cup sugar

First day:
Mix drained pineapple chunks with marshmallows. Refrigerate overnight in covered dish. Cook pineapple juice with flour, sugar, beaten egg, and vinegar until thick. Refrigerate overnight.

Second Day:
Combine Cool Whip with cooked dressing. Add rest of ingredients and refrigerate until served.

TRANSCONTINENTAL TOSS
Serves 10

1 cup peach slices
1 cup pear slices
1 cup pineapple chunks
1 cup green seedless grapes
2 cups strawberries
1 (11 ounce can) mandarin oranges
Combine fruits in bowl.

Dressing:
1 small can evaporated milk
1 (7 ounce jar) marshmallow creme
2 tablespoons orange juice

Toss fruit lightly with dressing before serving.

MYSTERY SALAD

1 can cherry pie filling
1 can crushed pineapple (drained)
1 can mandarin oranges (drained)
1 cup mini marshmallows
1 can Eagle Brand sweetened condensed milk
1-8 ounce container of whipped topping
1/4 cup walnuts coarsely chopped

Mix all ingredients together. Pour into large bowl or in a large pan. Put more nuts on top if desired. Cover and refrigerate until served.

Donna Coakley, Parrottsville, TN

FRUIT COCKTAIL SALAD

1 (5-5/8 ounce) package vanilla flavored Jell-O instant pudding mix
1-1/3 cups buttermilk
1 (8 ounce) container Cool Whip
1 (30 ounce) can fruit cocktail, well-drained
2 cans mandarin oranges, well-drained
1 cup miniature rainbow-colored marshmallows (optional)

Blend buttermilk into pudding mix using medium speed of mixer. When smooth, blend in Cool Whip. If consistency of mixture seems too thick, add a little more buttermilk.

Fold in fruit cocktail and mandarin oranges, reserving half a can of oranges for garnish. Swirl a design on top of salad with a tablespoon. Gently arrange balance of mandarin orange slices in the swirled design on top of the salad.

Add colored marshmallows to mixture before garnishing, if desired.

Lalla Fellows, Long Beach, CA

CHERRY COLA SALAD

1 (3 ounce) package (dark) cherry gelatin
1 cup hot water
1 bottle (16-ounce) cola
3/4 teaspoon lemon juice
4 ounces cream cheese (cut into small cubes)
1/2 cup chopped nuts
1 can dark sweet cherries (drained and cut)

Put gelatin into hot water and stir until dissolved. When it cools, add cola and refrigerate until gelatin begins to harden. Add cherries, nuts, and cream cheese. Pour into gelatin mold and chill.

Karin Shea Fedders, Dameron, Md.

DREAM SALAD

1 small box lime gelatin
1 (8-ounce) package cream cheese, softened
1/8 teaspoon salt
1/2 cup mayonnaise
1 cup chopped celery
1/2 cup finely chopped nuts
1 (8-ounce) can crushed pineapple, drained
1 cup whipped cream
1/2 pound mini marshmallows
1 cup cottage cheese
1-3/4 cups boiling water

Dissolve gelatin in boiling water. Beat cream cheese, salt, and mayonnaise until light and fluffy. Add gelatin, celery, nuts, whipped cream, marshmallows, cottage cheese, and pineapple. Put in 9 x 13 inch pan with a cover; chill.

Betty Brennan, Faribault, MN

CHERRY SALAD
Serves 15

2 (6-ounce) packages cherry gelatin
2 cups hot water
1 cup cold water
1 can cherry pie filling

1 (8-ounce) package cream cheese
1 cup crushed pineapple, drained
Cool Whip

Dissolve gelatin in hot water; add cold water and pie filling. Pour into 13x9-inch pan. When completely set, cover with the following topping: Whip together 1 large package cream cheese and 1 cup crushed pineapple, drained; spread on gelatin. A container of Cool Whip (whipped topping) may be folded into the whipped cream cheese layer and spread over the gelatin.

Marguerite Garvey, Boone, Iowa

APRICOT GELATIN MOLD

2 (6-ounce) packages apricot gelatin
3 cups boiling water
1 (9-ounce) container frozen whipped topping, thawed
2 cups cold water
2 bananas, sliced
1/2 cup pecans or walnuts
1 (13-1/4-ounce) can pineapple tidbits, drained

Dissolve gelatin in boiling water. Add whipped topping and let dissolve. Mix well. Add cold water. Refrigerate until thickened. Blend in sliced bananas, nuts, and pineapple tidbits. Chill overnight. Must be prepared a day ahead.

Leota Baxter, Ingalls, Kan.

GOLDEN GLOW SALAD

1 cup boiling water
1 package lemon gelatin
1 cup pineapple juice
1 cup diced pineapple
1 tablespoon lemon juice
1/3 cup chopped nuts
1/2 teaspoon salt
1 cup grated carrots

Canned pineapple and juice *must* be used. Dissolve gelatin in boiling water; add juice and salt. When slightly thickened, add pineapple, carrots, nuts, and lemon juice. Turn into mold and chill until firm. Unmold on bed of shredded lettuce.

Mrs. Larry Morris, Cedar Hills, TX

BROCCOLI SALAD

1 bunch broccoli, cut into bite-size pieces
1/2 cup raisins
1 small onion, chopped
1 cup Miracle Whip salad dressing
1/4 cup sugar
2 tablespoons vinegar
12 slices bacon, fried, and crumbled

Mix sugar and vinegar with salad dressing. Pour over broccoli, raisins, onion, and bacon. Mix well, set in refrigerator a couple hours to cool and blend flavors.

Mrs. Tom McNiel, Constantine, Mich.

CARROT-DATE SLAW
Serves 4

1/2 cup commercial sour cream
1/4 cup milk
1 tablespoon lemon juice
1 teaspoon sugar
1/4 teaspoon salt
3 cups shredded carrots
1/2 cup chopped dates

Combine all ingredients; stir well. Chill thoroughly.

Mrs. Bruce Fowler, Woodruff, S.C

COOL-AS-A-CUCUMBER SALAD
Serves 4

1 cup sour cream
2 tablespoons lemon juice
1/4 teaspoon dried dill weed
2 medium cucumbers, pared and sliced

Combine first 3 ingredients, stirring well. Add cucumbers and coat gently. Chill at least 2 hours before serving.

AMSTERDAM SPINACH SALAD

Serves 4

3 cups fresh spinach, cut into bite-size pieces
5 slices crisp bacon, crumbled
1 medium carrot, shredded
1 tablespoon minced onion
1/4 cup bottled Italian dressing
1/8 teaspoon dry mustard.
Dash of pepper

Combine spinach, bacon, carrots and onion in medium bowl. Heat Italian dressing with mustard and pepper in a small saucepan; pour over spinach and toss.

Sue Hibbard, Rochester, NY

CHINESE CABBAGE SALAD

Serves 6-8

1 large head Chinese cabbage, chopped
2 small purple onions, sliced in rings
1 (8 ounce) carton sour cream
1/2 cup chopped onion
2 tablespoons vinegar
2 tablespoons celery seed
1/2 teaspoon salt
1/4 teaspoon pepper

Combine chopped cabbage and onion rings. Set aside.

Combine sour cream, chopped onion, vinegar, celery seed, salt, and pepper. Stir well. Mix into cabbage and onion rings. Chill well before serving.

Lily Jo Drake, Satellite Beach, FL

CAULIFLOWER-BROCCOLI SALAD

1 head cauliflower
2 stalks broccoli
1/4 cup sliced green onions
1 pound bacon, cooked and crumbled
6 ounces Cheddar cheese, cubed
6 ounces Mozzarella cheese, cubed

2 tablespoons vinegar
2 cups mayonnaise
1/4 cup sugar
1/2 teaspoon salt

Cut up the cauliflower and broccoli into very small pieces. Add to diced cheeses and onion. Mix mayonnaise, sugar, salt, and vinegar together; stir into vegetables. Add bacon last.

This is an excellent salad and can be made ahead and kept for a day or two in the refrigerator.

Sharon Sisson, Longview, Wash.

MARINATED CARROTS

Serves 8

1 bunch large carrots
2 cloves garlic, sliced
1/2 teaspoon salt
1/2 teaspoon pepper
1/4 cup olive oil
2 tablespoons wine vinegar
1 teaspoon oregano

Scrape carrots and cut into thick slices. Boil carrots in water 10 minutes, or until tender, taking care not to overcook. Drain well and place in bowl with garlic, salt, pepper, oil, vinegar, and oregano. Stir; mix well. Let stand in marinade 12 hours before serving.

Helen V. Robiolio, Union City, N.J.

ELEGANT WHITE SALAD

2 envelopes plain gelatin
1/2 cup cold pineapple juice
1-1/2 cups hot pineapple juice
1/2 cup sugar
Juice of 1 lemon
1 teaspoon almond extract
1 cup half and half cream
1 cup heavy cream, whipped

Dissolve gelatin in cold pineapple juice. When dissolved, add hot juice, sugar and lemon juice. Let cool. Then add half and half; refrigerate. (Mixture looks curdled at this point.) When partly set, add extract and whipped cream. Pour into ring mold.

When ready to serve, unmold on large serving plate. Surround with pineapple chunks, mandarin oranges or any fruit combination. Place fruit in the center, too.

Mrs. Martha Mehloff, Eureka, SD

SPRING SPINACH SALAD

Serves 8-10

1 pound fresh spinach
1 medium sliced cucumber
1/4 cup diced celery
8 sliced radishes
1/4 cup sliced green onions
1/2 cup French dressing
2 tomatoes, quartered

Rub bowl with cut clove of garlic; remove garlic. Add spinach. (Use small spinach leaves whole; shred larger leaves.) Arrange other vegetables over spinach. (Score cucumber with fork before slicing.)

Pour on dressing. Garnish with tomato quarters. Also, if desired, cut one tomato into a "flower" and fill center with sieved hard-cooked egg yolk.

Amelia M. Brown, Pittsburgh, PA

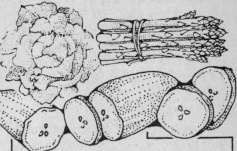

GARDEN FRESH CUCUMBERS

Makes 3 cups

1/4 cup vinegar
1 tablespoon lemon juice
1 teaspoon celery seeds
2 tablespoons sugar
3/4 teaspoon salt
1/8 teaspoon pepper
2 tablespoons chopped onion
3 cups sliced peeled cucumbers

Combine vinegar, lemon juice, celery seeds, sugar, salt, pepper, and onion. Pour over cucumbers. Chill.

Sharon M. Crider, Evansville, WI

PEANUT CRUNCH SALAD

Serves 12-15

4 cups shredded cabbage
1 cup finely chopped celery
1/2 cup sour cream
1/2 cup mayonnaise
1 teaspoon salt
1/4 cup chopped green onion
1/4 cup chopped green pepper
1/2 cup chopped cucumber
1 tablespoon butter
1/2 cup coarsely chopped dry roasted
   peanuts
2 tablespoons grated Parmesan
   cheese

Toss cabbage and celery together; chill. Combine sour cream, mayonnaise, salt, onion, green pepper and cucumber in small bowl; chill.

Just before serving, melt butter in small skillet. Add peanuts; heat until lightly browned and immediately stir in cheese.

Toss chilled vegetables with dressing. Sprinkle peanut mixture on top of salad and serve.

Sue Hibbard, Rochester, NY

GARDEN GATE SALAD

1/2 teaspoon grated onion
1/2 teaspoon vinegar
1/4 teaspoon paprika
1/2 teaspoon salt
1/2 cup mayonnaise or salad dressing
2 cups cubed cooked potatoes
1/2 cup diced celery
1/2 cup diced cucumbers
1/4 cup sliced radishes
1/4 cup chopped green peppers
Lettuce
Watercress

Mix onion, vinegar, paprika, salt and mayonnaise or salad dressing. Combine with potato, celery, cucumber, radishes, and green pepper. Chill and serve on lettuce and watercress. This is a very simple salad that is tasty and most attractive.

Lillian Smith, Montreal, QUE

SUPER DELICIOUS STRAWBERRY GELATIN SALAD

Serves 8

1-1/3 cups coarsely ground pretzels
3/4 stick margarine
4 ounces cream cheese
1/2 cup sugar
1/2 cup whipped cream
1 cup pineapple juice
1 package (3 ounce package) strawberry jello
1 (10 ounce package) frozen strawberries

Combine pretzels and margarine. Press into 8 x 8 x 2 inch pan. Bake at 400 degrees for 10 minutes. Cream sugar and cream cheese; fold in whipped cream. Pour over pretzel crust and refrigerate. Dissolve jello in hot pineapple juice; add partially thawed strawberries. When mixture starts to set, pour over other layers. Refrigerate until firm.

Lucille Roehr, Hammond, IN

MOLDED CHERRY SALAD

Serves 6

1 package apple gelatin
1 cup boiling water
1 cup cherry juice
1 tablespoon lemon juice
1-1/2 cups pitted white cherries
1 (3 ounce) package cream cheese
1 tablespoon mayonnaise
Lettuce leaves

Dissolve apple gelatin in boiling water; add cherry juice and lemon juice. Pour one-third of the mixture into bottom of a mold. Chill. Fill pitted cherries with cream cheese which has been whipped with mayonnaise; arrange on gelatin. Pour slightly thickened gelatin around the cherries and allow to set. When completely chilled and set, unmold and serve on lettuce leaves. Serve with additional mayonnaise, if desired.

Betty Slavin, Omaha, Neb.

BUTTERMINT SALAD

2 (13 ounce) cans crushed pineapple,
   undrained
1 package dry lime gelatin
1 (10 ounce) package miniature
   marshmallows
1 (7 ounce) package soft buttermints;
   crushed
1 (9 ounce) container Cool Whip

Mix pineapple, gelatin, and marshmallows in large bowl. Cover and refrigerate overnight. Add mints and Cool Whip in morning and serve one of three ways:

1) Pour into a 9 x 13 inch pan and freeze. Cut into squares and serve on lettuce leaves.

2) Pour into large bowl and refrigerate. Serve chilled. Salad will be soft.

3) Pour into individual aluminum foil muffin tins and freeze. Serve when solid.

Kathy Ericksen, Rockwell City, IA

VELVET SALAD

1 (3 ounce) package lemon gelatin
2 cups boiling water
1 pound marshmallows
1 medium can crushed pineapple,
   drained
1 (3 ounce) package cream cheese
1 cup whipping cream
1 cup mayonnaise
1 (3 ounce) package cherry gelatin
2 cups hot water

Dissolve lemon gelatin in boiling water. Add marshmallows; stir until dissolved. Mix together drained, crushed pineapple, cream cheese, whipping cream, and mayonnaise. Combine with lemon gelatin mixture. Chill. Dissolve cherry gelatin in hot water. Cool, then pour over lemon gelatin mixture.

This is a colorful and refreshing salad for the Christmas holidays.

Cathy Cecava, Lincoln, Neb.

MIXED SALAD
Serves 6

- ⅓ cup olive *or* vegetable oil
- 2 tablespoons fresh lemon juice
- 2 tablespoons white wine vinegar
- 1 small clove garlic, minced
- ¼ teaspoon salt
- ¼ teaspoon basil, crushed
- ⅛ teaspoon white pepper
- ½ head romaine lettuce
- ½ head Boston lettuce
- 1 cucumber, sliced
- ¼ cup shredded carrot
- 2 tablespoons sliced scallion

In small bowl, combine oil, lemon juice, vinegar, garlic, salt, basil and pepper. Cover and chill at least 1 hour.

At serving time, wash lettuce leaves and tear into bite-size pieces; place in a large bowl. Add cucumber, carrot and scallion. Pour dressing over salad and toss to coat evenly.

Mary Dale, Cincinnati, Ohio

LUNCHEON SALAD

- 1 cup sliced fresh mushrooms
- 1 cup chopped cooked shrimp
- 1 teaspoon tarragon leaves
- 1/2 cup Italian dressing
- 3 ripe avocados, chilled
- Red leaf or romaine lettuce

Combine all ingredients, except avocados and lettuce. Chill for 1 hour in refrigerator. Arrange lettuce leaves on individual salad plates. Peel and halve avocados. Place an avocado half on each salad plate and fill with marinated combination. Garnish with whole cherry tomatoes and radish roses, if desired. This is a great salad for company in the summertime!

Suzan L. Wiener, Spring Hill, Fla.

PEPPERONI SALAD
Serves 6–8

- 1 medium onion, thinly sliced
- 8 ounces pepperoni, thinly sliced
- ¼ cup crumbled bleu cheese
- ⅔ cup salad oil
- ⅓ cup cider vinegar
  Salt and freshly ground pepper to taste
- 10 ounces fresh spinach, washed thoroughly, dried and chopped
- ½ head iceberg lettuce, chopped

One day before serving, separate onion slices into rings and place in large bowl; add pepperoni slices and bleu cheese. Add oil, vinegar, salt and pepper. Toss in the spinach and lettuce. Chill salad overnight in covered bowl.

Agnes Ward, Erie, Pa.

TART APPLE SALAD
Serves 10

- 6 apples, sweet-tart and crisp
- ½ cup chopped English walnuts
- 1 cup finely chopped celery
- 1½ cups purple grapes, halved and seeds removed
- ¼ cup sugar
- 1 heaping tablespoon Miracle Whip
- ½ pint whipping cream, whipped

Prepare the fruit and celery. Combine fruit, nuts and celery. Sprinkle with sugar; stir in Miracle Whip. Stir well to cover all the fruit, nuts and celery with a light coating of the sugar/dressing mixture. Add stiffly beaten whipped cream. You can do everything except the cream ahead of time, and refrigerate for a couple of hours. Add whipped cream just before serving. Be sure to refrigerate immediately in a covered container.

Linda Taylor, Gravois Mills, Mo.

FROZEN PEA SALAD

- 1 (10–12-ounce) package frozen peas
- 1 (4-ounce) package Hidden Valley Original Ranch salad dressing
- 1 cup buttermilk
- 1 (8-ounce) carton sour cream
- 1 small onion, chopped
- 1 small head lettuce, cut in bite-size pieces
- 4 hard-cooked eggs, diced
- 8 to 10 strips bacon, fried and drained

Thaw peas; drain on paper towels. In a small bowl put dry dressing mix, buttermilk and sour cream; whip this mixture until creamy and smooth. Add onion, salt and pepper to taste. In a large bowl combine lettuce, diced eggs, drained bacon and drained peas. Add dressing mixture and toss lightly until salad ingredients are coated. Refrigerate until chilled; serve.

Rose Mary Dietz, Hoisington, Kan.

CELERY AND ORANGE SALAD
Serves 6

- 3 medium oranges
- 2 ribs celery
- 2 shallots, chopped
- 4 tablespoons oil
- 1 tablespoon lemon juice
  Salt and pepper
  Chopped parsley

Peel oranges, cutting just beneath the pith. Hold the fruit in one hand and cut out each segment, freeing it from its protective membranes as you cut. Cut the celery into 1½-inch julienne strips. Put the shallots, oranges and celery into a bowl; add the remaining ingredients and toss. Allow salad to rest for 1–6 hours before serving.

Marcella Swigert, Monroe City, Mo.

CHICK-PEA AND SPINACH SALAD

6 ounces dried chick-peas
1 pound fresh spinach
6 tablespoons olive oil
2 tablespoons wine vinegar
Salt and pepper
½ cup plain yogurt
2 tablespoons chopped parsley

Soak chick-peas in cold water overnight. Strain. Put in large saucepan and add about 4 cups fresh water. Bring to a boil; cover; simmer gently for 1½ hours, or until peas are tender but not mushy. Let peas cool in the cooking liquid, then drain.

Wash spinach; discard any coarse or damaged leaves, and pull off all stems. Cut large leaves into pieces; leave small leaves whole. Combine chick-peas and spinach in a salad bowl. Pour in oil and vinegar; add salt and pepper to taste. Toss ingredients together, but gently, so as not to break up peas. Chill salad until ready to serve. At serving time, arrange the mixture in a shallow bowl and top with yogurt. Sprinkle parsley over all.
Marcella Swigert, Monroe City, Mo.

ZUCCHINI–APPLE SLAW
Serves 6

4 cups coarsely shredded zucchini
1/4 cup green onions, thinly sliced on the diagonal
2–3 medium-size red or green tart apples (unskinned)
1/2 cup mayonnaise
3 tablespoons cider vinegar
1 tablespoon sugar
1 teaspoon poppy seeds
Salt and pepper to taste

In a large bowl combine zucchini and onions. Core apples and cut into 1/4- to 1/2-inch chunks. Add apples to zucchini mixture. Combine may-

onnaise, vinegar, sugar and poppy seeds until well-blended. Pour dressing over salad and mix lightly until well-coated. Season with salt and pepper to taste. Cover and refrigerate for 2–4 hours. Use a slotted spoon to transfer to serving bowl or individual plates.

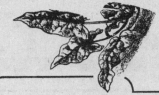

GREEN BEANS AND BACON SALAD
Serves 6

6 slices bacon, coarsely chopped
1-1/2 pounds fresh beans, trimmed and cooked crisp-tender, drained
or
2 (9-ounce) packages frozen whole green beans, thawed
1 medium yellow, red, or green bell pepper, coarsely chopped
3 tablespoons olive oil
1/4 teaspoon pepper

Cook bacon in skillet over medium heat until crisp, stirring at least twice. Remove bacon with a slotted spoon; transfer to paper towel to drain. Pour all but 1 tablespoon drippings from skillet. Add all remaining ingredients, except bacon. Cook about 3 minutes, stirring constantly until beans are heated through. Transfer to a large bowl. Stir in bacon. Cool completely. Cover and refrigerate overnight. Can be prepared at least 2 days before serving. Serve at room temperature. This salad is great with fried chicken!
Leota Baxter, Ingalls, Kan.

FIVE-CUP FRUIT SALAD

1 cup flaked coconut
1 cup mandarin oranges
1 cup miniature marshmallows
1 cup pineapple bits, well-drained
1 cup commercial sour cream

Toss fruit, coconut and marshmallows with sour cream. Chill and serve.
Dovie Lucy, McLoud, Okla.

GOURMET FRUIT MOLD

1 (3-ounce) package raspberry gelatin
1-1/4 cups Dr. Pepper beverage, boiling
1 (10-ounce) package frozen raspberries
3/4 cup canned crushed pineapple, drained
1 large banana, sliced
1/4 cup chopped pecans

Dissolve gelatin in boiling Dr. Pepper. Add partially thawed raspberries. Stir until berries are separated. Chill until mixture is thickened. Fold in remaining ingredients. Pour into molds. Chill until firm; unmold. Garnish with salad greens. Serve with Sour Cream Fruit Dressing (recipe follows).

Sour Cream Fruit Dressing:
Combine 1 cup sour cream with 1-1/2 cups miniature marshmallows, 1 tablespoon sugar, and 2-1/2 tablespoons lemon juice. Chill several hours. Stir well before serving.
Mrs. Bruce Fowler, Woodruff, S.C.

ORIENTAL SLAW
Serves 6

1 small to medium head of Ñappa or Chinese cabbage, washed and crisped (reserve 6 outer leaves)
1 cup pineapple tidbits, drained (fresh, if possible)
1 large tart apple, diced and unskinned
1 cup plain low-fat yogurt
1/4 cup mayonnaise
Juice of 1 lemon
1 tablespoon honey (more, if desired)

Cut cabbage crosswise into thin 1/8- to 1/4-inch slices. Combine with pineapple and apples. Mix yogurt, mayonnaise, lemon juice and honey; pour over cabbage mixture. Chill. When ready to serve, place whole cabbage leaf on plate, mound slaw on top and serve.

Sensational
SOUPS & STEWS

SAVORY TOMATO-SPINACH SOUP
Serves 4

1 pound lean beef, cut into 1-inch cubes
4 cups beef bouillon
¼ teaspoon salt
4 potatoes, cubed
3 green onions, sliced
1½ pounds fresh spinach, washed and coarsely chopped
4 tomatoes, peeled and cut into wedges
¼ teaspoon nutmeg

Combine beef, bouillon, salt, potatoes and onions; cover; cook 20 minutes. Add spinach and tomatoes; cook 5 minutes. To serve: Sprinkle each serving lightly with nutmeg.

Gwen Campbell, Sterling, Va.

TORTILLA SOUP
Serves 4–6

1 (18-ounce) jar Ortega Mild Green Chile Salsa
1 (13¾-ounce) College Inn Chicken Broth
1 small zucchini, halved and sliced
1 cup cooked garbanzo beans
2 tablespoons Ortega Diced Jalapeños Tortilla Chips, coarsely broken
¾ cup shredded Monterey Jack cheese

In saucepan, combine first 5 ingredients; simmer 5–7 minutes. Arrange a shallow layer of chips in serving bowls. Ladle in soup; top with cheese. Serve immediately.

Tina Peters, Seattle, Wash.

GRANDMA'S BEEF RIVEL SOUP
Serves 4

1 pound rib boiling beef *or* chuck roast, cut in chunks
1 medium onion, finely chopped
2 quarts cold water
2 teaspoons salt
½ teaspoon pepper
1 large egg
¼ cup (or more) flour

Slowly boil beef with water, onion, salt and pepper until tender. Mix flour and egg with your fingers until in small chunks, called rivels. Add to broth and cook for 5 minutes. Serve in soup bowls with crackers or croutons. Beef could be cooked in Crockpot for convenience.

Marjorie W. Baxla, Greenfield, Ohio

EGG DROP SOUP
Serves 4

2 (13¾-ounce) cans chicken broth
1 tablespoon cornstarch
1 egg, well-beaten
2 tablespoons chopped green onion

In saucepan slowly stir chicken broth into cornstarch. Cook, stirring constantly, until slightly thickened. Slowly pour in the well-beaten egg; stir once gently. Remove from heat. Garnish with green onion.

Annie Cmehil, New Castle, Ind.

YANKEE CHOWDER
Serves 6

1 can condensed cream of mushroom soup
3 soup cans water
1 can condensed turkey noodle soup
1 can condensed vegetarian vegetable soup

Stir mushroom soup until smooth in a large saucepan; gradually stir in water. Add remaining soups. Heat thoroughly, stirring often. (115 calories per serving)

Shari Crider, Stoughton, Wis.

VEGETABLE SOUP
Serves 6–8

3 cups beef or vegetable stock
1 diced onion
3 medium carrots, sliced
2 stalks celery, diced
2 cups cooked noodles
2 cups tomatoes, chopped
2 tablespoons minced parsley
1/2 teaspoon dried basil

Simmer until vegetables are tender; add noodles, tomatoes, parsley and basil. So quick to make—and so good to taste!

Mrs. D. Garms, Anaheim, Calif.

SPINACH-POTATO SOUP
Serves 7

2 tablespoons butter *or* margarine
1 cup sliced leeks
1½ pounds potatoes, peeled and cubed (4 cups)
2 (14½-ounce) cans Swanson clear ready-to-serve chicken broth *or*
3 (10½-ounce) cans Campbell's ready-to-serve low-sodium chicken broth
¼ cup water
4 cups coarsely chopped spinach leaves
1 teaspoon lemon juice
¼ teaspoon pepper
Sour cream *or* plain low-fat yogurt for garnish

In 3-quart saucepan over medium heat, in hot butter, cook leeks until tender, stirring often.

Add potatoes, broth and water. Heat to boiling; reduce heat to low. Cover; simmer until potatoes are tender, stirring occasionally.

Stir in spinach, lemon juice and pepper; simmer 5 minutes. Garnish with sour cream. (21 calories per serving)

Fran Sievers, Atlanta, Ga.

CREAMY CHICKEN LEEK SOUP

1 package Knorr Leek Soup Mix
2 cups water
2 cups milk
1 cup instant rice
1 (6-ounce) can chicken, chopped

Heat soup mix, water, milk and chicken over medium heat. Simmer 10 minutes. Add rice. Remove from heat; cover and let stand 5 minutes.

J.L. Rede, Tucumcari, N.M.

SAUSAGE STEW
Serves 6–8

1 can condensed beef broth
1 cup water
1/8 teaspoon pepper
1 bay leaf
2 medium onions, quartered
6 carrots, cut in julienne pieces
1-1/2 cups celery, diced
2 potatoes, diced
2 tablespoons water
1 tablespoon flour
1 pound smoked sausage, cut in 1/2-inch pieces
Salt to taste
Grated Parmesan cheese

Combine broth, 1 cup water, pepper, bay leaf and vegetables, except potatoes, in a 4-quart pot. Simmer, covered, for 10 minutes. Add potatoes; cook until vegetables are tender. Remove bay leaf. Mix 2 tablespoons water with flour; stir into vegetables. Add sausage; heat. Add salt. Top each serving with cheese.

Laura Hicks, Troy, Mont.

CREAM OF VEGETABLE SOUP
Serves 4–6

2 medium carrots, cut in chunks
1 medium potato, cut in chunks
1 rib celery, cut in chunks
1 large onion, cut in chunks
2 vegetable bouillon cubes
2 cups water
1 teaspoon salt
Dash pepper
2 cups milk

In a 2-quart saucepan, combine all ingredients, except milk, and cook, covered, until vegetables are tender.

Put half of milk and half of vegetable mixture (including liquid) in blender. Blend until vegetables are puréed. Repeat with remaining half of milk and vegetables. Return all of puréed mixture to saucepan and cook until soup is bubbly and hot.

CHEESY CHICKEN CHOWDER
Serves 8

8 tablespoons butter
2 cups carrots, shredded
½ cup onion, chopped
½ cup flour
3 cups chicken broth
4 cups milk
2 cups diced cooked chicken
1 cup corn, fresh *or* frozen
1 teaspoon Worcestershire sauce
8 ounces cheddar cheese, shredded
2 tablespoons white wine (optional)
1 teaspoon salt
½ teaspoon pepper

Melt butter in a skillet. Add carrots and onion; sauté until tender. Blend in flour. Add broth and milk. Cook and stir until thick and smooth. Add remaining ingredients and stir until cheese is melted.

Diantha Susan Hibbard, Rochester, N.Y.

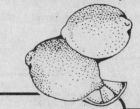

CHICKEN-LEMON SOUP
Serves 4

1 quart chicken broth
1/4 cup uncooked rice
Pinch of mace or nutmeg
3 egg yolks
Juice of 1 lemon
Salt and pepper

Place broth, rice and mace in a large saucepan. Cover, and simmer 25–30 minutes until rice is tender. Beat yolks with lemon juice. Spoon a little hot broth into egg mixture; return to pan and heat over lowest heat for 1–2 minutes, stirring constantly, until no taste of raw egg remains. Do not boil. Season with salt and pepper to taste.

QUICK AND EASY CHILI CON CARNE
Serves 12

- 1 cup onion, finely chopped
- 1 cup green pepper, finely chopped
- ½ cup celery, finely chopped
- 2 cloves garlic, finely chopped
- 2 pounds ground beef
- 2 cups canned tomatoes
- 4 teaspoons sugar
- 4 teaspoons salt
- 2 tablespoons chili powder
- 5 cups kidney beans
- 30 sticks vermicelli, broken in small pieces

Sauté onions and green pepper, celery and garlic until lightly browned. Add meat and fry only until browned. Add tomatoes, sugar, salt and chili powder. Cover and bring to a boil. Simmer for 30 minutes; then add kidney beans and vermicelli. Cook for 15 minutes.

Suzan L. Wiener, Spring Hill, Fla.

AUNT DOT'S BRUNSWICK STEW

- 1 (3-pound) chicken, cooked, boned and cut up

To chicken broth add:
- 1 (20-ounce) can tomatoes
- 1 (16-ounce) package frozen mixed vegetables
- 1 (16-ounce) can creamed corn
- 1 (16-ounce) can tomato sauce
- 3–4 stalks celery, sliced
- 3–4 potatoes, diced
- 1 small can butter beans

Cook all ingredients until vegetables are done. Add salt and pepper to taste. You can eat this right away or

simmer it on the back of the stove while you do other chores!

It also freezes well and tastes better after a day or two of "sitting" in the refrigerator.

Phyliss Dixon, Fairbanks, Alaska

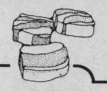

BURGOO
Serves 2
(A low-sodium stew)

- 1/4 pound lean hamburger
- 1 onion, chopped
- 1 small or medium red potato, chopped with skin
- 1 carrot, chopped
- 2 tablespoons celery, chopped
- 1 clove garlic, chopped
- 1/4 cup frozen peas
- 1 teaspoon low-sodium beef bouillon
- 1/4 teaspoon thyme
- 1/4 teaspoon basil
- 1 bay leaf
- 1/8 teaspoon black pepper
- Few grains hot pepper, if desired

Brown hamburger with onion and garlic over moderate heat. Add potato, carrot, peas and celery with enough boiling water to barely cover. Add remaining seasonings and spices. Simmer over low heat for about 15 minutes. No salt is needed. Vegetables and herbs may be varied according to taste and season.

Mrs. Olen Begly, West Salem, Ohio

CREAMY BROCCOLI SOUP
Makes 2 quarts

- 2 tablespoons chopped onions
- 3 tablespoons butter *or* margarine
- 3 tablespoons flour
- 1½ teaspoons salt
- 3 cups milk
- 3 cups chicken broth *or* 3 chicken bouillon cubes dissolved in 3 cups boiling water

- 1 (10-ounce) package chopped broccoli, slightly thawed
- 2 cups carrots, finely sliced
- Pepper

In large saucepan sauté onion in butter until tender. With a whisk, stir in flour, 1½ teaspoons salt and milk.

Gradually add broth, stirring constantly. Bring to a boil. Add broccoli and carrots; cook over low heat (do not boil), stirring occasionally, about 25 minutes, or until carrots are tender. Add pepper and salt to taste. Serve hot.

Elizabeth Dunn, Harrisonville, N.J.

ITALIAN MINESTRONE SOUP

- 3 strips bacon, diced
- 1 cup chopped onions
- 2 small stalks celery, thinly sliced
- 1 small carrot, thinly sliced
- 4 cups water
- 1 (15-ounce) can kidney beans, drained
- 1 (14-1/2-ounce) can Italian-flavored whole tomatoes, undrained and chopped
- 2 small potatoes, pared and diced
- 1 small zucchini, diced
- 1/2 cup macaroni
- 2 beef bouillon cubes
- 1/2 teaspoon garlic salt
- 1/4 teaspoon pepper

In large Dutch oven or kettle, sauté bacon until crisp; remove and reserve drippings. Sauté onions, celery and carrot until tender. Add remaining ingredients and bring to a boil. Simmer, covered, for 30 minutes.

I usually double this recipe for my family of four. The leftovers are great heated up for a fast, healthful lunch. Serve for dinner with tossed green salad and whole-wheat rolls.

Phyliss Dixon, Fairbanks, Alaska

CORNED BEEF CHOWDER
Serves 5

3 cups milk
1 can cream of potato soup
1 (10 ounce) package frozen
 Brussels sprouts, thawed
1 can corned beef, broken up

In a large saucepan, blend 1-1/3 cups milk and soup. Cut up Brussels sprouts and add to soup. Bring to boil. Reduce heat; simmer 15 minutes. Add remaining milk and beef. Heat through.

Kenneth McAdams, El Dorado, Ark.

POTATO HAM CHOWDER
Serves 6

4 potatoes
2 tablespoons margarine
1/2 cup diced onions
2 cups water
1 teaspoon salt
1/8 teaspoon pepper
4 tablespoons flour
1/3 cup water
2 cups milk
1 (12 ounce) can whole kernel corn
2 cups diced cooked ham

Peel and dice potatoes. In large saucepan, melt margarine. Add onion, and cook until tender. Add potatoes, 2 cups water, and seasonings. Cover; simmer until potatoes are done. Make a paste of flour and 1/3 cup water; add to potato mixture. Add milk and cook until slightly thickened. Stir in corn and ham. Heat thoroughly, but do not boil.

MAINE CORN CHOWDER
Makes 9 cups

5 slices bacon
2 medium onions, sliced
3 cups diced, pared potatoes
2 cups water
1 teaspoon salt
1/2 teaspoon pepper
1 (1-pound,1-ounce) can cream-
 style corn
2 cups milk

Cook bacon in Dutch oven until crisp. Drain on paper towels. Set aside. Sauté onion in bacon drippings until soft. Add potatoes, water, salt, and pepper. Bring to a boil. Reduce heat; cover and simmer about 15 minutes until potatoes are tender. Add corn and milk. Heat thoroughly. When serving, garnish with crumbled bacon.

Helen Weissinger, Levittown, Pa.

CHILI

1 pound chunk beef
1-1/2 pounds ground beef
1 pound pork, cut into 1/4-inch
 cubes
1 large onion
1 can beer
Chili powder to taste
1 teaspoon salt
Sugar to sweeten
1 tablespoon oregano
1 (16 ounce) can kidney beans
1 (16 ounce) can butter beans
1 (16 ounce) can garbanzo beans
1 (No. 2-1/2) can tomatoes
1 (15 ounce) can tomato sauce
1 (6 ounce) can tomato paste
1 (16 ounce) can mushrooms
 (optional)
1 (16 ounce) can northern beans
1 cup beef broth made from bouillon
Garlic powder to taste
Add more tomato juice, as needed

Brown beef, pork, and onion; place in large kettle. Add all the rest of ingredients. If very thick, add water and tomato juice; simmer several hours until flavors are blended and meat is tender.

Arthur J. Gatton, Lake Mills, Wis.

LUMBERJACK CHILI

2 pounds ground beef
1 large onion, diced
1/2 green pepper, diced
4 stalks celery, diced
1 large can tomato juice
1 can whole tomatoes
2 cans red kidney beans
2 tablespoons chili powder
1 teaspoon garlic powder
1 teaspoon celery salt
1 teaspoon Italian seasoning
1/2 teaspoon pepper

Brown beef and drain well. Sauté onion, green pepper, and celery. Combine all in large saucepot with remaining ingredients. Simmer for about 1 hour. Freezes well, and is very good reheated.

Ida Bloedow, Madison, Wis.

CHI CHI CHILI

1-1/2 pounds chopped meat or
 ground chuck
1-1/2 cups onion, cut up
1-1/2 celery, chopped
2 cloves garlic
2 teaspoons salt
1 teaspoon sage
2 tablespoons chili powder
1 tablespoon paprika
1 teaspoon thyme
1 bay leaf
2 cans kidney beans or chili beans (if
 you like it hotter)
1 large can tomatos
1 small can tomato paste

Brown meat, onion, garlic and celery. Add remaining ingredients and simmer 1 to 2 hours.

Mrs. Kit Rollins, Cedarburg, WI

FAMILY FARE CHICKEN VEGETABLE SOUP

1 cup potatoes, cut into small squares (diced)
4 cups chicken stock or broth
1 teaspoon salt
1/8 teaspoon pepper
1 cup onions, thinly sliced
1 cup carrots, diced
1 cup celery, chopped
1 cup fresh green beans, cut in 2-inch pieces
2 cups cooked chicken, diced
1 cup zucchini, sliced

In saucepan over medium heat, bring potatoes to boiling point in enough salted water to cover. Cook potatoes 5 minutes; drain and set aside. In large saucepan, heat stock to boiling. Season with salt and pepper. Add onion, carrots, and celery; simmer 5 minutes. Stir in green beans and chicken; heat soup to boiling. Add zucchini and potatoes; simmer 1 minute longer.

Gwen Campbell, Sterling, Va.

COCK-A-LEEKIE SOUP

Serves 4
(dates back to the 14th century)

1 dozen leeks
1 ounce butter
2 stalks celery, chopped
1 carrot, chopped
1-1/2 quarts chicken broth
1 cup cooked chicken, diced
Salt and pepper to taste
1 egg yolk

Wash and trim leeks. Cut into 1/2-inch-long pieces. Discard roots and tops. Fry in butter with celery and carrot. When brown, add 1 quart broth and chicken. Cover and simmer for 2 hours. Salt, pepper, and stir in egg yolk which has been blended with remaining broth. Heat thoroughly.

CREAMY ASPARAGUS SOUP

Serves 4

1 (10-ounce) package frozen asparagus
1/2 cup chicken broth
2 egg yolks
1/4 cup whole milk
1/2 teaspoon salt
1/4 teaspoon pepper
2 drops Worcestershire sauce
Parsley for garnish
Paprika for garnish

In large pan, combine asparagus and chicken broth; heat to simmer and cook, covered, for 8 minutes. Cool. Put in blender or food processor, and blend until smooth. Add egg yolks and blend well. Return asparagus mixture to pan; stir in milk, salt, and pepper; add Worcestershire sauce. Heat well, but do not boil. Top with parsley and paprika.

CREAMY TOMATO SOUP

Serves 4

1 diced potato
2 diced carrots
2 diced celery stalks
1 medium onion, chopped
2 bay leaves
1-1/2 teaspoons dried basil
3/4 teaspoon oregano
1/4 teaspoon chili powder
1/4 teaspoon pepper
1-1/2 cups stock

Place all ingredients in saucepan. Bring to a boil; reduce heat; and simmer, covered, for 10 minutes or until tender.
Then stir in:
1 (16-ounce) can undrained tomatoes
2 tablespoons tomato paste
1/3 cup tiny pasta, cooked

Simmer 5 minutes more; remove from heat and stir in 1 cup low-fat yogurt. Serve immediately.

Dorothy E. Snyder, Pine Grove, Pa.

TACO SOUP

(teenage favorite)
Makes 3-1/2 quarts

1 pound lean ground beef
2-1/2 quarts chicken stock
1 (2-1/2-ounce) package taco seasoning mix
1/2 teaspoon cumin
1/2 teaspoon salt
1/4 teaspoon pepper
2 cups green onions, thinly sliced
2 cups tomatoes, chopped
1 (18-ounce) can pitted black olives, drained and sliced
1 (14-ounce) package corn chips
4 cups iceberg lettuce, shredded
2 cups cheddar cheese, shredded

In medium-size skillet, brown ground beef. Drain well and set aside. In large skillet, combine the chicken stock, taco seasoning mix, cumin, salt, pepper, and ground beef. Bring to a boil. Reduce heat and simmer covered for 10 minutes. Add green onions, tomatoes, and black olives. Simmer another 10 minutes. Ladle into bowls; top with chips, lettuce, and cheese.

VEGETABLE BEEF SOUP

Serves 8

1 pound ground beef
1 large can tomatoes, whole
1 can tomato soup
1 small onion, chopped
2 cups water
1 can lima beans, drained
1 can whole-kernel corn, undrained
1 cup sliced carrots
1 cup potatoes, cut up
1 cup diced celery
1/4 teaspoon salt
1/4 teaspoon pepper

Combine beef, tomatoes, soup, and onion in cooker. Add water, beans, and vegetables. Add salt, pepper, and other spices of preference. Stir well. Cook at lowest setting, 4 to 6 hours.

GOLDEN PUMPKIN SOUP

Serves 4-6

1 cup onion, chopped
1/2 cup celery, chopped
2 tablespoons butter or margarine
2 cups chicken broth
1-1/2 cups mushrooms, sliced
1/2 cup rice, uncooked
1/4 teaspoon salt
1/4 teaspoon curry powder
1/4 teaspoon tarragon
1 (16 ounce) can pumpkin
2 tablespoons margarine
Salt and pepper to taste

Sauté celery and onion in margarine, while potatoes are cooking. Mash potatoes and add all ingredients. Add more milk, if a thinner soup is desired. Bring to a boil and remove from heat. This is a delicious and rich-tasting soup made with evaporated milk. Try it, you'll like it!!

Betty Perkins, Hot Springs, Ark.

CASSEROLE PORK STEW

Serves 6

1   pound lean pork pieces, 1 inch square (fat trimmed off)
3   medium potatoes (about 1 pound), cut in 1½-inch pieces
1   (16-ounce) bag carrots, cut into ½-inch pieces
1   medium green pepper, cut into thin strips
1   medium onion, sliced
1   medium tomato, cut in thin wedges
2   beef bouillon cubes
1   cup water
1   tablespoon flour

Place all ingredients, except flour, in 2½-quart or larger casserole. Evenly sprinkle flour over top of pork mixture. Cover casserole and bake in a 350-degree oven for 1¾ hours, or until pork and vegetables are tender. Stir occasionally. (235 calories per serving)

Margaret Rhone, Arroyo Grande, Calif.

EASY CREAM OF BROCCOLI SOUP

Makes 8 cups

2 (10 ounce) packages frozen chopped broccoli
2 cans cream of mushroom soup
2-2/3 cups milk
3 tablespoons butter
1/2 teaspoon tarragon
Dash pepper

Cook broccoli; drain well. Add remaining ingredients and simmer over low heat until thoroughly heated.

Cheryl Santefort, Thornton, Ill.

CREAMY CARROT SOUP

2 tablespoons butter
1/4 cup chopped onion
1 rib celery, chopped
2 cups carrots, pared and sliced
2 cups chicken broth
1 cup milk or half-&-half
1 teaspoon salt
1/4 teaspoon nutmeg
1/8 teaspoon pepper

Melt butter; add onion and celery; cook until tender. Add carrots; cook 5 minutes. Add broth and bring to boil. Cover; cook over medium heat for 20 minutes until carrots are tender. Puree in blender. Add milk, salt, nutmeg, and pepper. Simmer 5-10 minutes, but do not boil.

Laura Hicks, Troy, Mont.

CREAM OF MUSHROOM SOUP

Serves 4-6

1 cup (1/4 pound) mushrooms
2 tablespoons chopped onion (1 medium)
2 tablespoons butter
2 tablespoons all-purpose flour
2 cups chicken stock or beef broth
1/2 cup light cream
1/4 teaspoon salt

1/4 teaspoon ground nutmeg
1/8 teaspoon white pepper

Slice mushrooms through cap and stem; cook with 2 tablespoons onion in butter for 5 minutes. Blend in flour; add broth. Cook; stir until slightly thickened. Cool slightly; add cream and seasonings. Heat through; serve at once.

Agnes Ward, Erie, Pa.

ITALIAN RICE AND PEA SOUP

1/3 cup olive oil
1 slice bacon, chopped
1 slice ham, chopped
1 small onion, chopped
1 tablespoon parsley, minced
1 package frozen peas
1 quart soup stock or water
1/2 cup uncooked rice
Salt and pepper
3 tablespoons grated Parmesan cheese

Sauté onion, bacon, ham and parsley in oil until light brown. Add peas; cook 5 minutes, stirring frequently. Add liquid and bring to a boil. Add washed rice, seasonings, and cheese; cook over medium heat until rice crushes easily between fingers. Serve very hot.

Leona Teodori, Warren, Mich.

NOODLE EGG DROP SOUP

Serves 4

2 cans (10-3/4 ounce each) chicken broth
4 cups water
1-1/2 cups fine egg noodles, uncooked
2 eggs, beaten
2 tablespoons chopped parsley
2 tablespoons butter

Bring chicken broth and water to boil; gradually add noodles, stirring occasionally; cook 8 minutes. Reduce heat to low, stir in eggs. Simmer 3 minutes longer. Remove from heat; stir in parsley and butter.

Sharon M. Crider, Evansville, WI

Turkey
TREATS

TURKEY MEATBALLS
Serves 4

1 pound ground turkey
1 small onion, finely chopped
½ cup bread crumbs
1½ tablespoons cold water
1 egg, slightly beaten
Salt and pepper to taste
½ teaspoon Mrs. Dash salt-free seasoning
2 tablespoons cooking oil
1 package brown gravy mix

In bowl, combine all ingredients, except cooking oil and gravy mix; mix thoroughly. Shape mixture into 1½–2-inch meatballs. In hot skillet with 2 tablespoons cooking oil, brown meatballs. In large saucepan mix 1 package brown gravy mix according to package directions. Add meatballs, and simmer for 1 hour. Serve with cooked noodles or rice.

Catherine Murphy, Eliot, Mass.

TURKEY BAKE

1 pound ground turkey, browned
2 cans Rotel tomatoes
1 can cream of celery soup
1 can cream of chicken soup
1 cup Minute Rice, uncooked
1 cup grated cheddar cheese
2 cups tortilla chips, crushed
2 tablespoons butter

Mix together all ingredients, except tortilla chips and cheddar cheese. Spread butter in bottom of 13 x 9-inch pan and cover with 1 cup crushed tortilla chips. Pour in ground turkey mixture. Sprinkle grated cheddar cheese on top and cover with 1 cup crushed tortilla chips.

Bake at 350 degrees for 45 minutes to 1 hour.

Germaine Tank, Oshkosh, Wis.

BARBECUED TURKEY STEAKS
Serves 4

1/2 cup oil
3 tablespoons vinegar
2 tablespoons ketchup
3/4 teaspoon onion salt
1/8 teaspoon garlic powder
1/4 teaspoon dill weed
1/4 teaspoon savory, crushed
1/4 teaspoon pepper
1 tablespoon chopped parsley
1 pound turkey breast steaks, 3/8- to 1/2-inch thickness

Combine oil, vinegar, 1 tablespoon ketchup, onion salt, garlic powder, dill weed, savory, pepper, and parsley. Pour over turkey steaks in shallow pan. Refrigerate steaks, turning occasionally, for several hours. Drain well; stir remaining ketchup into the marinade. Grill over hot coals about 6-8 minutes, depending on thickness of meat, brushing with the reserved marinade as meat is turned.

Leota Baxter, Ingalls, Kan.

AFTER-HOLIDAY HOT TURKEY SANDWICH

8 bread slices
4 slices white meat
4 slices dark meat
2–3 cups prepared dressing from turkey
Gravy (prepared or purchased)

Butter the bread slices. Put 1 slice of bread on each of 4 plates. Cover bread with hot dressing. Top with 1 slice of white meat and 1 slice of dark meat. Pour hot gravy over turkey. Cut remaining bread slices diagonally. Arrange 2 on each plate.

Sarah Burkett, Centralia, Ill.

LOW-CAL TURKEY LOAF
Serves 6

1½ pounds ground turkey
1 large carrot, grated
1 small onion, chopped
½ cup dry bread crumbs
2 large eggs, slightly beaten
1 (8-ounce) can tomato sauce

Combine all ingredients. Mix lightly and press into greased 9 x 5-inch loaf pan. Bake 1 hour in a 350-degree oven. (180 calories per serving.)

Mrs. D. Garms, Anaheim, Calif.

Vegetables
GARDEN-FRESH

GOLDEN CARROTS SUPREME
Serves 6

¼ cup butter *or* margarine
¾ cup chicken broth *or* bouillon
2 teaspoons salt
⅛ teaspoon pepper
2 teaspoons sugar
5 cups carrots, diagonally sliced (¼ inch)
2 teaspoons lemon juice
¼ cup chopped parsley

Add butter or margarine to boiling chicken broth. Stir in salt, pepper, sugar and carrots. Simmer, covered, until carrots are tender-crisp, about 10 minutes. Stir in lemon juice and parsley.

Marie Franks, Millerton, Pa.

CORN FROM THE ISLANDS

A Hawaiian recipe that is an excellent way to prepare corn on the cob that is a little past its prime.

2 cups milk
2 cups water
1 tablespoon butter
2 tablespoons sugar
6 ears corn, cleaned and rinsed

In a large saucepan, combine milk and water. Add butter and sugar. Stir. Bring just to a boil; add corn and return to almost boiling. Cover and simmer 3–5 minutes. Serve with salt and butter.

Marsha Miller, Hilliard, Ohio

SUMMER GARDEN RICE
Serves 4—6

1 tablespoon vegetable or olive oil
2 onions, chopped
1 zucchini, sliced into rings
1/2 cup yellow corn
1/2 cup white corn
1 green pepper, diced
2 garden-fresh tomatoes, chopped
2 radishes, thinly sliced
2 cups cooked rice

Salt and pepper to taste
1 teaspoon fresh dill

In a saucepan combine all ingredients, except rice and dill; sauté until tender. Add cooked rice; sprinkle dill over individual servings. Can be served hot or cold.

Gwen Campbell, Sterling, Va.

SQUASH-MADE-CHEESY

3 or 4 summer squash
1 onion, chopped
1 can mushroom soup
1/2 small box Velveeta cheese, cubed
1/2 stick butter, melted
Saltine crackers, crumbled

Slice and boil squash until tender; drain. Add onion, cheese and soup. Pour into buttered casserole. Cover top with cracker crumbs and drizzle butter over all. Bake at 350 degrees for 30 minutes.

Brenda Peery, Tannersville, Va.

CORN PUDDING

2 cups corn
1/2 cup milk
1 tablespoon butter
1/2 teaspoon baking powder
1/8 teaspoon pepper
2 eggs, separated
1 tablespoon flour
1/2 teaspoon salt

Mix baking powder with flour; stir milk, egg yolks, and flour into corn. Add seasoning. Add egg whites, beaten stiff. Pour into greased baking dish and dot with butter. Bake 30 minutes in a 325-degree oven. Serve at once.

Suzan L. Wiener, Spring Hill, Fla.

WINTER SQUASH

2 cups squash, cooked
1 cup sugar
1 cup milk
3 eggs
¾ stick margarine
1 teaspoon coconut extract
4 tablespoons coconut Ritz crackers

Place all ingredients, except crackers, in blender; blend well. Pour into a casserole dish; set in a shallow pan of water. Bake at 350 degrees for 45 minutes. Top with crushed Ritz crackers and brown.

Villa Zicafoose, Humansville, Mo.

CARROT SOUFFLÉ
Serves 4

2 cups sliced carrots
  Water, unsalted
¼ cup butter
1 medium onion, chopped
3 tablespoons flour
1 cup milk
1 teaspoon salt
3 eggs, separated

Cook carrots in a small amount of water (just barely enough to cover) until fork-tender. Drain, if necessary. Set aside to cool slightly.

Melt butter in a 10-inch skillet; add onion and sauté until onion is tender. Stir in flour and cook for several minutes, stirring with fork, until flour browns.

Meanwhile, put milk in blender and add cooked carrots. Whirl until carrots are finely grated. Add milk-carrot mixture all at once to the onion-flour mixture. Cook, stirring frequently, until mixture is bubbly and thickened. Remove from heat and stir in salt. Cool slightly.

Beat egg whites until stiff peaks form. Beat egg yolks until thick and lemon-colored. Stir yolks into carrot mixture. Fold in egg whites. Pour into a greased 1½-quart casserole and bake at 350 degrees for 25–30 minutes, or until soufflé is puffed and golden.

SAUCY ONIONS
Serves 6

6 medium onions, peeled and
  washed
1/3 cup strained honey
1/4 cup water
3 tablespoons butter

Arrange onions in single layer in baking dish. Mix honey and water together; pour over onions. Dot with butter; cover. Bake at 400 degrees for 1 hour.

Diantha Susan Hibbard, Rochester, N.Y.

SOUTH–OF–THE–BORDER STUFFED LETTUCE
Serves 6

1 large head iceberg lettuce
1 teaspoon unflavored gelatin
2 teaspoons cold water
4 ounces cream cheese
1 packet dry onion soup mix
1 tablespoon vegetable oil
1/4 teaspoon salt
1 tablespoon chili sauce
1 tablespoon fresh lemon juice
1 cup red kidney beans
1/2 cup corn chips, crushed

Remove core from lettuce; rinse with cold water. Hollow out center; turn upside down; drain thoroughly. Add gelatin to cold water; dissolve over hot water. In mixer bowl, mix together cream cheese, onion soup mix, oil, salt, chili sauce, lemon juice, and dissolved gelatin. Fold in beans and half the corn chips; pack into the hollow of the lettuce. Cover; refrigerate 1-1/2 hours.

Cut into slices to serve; garnish with remaining chips.

Gwen Campbell, Sterling, Va.

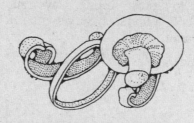

BAKED SHREDDED CARROTS
Serves 6

4 cups shredded carrots
1 medium onion, finely
  chopped
1 tablespoon sugar
¼ teaspoon salt
2 tablespoons butter

Lightly toss together the carrots, onion, sugar and salt until well-combined. Spread evenly in a shallow 1-quart casserole and dot with butter. Bake, covered, at 325 degrees for 1 hour.

SEASONED BRUSSELS SPROUTS
Serves 6

2 (10-ounce) packages frozen
  brussels sprouts *or* cut broccoli
1 or 2 chicken bouillon cubes
2 (10 1/2-ounce) cans condensed
  cream of celery soup
1/2 cup grated sharp cheese
Pimiento strips

Cook brussels sprouts with bouillon cubes and water until just tender. Heat soup to boiling; pour over sprouts. Garnish with cheese and pimiento. Serve at once.

Ida Bloedow, Madison, Wis.

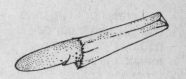

BROCCOLI PARMESAN
Serves 8

2-1/2 pounds broccoli, cut into
  flowerets
1 small onion, minced
6 tablespoons butter
4 tablespoons flour
2 cups milk
1/2 teaspoon salt
1/8 teaspoon pepper
1/2 teaspoon dry mustard
1 egg yolk, beaten
1 cup Parmesan cheese
1/4 cup dry bread crumbs *or*
  1/4 cup cracker crumbs

Cook broccoli until crisp-tender. Sauté onion in 4 tablespoons butter. Stir in flour and stir until smooth. Slowly add milk. Cook until thick and bubbly. Add salt, pepper, dry mustard, egg yolk, and cheese. Pour half of the sauce into a 9x11-inch pan. Place broccoli in pan with stems in center. Pour remaining sauce over broccoli. Brown 1/4 cup bread or cracker crumbs in 2 tablespoons butter and sprinkle down center. Bake at 400 degrees for 20 minutes.

Ida Bloedow, Madison, Wis.

SCALLOPED ASPARAGUS

Serves 4-6

4 cups fresh asparagus, cut into 1-
  inch pieces
1-1/2 cups milk
2 tablespoons flour
1 teaspoon salt
1/2 teaspoon pepper
1/2 cup grated American cheese
1 cup bread crumbs
2 tablespoons butter

Preheat oven to 325 degrees. Cook asparagus in a little water until tender, then transfer to a buttered baking dish. Combine milk, flour, salt, and pepper together. Add to the asparagus. Add the remaining cheese and half the remaining bread crumbs; stir again. Dot with butter; sprinkle remaining bread crumbs on top. Bake 30 minutes, or until brown on top.

SPINACH RING

Serves 6

1 (10-ounce) package frozen
  spinach
2 eggs, beaten
1-1/2 cups dairy sour cream
2 tablespoons flour
2 tablespoons grated Parmesan
  cheese
1/2 teaspoon salt
1/8 teaspoon onion powder
1/8 teaspoon pepper
6 hard-cooked eggs, chopped

Remove outer wrapper from package of spinach. Place unopened carton in dish in microwave and cook 5 minutes on HIGH. Turn out into strainer and drain well, pressing out excess moisture with back of spoon. Set aside. Combine all remaining ingredients, except hard-cooked eggs; blend well. Stir in reserved spinach. Fold in chopped eggs. Pour into well-greased 1-quart ring mold. Cook on 50 percent or 30 percent power, 20-30 minutes, or until knife inserted halfway between center and outer edge

comes out clean. Let stand, uncovered, 10 minutes. Unmold onto serving platter. Use a reduced-power setting for best results.

Suzan L. Wiener, Spring Hill, Fla.

GOLDENROD BEANS

Serves 6

1-1/2 pounds whole green beans
1-1/2 tablespoons butter or margarine
2 tablespoons flour
1/2 teaspoon salt
1/8 teaspoon pepper
3/4 cup evaporated milk
3 hard-cooked eggs, separated
3/4 cup mayonnaise

Cook beans in boiling, salted water until tender. Save 1/2 cup of the liquid. Melt butter. Blend in flour, salt, and pepper. Add bean stock and cook until thickened, stirring constantly. Add milk and chopped egg whites. Heat thoroughly. Remove from heat and add mayonnaise. Drain beans. Cover with sauce and sprinkle with sieved egg yolks.

BAKED SUMMER SQUASH

Serves 16–20

1/2 cup butter *or* margarine, melted
1 (6-ounce) package herbed stuffing
  mix
2 pounds summer squash *or*
  zucchini, sliced (not too thin)
1/4 cup chopped onion
1 cup carrots, shredded
Salt to taste
1 can cream of chicken soup
1 cup sour cream

Pour melted butter or margarine over stuffing mix; toss well. Cook squash and onion together in small amount of water for 5 minutes; mix in carrots. Drain. Season with salt. Combine soup and sour cream; mix with vegetables. Line 9 x 13-inch casserole dish with 1/2 of the stuffing mixture. Add vegetable mixture.

Cover with remaining stuffing mixture. Bake at 350 degrees for 25 minutes, or until brown.

Good "make-ahead" recipe.

Marty Grant, Marquette, Mich.

BAKED LIMA BEANS IN TOMATO SAUCE

1 (1-pound) package dried lima
  beans
9 slices bacon
2 (8-ounce) cans tomato sauce
1 cup chopped onion
1/4 cup light brown sugar, firmly
  packed
2 teaspoons mustard
2 teaspoons Worcestershire sauce
1/2 teaspoon oregano

Cook beans until just tender. Drain, reserving 1/2 cup liquid. Cut bacon into 1/2-inch pieces. Sauté lightly. Add onion and sauté until it is tender and bacon is browned. Combine all ingredients and mix until well-blended. Turn into 2-1/2-quart shallow baking dish. Bake at 350 degrees for 45 minutes.

Betty Ireton, Kingston, Ohio.

CABBAGE AU GRATIN

1/2 large head cabbage, chopped
3/4 cup grated cheese
Paprika
Salt
2 cups medium white sauce
1/2 cup cracker crumbs
3 tablespoons melted butter

Put a layer of chopped cabbage into a buttered baking dish; sprinkle with grated cheese, paprika, and salt. Cover with a layer of medium white sauce. Repeat the layers until all ingredients have been used.

Cover with cracker crumbs mixed with melted butter. Bake in moderately hot oven at 350 degrees, until bubbling hot and evenly browned.

Betty Slavin, Omaha, Neb.

GOLDEN CROWN CARROT SOUFFLÉ
Serves 7

5 carrots, cooked and mashed
1 cup milk
1 onion (whole)
1 whole clove inserted into onion
1 bay leaf
1/2 cup butter or margarine
3 tablespoons flour
3 egg yolks, slightly beaten
1/4 teaspoon salt
1/4 teaspoon pepper
1/8 teaspoon paprika
1/8 teaspoon nutmeg
1/8 teaspoon marjoram
3 tablespoons Parmesan cheese, grated
3 egg whites, beaten

Cook carrots; drain; place in buttered 2-quart soufflé mold or round dish. Heat milk with onion and clove; add bay leaf. Simmer 8 minutes; strain; set aside. In a saucepan melt butter; add flour; slowly add strained milk mixture; cook until smooth and thick. Remove from heat; blend in egg yolks slowly; add salt, pepper, spices, and cheese. Beat egg whites until stiff; fold into sauce mixture. Pour over carrots; bake at 350 degrees, until golden crown is well-puffed and firm.

Gwen Campbell, Sterling, Va.

ASPARAGUS– PEANUT BAKE
Serves 4-6

4 cups fresh asparagus, cut in 1-inch pieces
1 (10-3/4-ounce) can cream of mushroom soup
1/2 cup peanuts, crushed
1 cup grated cheddar cheese
Salt and pepper to taste
1/2 stick butter or margarine

Cook asparagus in small amount of water until tender-crisp. Arrange layers of asparagus, soup, peanuts, and cheese in a greased casserole; season with salt and pepper. Dot with butter. Bake at 350 degrees for 30 minutes, or until heated through and bubbly.

CURRIED ASPARAGUS SALAD
Serves 4

1 pound hot steamed asparagus, drained
1/2 cup French dressing
8 lettuce leaves, washed and crisped
1 pimiento, drained and cut into 1/4-inch strips

Curry Dressing:
1/2 cup mayonnaise
1 tablespoon sour cream
1/2 teaspoon curry powder
1/2 teaspoon lemon juice

Marinate asparagus in French dressing for 3 to 4 hours in the refrigerator, turning occasionally. Shortly before serving, mix Curry Dressing. Drain asparagus (reserve French dressing for other salads later) and arrange on lettuce. Top with Curry Dressing. Garnish with pimiento.

FRESH SPINACH AND LETTUCE PIE
Serves 5

1 pound spinach, chopped (or 1 package frozen spinach, thawed)
1 cup onions, finely chopped
1/2 cup green onions, finely chopped
1 cup fresh lettuce, chopped
1 cup fresh parsley, chopped
2 tablespoons flour
1 teaspoon salt
1/4 teaspoon pepper

1/4 teaspoon nutmeg
1/2 cup walnuts, chopped
8 eggs, well-beaten
4 tablespoons butter or margarine

Wash spinach; drain well. Mix together next 10 ingredients. Melt butter in an 11-inch pie plate; pour vegetable mixture into it. Bake at 325 degrees for 1 hour, or until top is golden and crisp. Can be served hot or chilled.

Gwen Campbell, Sterling, Va.

ASPARAGUS– CHEESE PIE
Serves 6

1 (9-inch) pastry shell
6 slices bacon
1 medium-size onion, thinly sliced
1 cup shredded Swiss cheese
2 tablespoons grated Parmesan cheese
2 cups heavy cream
4 eggs, well-beaten
1 teaspoon salt
1/4 teaspoon grated nutmeg
6 stalks asparagus, partly cooked

Bake pastry shell in 350-degree oven for 5 minutes. Sauté bacon until crisp; drain off fat, leaving about 1 tablespoon. Sauté onion in remaining fat until transparent. Combine bacon, onion, and cheeses; place in pastry. Mix cream, eggs, salt, and nutmeg; pour into pie shell. Arrange asparagus in a wagon wheel design on top of pie. Bake for 35-40 minutes in a 375-degree oven, or until golden.

ELEGANT EGGPLANT
Serves 12

3 large eggplants
1/2 pound spicy bulk sausage
3 green onions, chopped
1 cup celery, chopped
1 (6 1/4-ounce) package corn bread stuffing mix
1/2 teaspoon black pepper flakes
1/2 teaspoon salt
2 cups grated cheddar cheese

Peel and dice eggplants; cook in salted water until tender. Drain well and set aside. Sauté sausage in skillet until well-done; remove to paper towels; set aside. Sauté green onions and celery in skillet until transparent; set aside. Prepare stuffing mix according to package instructions. Combine eggplant, sausage, onion/celery mixture, salt, pepper and stuffing mix. Transfer to shallow baking dish. Top with cheese; broil until cheese is melted. Serve hot.

Marcella Swigert, Monroe City, Mo.

RICE PILAF
Serves 8

- 4 cups chicken broth
- 2 cups long-grain rice, uncooked
- 2 tablespoons butter *or* margarine
- 1 teaspoon salt, optional
- ¼ teaspoon thyme *or* marjoram
- 2 tablespoons chopped parsley

In large saucepan heat broth to boiling. Add rice, butter or margarine and salt, if desired, and thyme or marjoram. Return to boiling. Cover; reduce heat and simmer 20 minutes until rice is tender and broth is absorbed. This recipe can be made ahead up to this point. Cover and keep at room temperature for up to 3 hours. To reheat, place covered pan over low heat. Toss with fork after 10 minutes. When hot, garnish with parsley.

M. Manson, Castle Rock, Wash.

CELERY SUPREME
Serves 4-6

- 4 cups celery, cut in 1-inch lengths
- 1 (10-ounce) can condensed cream of chicken soup
- 5 ounces water chestnuts, sliced
- 1/4 cup chopped pimiento
- Buttered bread crumbs

Cook celery in salted water until tender-crisp. Drain and put into a greased 1-1/2-quart casserole.

Mix the soup, water chestnuts, and pimiento together and spoon over top. Melt a small amount of butter in a saucepan and stir in bread crumbs to coat. Spread over top of casserole.

Bake, uncovered, in 350-degree oven for 30 minutes or until celery is tender.

Millicent Corbeene, St. John's, New Foundland., Canada

SIX-LAYER BAKE
Serves 4-6

- 2 cups sliced potatoes
- 2 cups chopped celery
- 2 cups sliced carrots
- 1 cup sliced onions
- 2 cups ground beef
- 2 cups canned tomatoes
- 2 teaspoons salt
- 1/4 teaspoon pepper

In a greased casserole make a layer of each ingredient in the order given. Season each layer. Bake for 2 hours at 350 degrees.

Dorothy E. Snyder, Pine Grove, Pa.

STUFFED ZUCCHINI CURRY
Serves 2

- 1 large zucchini
- 1 apple, peeled and finely chopped
- 1/4 cup mozzarella cheese, grated
- 1/4 cup bread crumbs
- 1 egg, beaten
- 1/2 teaspoon curry powder
- 1/4 teaspoon ginger
- 3 tablespoons golden raisins

Cut zucchini down the middle, lengthwise. Scoop out pulp; leave 1/2 inch of shell. Place pulp in a bowl; drain off excess water. Add remaining ingredients; place in zucchini shells. Place stuffed zucchini in an ovenproof baking dish; add just enough water to cover the bottom of the dish. Bake at 350 degrees for 20 minutes, or until the zucchini is tender.

Gwen Campbell, Sterling, Va.

MARVELOUS MARINATED MUSHROOMS

- 3 pounds fresh button mushrooms
- 1 (½-ounce) package garlic salad dressing mix
- 1½ cups oil
- ½ cup lemon juice
- Salt and pepper to taste
- 2 tablespoons Accent
- 2 tablespoons parsley flakes
- 2 tablespoons garlic powder (optional)

Wash and cap mushrooms. Cover in salt water and boil 1 minute. Drain. Prepare marinade from rest of ingredients. Pour over caps and chill at least 24 hours. Drain and serve cold.

Diantha Susan Hibbard, Rochester, N.Y.

COPPER PENNIES
Serves 16

- 2 pounds carrots, peeled and sliced
- 1 cup diced green pepper
- 1 cup chopped onions
- 1 cup tomato soup
- 1 tablespoon Worcestershire sauce
- 1 cup sugar
- 3/4 cup vinegar
- 1/2 cup salad oil
- 1 teaspoon dry or prepared mustard
- Salt and pepper to taste

Cook carrots until tender; drain. Add green pepper and onions. Combine remaining ingredients; pour over carrot mixture. Mix well. Refrigerate until ready to use. This will keep well for 2 weeks in the refrigerator.

Lorraine Michalski, West Seneca, N.Y.

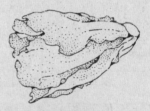

OVEN-COOKED ASPARAGUS
Serves 6

- 3 tablespoons melted butter
- 3 tablespoons flour
- 1 cup milk
- 3/4 teaspoon salt
- 1/4 teaspoon pepper
- 1-2/3 cups finely chopped, cooked asparagus
- 2 eggs, beaten

In a pot combine butter and flour thoroughly. Add the milk gradually. Cook, stirring constantly, until thick and smooth. Add salt, pepper, and asparagus. Fold eggs into mixture. Spoon mixture into greased custard cups. Set in a pan of hot water. Bake at 375 degrees for 15 minutes.

VEGETABLE PIZZA

1 package crescent dinner rolls
1 (8-ounce) package cream cheese
1 (8-ounce) container plain yogurt
1/2 package Hidden Valley ranch
  dressing
3/4 cup shredded cheddar cheese
3/4 cup carrots, very finely chopped
3/4 cup tomatoes, very finely
  chopped
3/4 cup onions, very finely chopped
3/4 cup broccoli, very finely
  chopped
3/4 cup cauliflower, very finely
  chopped
3/4 cup celery, very finely chopped

Cover bottom of cookie sheet with crescent rolls. Press in the separations. Bake at 350 degrees until light brown. Cool. Mix yogurt, cream cheese and flavoring until smooth and spread over crust. Cover with vegetable toppings and cheddar cheese.

Kristy Schemrich, Shreve, Ohio

ZUCCHINI–CORN PUDDING
Serves 8

1-1/2 pounds zucchini, thinly sliced
1 medium onion, thinly sliced
1 green pepper, minced
1 clove garlic, minced
1/4 teaspoon rosemary
1/4 cup salad oil
1 (No. 2) can cream-style corn
3/4 cup grated cheese
3 eggs, well-beaten
Salt and pepper to taste

Cook zucchini in boiling, salted water until tender. Drain; squeeze out all liquid. Sauté onion, green pepper, garlic, and rosemary in oil until tender. Add zucchini, corn, cheese, eggs, salt, and pepper. Mix; turn into greased 2-quart casserole. Bake 45 minutes at 350 degrees, or until firm.

June Harding, Ferndale, Mich.

GLAZED ACORN SQUASH
Serves 12

3 acorn squash
1/4 cup margarine
1/4 cup firmly packed brown sugar
2 tablespoons maple-flavored syrup
1/2 cup coarsely chopped walnuts

Heat oven to 350 degrees. Cut squash in half lengthwise; remove seeds. Cut squash halves, crosswise, into 1-inch-thick pieces. Arrange in 13 x 9-inch (3-quart) baking dish; cover. Bake at 350 degrees for 35–40 minutes, or until nearly tender. In small saucepan, melt margarine. Stir in brown sugar, syrup and walnuts; cook over medium heat until sugar dissolves. Spoon over squash and continue baking an additional 10–15 minutes, or until squash in tender. Baste occasionally. (140 calories per serving)

Mrs. Sherwin Dick, Inman, Neb.

FILLED BEET BASKETS
Serves 6

6 medium-size beets, cooked
1 cup beet greens (tops), cooked
  and chopped
1 hard-cooked egg, chopped
1 slice bacon, cooked crisp and
  crumbled
1 tablespoon onion, chopped
1/4 teaspoon salt
1/4 teaspoon pepper
1 tablespoon butter or margarine,
  melted
Parsley

Scoop out centers of cooked beets to form baskets. Chop centers, green tops and egg. Add crumbled bacon, onion, salt, pepper and butter. Heap mixture carefully into beet baskets; garnish with parsley. Can be served on crisp lettuce, as a side dish, or placed around edge of platter with any baked meat, chicken or turkey.

Gwen Campbell, Sterling, Va.

SQUASH BAKE
Serves 6

1 pound yellow squash, finely sliced
1/2 cup almonds, chopped
2–3 white onions, finely sliced
Salt and pepper to taste
1 stick butter
1 cup bread crumbs, toasted
1 egg, beaten
6 tablespoons cream

Cook squash and onions in saucepan with butter over medium heat until mixture is soft. Remove pan from heat and add egg, cream and almonds. Mix well; add salt and pepper. Place in a 1-1/2-quart casserole and top with bread crumbs. Bake at 350 degrees for 30 minutes, or until bubbly.

June Harding, Ferndale, Mich.

LEMON-GLAZED CARROTS
Serves 6

1-1/2 pounds small carrots, peeled
1/2 teaspoon salt
1/2 cup boiling water
1/3 cup brown sugar
2 tablespoons butter
1 teaspoon grated lemon peel
1 tablespoon lemon juice

Cook carrots, covered, in salted water until tender for about 20 minutes; drain. Combine remaining ingredients; heat and pour over carrots.

Melba Bellefeinlle, Libertyville, Ill.

CARROTS IN CUMIN BUTTER
Serves 4

3 cups sliced carrots
  Salted, boiling water
1 tablespoon butter
½ teaspoon ground cumin

Cook carrots in salted, boiling water just until tender. Drain well. Add butter and cumin; stir until butter is melted and cumin is evenly distributed.

MUSHROOM SUPREME

1 (12 ounce) can whole mushrooms
2 beef bouillon cubes
1/2 cup hot water
4 tablespoons butter
2 tablespoons flour
1/2 cup light cream
Pinch of salt and pepper
1/2 cup bread crumbs
1/2 to 1 cup Parmesan cheese.

Saute mushrooms in butter gently for two minutes. Dissolve beef cubes in hot water. Melt butter and blend with flour in another saucepan. Add cream, salt, pepper, beef broth, and mushrooms to butter and flour mixture. Pour into buttered casserole. Top with cheese and bread crumbs, mixed together. Bake for 30 minutes at 350 degrees.

Great for mushroom lovers.
Helen MacFarlane, Monaca, PA

ASPARAGUS-TOMATO STIR FRY
Serves 4

1 pound fresh asparagus
1 tablespoon cold water
1 teaspoon cornstarch
2 teaspoons soy sauce
1/4 teaspoon salt
1 tablespoon cooking oil
4 green onions, bias sliced in 1-inch lengths
1-1/2 cup sliced fresh mushrooms
2 small tomatoes, cut in thin wedges
Hot cooked rice

Snap off and discard woody base of asparagus. Bias slice the asparagus crosswise into 1-1/2 inch lengths and set aside. If asparagus spears are not slender and young, cut up pieces, cook uncovered in small amount of boiling salted water about 5 minutes; drain well. (Celery, green beans, broccoli, etc., may be used in place of asparagus.) In small bowl, blend water into cornstarch. Stir in soy sauce and salt; set aside. Stir-fry asparagus and green onions in hot oil 4 minutes. Use a long-handled spoon to turn and lift the food with a folding motion. Add mushrooms; stir-fry 1 minute more. Stir the soy mixture again. Push vegetables up the sides of the wok; add soy mixture to center of wok. Let mixture bubble slightly, then stir into vegetables. Cook and stir till mixture is thickened and bubbly. Add tomatoes and heat through. Serve at once with cooked rice.

COMPANY ASPARAGUS
Serves 4-6

14-1/2 - ounce can green asparagus
10-1/2 - ounce can Cheddar cheese soup
2 hard-boiled eggs, chopped
1/2 cup toasted slivered almonds
1 cup buttered bread crumbs, divided

Combine asparagus, soup, eggs, almonds and 1/2 cup bread crumbs in buttered 1-quart casserole dish. Spread 1/2 cup bread crumbs over mixture. Bake uncovered at 375 degrees for 20 minutes.
Mrs. E. O'Brien, Richmond, VA

ASPARAGUS WITH YOGURT DRESSING
Serves 4

1 pound fresh asparagus
1/2 cup plain yogurt
1 small clove garlic, crushed
1 tablespoon chopped parsley
1/4 teaspoon salt
1 small head Boston or Bibb lettuce
1 hard-cooked egg yolk; sieved

Snap off tough ends of asparagus. Remove scales with knife or peeler. Cook asparagus in boiling water about 10 minutes or until crisp-tender. Drain. Cool and place in refrigerator to chill. Combine yogurt with garlic, parsley, and salt; stir well. Chill. Place asparagus on bed of lettuce; top with yogurt dressing and sprinkle with egg yolk.
Peggy Fowler Revels, Woodruff, SC

ASPARAGUS VINAIGRETTE
Serves 4

1 pound fresh asparagus (or 1 pound fresh whole green beans)
1 head fresh cauliflower (or 1 package frozen cauliflower)
1 can (7 ounce) artichoke hearts
Vinaigrette Dressing (below)

Cook asparagus or beans and cauliflower. Drain artichokes. Pour 1/4 cup Vinaigrette Dressing over each vegetable. Chill at least 1 hour. Arrange the three vegetables artistically on individual serving plates or on one large platter. Garnish with cherry tomatoes or parsley.

ASPARAGUS LOAF

1 carton half & half
1 sleeve package soda crackers, crumbled
3 eggs, beaten
2 tablespoons butter
2 cans green asparagus spears, cut
Pinch of salt

Mix all ingredients together. Pour into buttered casserole. Bake at 350 degrees for 1 hour.
Ann Fischer, Clarksville, Ind.

ASPARAGUS WITH HERBS
Serves 3 - 45 calories per serving

1-1/4 cups asparagus
1 tablespoon diet margarine
1/2 teaspoon salt
1/4 cup water
2 tablespoons chives, chopped
1/8 teaspoon seasoned salt
1/16 teaspoon pepper

Separate asparagus. Place margarine, salt, water, and chives in skillet; cover tightly. Bring to boil, add asparagus and cover again. Gently boil until asparagus is tender. Sprinkle with seasoned salt and pepper.

Home Cooking

INDEX

INDEX

Fresh recipes ...
for today's busy cooks!

NOTHING TASTES BETTER THAN *HOME COOKING!*

♥ Delight your family and friends with easy-to-fix, great-tasting meals from the pages of *Home Cooking* magazine!

♥ Each new issue brings you scores of tasty, tried-and-true recipes guaranteed to please – over 1,000 a year!

♥ From savory entrees to tempting desserts – it's all in *Home Cooking!* The proof is in the pudding, so mail this coupon today to start your one-year subscription. You'll get an issue each month with a hundred or more great recipes for **only $12.⁹⁷**! That's a savings of over 26% off the newsstand price!

Subscribe TODAY!

ONLY $12.⁹⁷ FOR 12 GREAT ISSUES!

26%
SAVINGS
OFF THE NEWSSTAND PRICE!